The Cramoisy Queen

The Cramoisy Queen

A Life of Caresse Crosby

Linda Hamalian

Southern Illinois University Press · Carbondale

Printed in the United States of America
08 07 06 05 4 3 2 1

Library of Congress Cataloging-in-Publication Data

Hamalian, Linda.
The Cramoisy queen : a life of Caresse Crosby / Linda Hamalian.
p. cm.
Includes bibliographical references and index.
1. Crosby, Caresse, 1892– 2. Poets, American—20th century—Biography. 3. Publishers and publishing—France—Biography. 4. Americans—France—Paris—History—20th century. 5. Literature publishing—France—Paris—History—20th century. 6. Paris (France)—Intellectual life—20th century. I. Title.
PS3505.R865Z69 2004
811'.52—dc22
ISBN 0-8093-1865-2 (alk. paper)

The paper used in this publication meets the minimum requirements of American National Standard for Information Sciences—Permanence of Paper for Printed Library Materials, ANSI Z39.48-1992. ∞

For Leo

Contents

Illustrations

Preface

Caresse Crosby (1892–1970) and her husband Harry Crosby (1898–1929) founded the Black Sun Press in Paris in 1924. As patrons of expatriate writers, they befriended and published such influential figures as D. H. Lawrence, Hart Crane, Kay Boyle, Ernest Hemingway, and James Joyce and reprinted literary classics in letterpress editions. After Harry's death in 1929, Caresse directed the press for the next thirty years, adding to its list works by Marcel Proust, William Faulkner, Dorothy Parker, and Paul Eluard. She published four volumes of Harry's poetry, introduced by T. S. Eliot, D. H. Lawrence, and Ezra Pound. Her own first volume of poetry appeared under the Houghton Mifflin imprint in 1926, and Dial Press published her autobiography, *The Passionate Years,* in 1955. After she returned to the United States, her life intersected with such figures as Henry Miller, Romare Bearden, Salvador Dalí, Buckminster Fuller, and Anaïs Nin. She published several volumes of *Portfolio,* an international journal of literature and the arts. Furthermore, she spent a small fortune advocating world peace and women's rights.

My principal research has been conducted at the Crosby archives at Morris Library, Southern Illinois University. The Crosby collection totals 72 boxes, 172 books, and 7 packages of materials related to the Black Sun Press. Included are Harry's letters to Caresse and his mother; letters to and from D. H. Lawrence, Hart Crane, Kay Boyle, James Joyce, and Eugene Jolas; and unpublished notebooks, manuscripts, newspaper clippings, and a nearly complete collection of Black Sun books. There is a massive exchange of letters between Crosby and her family and friends, and materials concerning her literary and political activities from 1948 to 1970. An unpublished sequel to her popular and highly praised autobiography throws light on how she viewed her achievements and failures.

The Harris Collection in John Hay Library at Brown University houses a smaller Crosby archive, including ten volumes of Harry Crosby's holograph notebooks. Additional materials exist in the Berg Collection of the New York Public Library, the Beinecke Library at Yale University, the University of Connecticut at Storrs, and the Harry Ransom Humanities Research Center at the University of Texas in Austin.

Crosby was a dedicated patron of the arts, an innovative and creative publisher, a skillful writer of memoir (less so of poetry and drama), an active promoter of world peace, a person who enjoyed her sometimes embattled career. The life of Caresse Crosby is a story about a woman who first achieves recognition as a famous person's wife, about a woman who suffers criticism from family and friends because she pursues interests conventionally restricted to the men of her class. It is about a woman who believes in her own moral agency. Caresse Crosby found her own way to reconcile herself to living in the shadow of Harry Crosby's death. In the process, she far surpassed her programmed role as the mirror companion of her husband. She paid a high price to pursue the life of a defiant, spirited, and talented woman, but she never lost her sense of humor.

I would like to thank David Koch, Associate Dean of Special Collections; Shelley Cox, Rare Books Librarian; Katharine Salzmann, Archivist/Manuscripts Curator; Sheila Ryan, Interim Manuscripts Curator; and Diane Worrell, Photographs Librarian, all of Morris Library, for their graciousness, generosity, and erudition. As research assistant, Levi Burkett was meticulous in navigating the photo collection.

I would also like to thank Jim Simmons, former editorial director of Southern Illinois University Press, for his enthusiasm during the early days of this project. I extend much gratitude to former press director Rick Stetter and to editor-in-chief Karl Kageff for their continued support, patience, and encouragement.

I am grateful to the following libraries, trusts, and individuals for permission to consult and/or reprint from materials in their private collections and/or under their jurisdiction:

Special Collections Research Center, Morris Library, Southern Illinois University Carbondale, Caresse Crosby Papers, Collection 140, Photo Collection 49

Brown University Library, John Hay Library, Harris Collection, Black Sun Press Archive

National Library of Canada and National Archives of Canada

Andrea Mihalovic-Lee, the Romare Bearden Foundation
Bob Rosenthal, the Allen Ginsberg Trust
Ian von Franckenstein and the Estate of Kay Boyle and the Watkins/Loomis Agency
Carole Cleaver Rodman, the Estate of Selden Rodman
Barbara W. Stuhlmann, the Estate of Anaïs Nin
Allegra Fuller Snyder, the Estate of Buckminster Fuller
Fred Dennis, the Estate of Sylvia Beach
Stephen James Joyce, the Estate of James Joyce
Frances Lee Pearson, the Estate of Canada Lee
Pollinger Limited, the Estate of D. H. Lawrence
Penguin Group (U.S.A.), Inc., the Estate of Malcolm Cowley
Declan Spring, New Directions Publishing Corporation, the Estate of Ezra Pound
Bradford Morrow, the Kenneth Rexroth Trust
John Ferry, Masters and Masterworks Production, Inc.

For generously granting interviews, allowing me to quote from their correspondence, and providing me with vital information I would like to thank Walter Phelps Jacob, R. J. Palcho, Charles Henri Ford, William Watt, Richard Melville, Sharon Cowling, Stephen Kraft, William Jay Smith, Anne Conover, Millicent Bell, Lilace Hatayama, Mark Brown, Barbara LaBorde, Isabelle Fernandes, George deZwaan, Paul Schleuter, Timothy Engels, and Holly Snyder. I am most grateful to Bill Barker for the afternoon in Hudson, New York, when he shared with me his memories of Caresse and re-created her aura.

For professional advice, hard to find addresses, and sharing remote literary sources, I would like to thank Camille Billops and James V. Hatch, Marjorie and Harry Keyishian, Donna Perry and Neill Rosenfeld, Alice Deakins, Edward Burns, Amy Cherry, Bob Rosen, Marjorie and Jeffrey Appel, Debbie Lennartsson, Sheila Feig Brown, Virginia Ramey Mollenkott, Kathleen Kageff, Judith Jobin and Daniel Leary, and Valerie and Kumar Krishna.

I also wish to thank the National Endowment for the Arts for a Travel to Collections Grant, and William Paterson University for awarding me a sabbatical and released time for research and writing.

My friends, colleagues, and family, especially my parents, Adele and Edward Bearman, kept me afloat following the death of my husband, Leo Hamalian. Without their support, love, and wisdom, I would not have had the heart to finish this work.

The Cramoisy Queen

Spunky Little Rich Girl

Caresse Crosby was born at home in New York City on April 20, 1892, and christened Mary Phelps Jacob. Polly, as she was called by her family, was a headstrong little girl with large blue eyes set far apart, brown hair, a square forehead, a full chin, and a mouth that smiled halfway. She was the oldest of three children, the only daughter, and the first grandchild. Among her paternal ancestors were a knight of the Crusades and a great-grandfather whose stag hunts were featured in the *Sporting Magazine.* Grandfather Jacob (the name was changed from Allardyce after the War of the Roses) had come to the United States and made a fortune in real estate. Grandmother Emma Lawrence Jacob had contributed a handsome dowry to his ventures: her affluent father manufactured Broughams, four-wheeled, one-horse carriages originally designed by the former lord chancellor of England.

The maternal side of Caresse's family descended from William Bradford, who sailed on the *Mayflower* to Massachusetts and became its first governor, and from Robert Fulton, the inventor of the steamboat. Her great-grandfather was the first ambassador from the United States to Great Britain. Her grandfather, Walter Phelps, for whom her youngest brother was named (he was called Buddy), was a coal and iron magnate who as General Phelps led the Union Army to victory at the Battle of Antietam. The women of the family, all Daughters of the American Revolution, exerted on their family and friends a kind of domestic autocracy. True to her upbringing,

Mary Phelps, Caresse's mother, was bossy but benevolent, a combination of qualities Caresse learned to appreciate in retrospect.

Caresse did not regard her parents as wealthy. "My mother and father were never rich or even well off. They married on an allowance provided by my grandparents."[1] She liked to emphasize that her father, William, was cursed by a poor business sense and, unlike her mother, seven years his junior, was easily duped by sharper types. Nor was he capable of curbing his aristocratic predilections, so that "to eat duck without Burgundy or ices without champagne seemed utterly foolish, and not to eat them at all, impossible,"[2] especially when he was dining out with Caresse's mother. In Caresse's opinion, his high style of living was more a function of habit than choice. Although she eventually cast off the trappings of that precious world, Caresse remained at heart an aristocrat. Her assessment of her parents' position in the world as "not well off" suggests as much.

Indeed the Jacob family could have fit neatly into the society that Edith Wharton depicts in *The Age of Innocence,* not so much as objects for satire but as paradigms of a class. The family lived at 36 West Fifty-ninth Street, an elegant brownstone, and the present site of the Plaza Hotel. Caresse's grandparents lived seven blocks south; Rockefeller Center stands there now. This was a neighborhood where fathers left for their leather-desktop offices every morning, and where after breakfast, mothers gave the day's instructions to servants who kept home and heirlooms in pristine condition. Meanwhile in plush nurseries far removed from drawing and dining rooms, nannies and governesses taught the children to read and write English and French, and to learn the etiquette for passing through the shops of European dressmakers and haberdashers, the halls of Exeter and Andover, Harvard and Yale, and the reception lines at cotillions and charity balls. The atmosphere was serene; everyone was polite; no one aired dirty laundry. In her own words, Caresse grew up "in a world where only good smells existed."[3]

The Jacobs would leave New York City, first during the summers only to East Island on Long Island Sound, a real estate investment of her father's, and then in 1897 to a year-round expansive home in New Rochelle. Polly was five, her brother Len was three (born June 12, 1894), and Buddy was a little more than a year old (born March 1, 1896). Delighted with the move, Polly enjoyed idyllic days divided between acting out adventure fantasies in her own tree house and dressing up in her mother's discarded finery stored in the attic. At the end of the day, she awaited the return of her father, who found just enough time for a game of "catch the fox" before supper. Subsequent summers were spent on East Island or at Keyport, New Jersey, where Polly played hard on the family's private beach, unless her grandmother had come for a visit and she was required to sit demurely in a pretty pinafore while her brothers ran free. Clever and defiant, she often got into dangerous scrapes, feeling challenged rather than guided by the wisdom of her parents' rules and restrictions. Once, she nearly drowned because she seized upon a bait hook more than twice her size in order to catch minnows that were eluding her brothers.

There was as yet no formal schooling for Polly. When she turned eight, she was called upon to provide company for Ben Barnum, a first cousin on her mother's side, who lived a few miles away in Quaker Ridge at Windward. Because he was a fragile child, his parents had imported a private tutor from England, rather than have him attend boarding school as most boys in his circle did. The Barnums felt, however, that such an arrangement would be too lonely for the boy and proposed that Polly live at Windward Monday through Friday so that they could be classmates. Amenable to the idea, the Jacobs packed off their daughter to this grand home overlooking Long Island Sound, complete with stables, greenhouses, and cow barns. Pleased with this arrangement herself, Polly left her parents at the beginning of each week. She showed no signs of being homesick.

A room at Windward had been decorated exclusively for Polly, an indulgence usually reserved for adults in her family. Polly reveled in a special new status. She felt cozy, protected in her privacy but also courageous and ready for adventures real and imaginary. Twenty years later, Caresse would try to replicate this experience for her daughter: at home in Paris, she decorated a bedroom for Polleen in a similar fashion. However, Hart Crane slept in it a few days before her arrival and destroyed it during a drunken tryst with a young lover.

Polly was busy at Windward. Oddly enough, she had not been taught to read at home, but she made up for lost time under the instruction of Blanche Kimber, her English tutor. When the headaches she developed were blamed on constant reading, she was forced to engage in other activities, like dance classes at Dodsworth's (with its restricted clientele), and after a proper riding habit was made by de Pinna, riding lessons at Dorland's. As a member of the Saturday Club, she visited the country homes of people like Natica Nast, daughter of publisher Condé Nast. She was photographed by Charles Dana Gibson, creator of the legendary "Gibson girl," on one of these occasions, and another time, with the permission of her parents, at his studio. A drawing that he made of her was published in a 1904 volume of his work. Apparently, Polly took her turn as hostess to the Saturday Club at Windward even though beforehand she suffered "agonies of apprehension."

At Windward, Polly also practiced her skills at drawing, composing poetry, and writing editorials and society and sports columns (one on the joys of skating) for four issues of a "gazette" that she and Cousin Ben produced by mimeograph (actually Ben lost interest after two issues). Although for a good part of the time, Polly was separated from her immediate family during these early years, she was, nevertheless, happy, stimulated, and secure. Two decades later, when for the sake of saving her marriage she sent her own young daughter and son to boarding school, she drew on the good memories of her childhood to assuage whatever guilt she felt over the arrangement.

Meanwhile, the Jacob family moved back to New York City. At home on weekends, Polly attended St. Thomas Church at Fifth Avenue and Fifty-fourth Street twice every Sunday, preferring the aisle seat in the family pew because she had developed a crush on a choir boy who gave her a gentle nudge every time he filed by.

Eventually, Cousin Ben was deemed strong enough to withstand the rigor of living away from home and was sent to prep school. Polly returned to Manhattan in 1903. She attended Miss Chapin's in New York City for the next three years, a period marked by Yale and Harvard proms and golf tournaments. Her social skills were finely tuned by the time she was fourteen. She was reunited with the Barnums the summer of 1906 when they invited her to join them at a fantastically luxurious "camp" on upper St. Regis in the Adirondacks that they had rented. She easily fell into the convivial scene around her.

Among all the rich young men on vacation, Polly preferred Dick Peabody, whom she had seen win the Idem class race for junior skippers, an exciting event that showed off his ability to maneuver a small craft built for speed. A scion from a wealthy Massachusetts family, he was Polly's age, and in her estimation enormously attractive, full of "great charm and grace. His middle was slender, his hips were tightly set. . . . One of his front teeth was broken on the bias, and although he looked shy, he spoke with perfect poise and a fascinating indifference."[4]

Dick was equally smitten, and at a Saturday night dance, with "The Blue Danube Waltz" playing in the background, he proposed marriage. Still a student at Groton with four years at Harvard down the pike, he hoped that Polly would wait for him. Undaunted by the prospect of a seven-year delay, she accepted, a romantic, spontaneous gesture that at the time carried no formal commitment. They were, after all, too young for such an agreement to be taken seriously by either family.

A year later, when she was fifteen, Polly was packed off to Rosemary Hall, the exclusive girls' boarding school in Greenwich, Connecticut. Summers were spent either in the Adirondacks or on Long Island, in fashionable Southampton, swimming and playing tennis and golf. She became infatuated there with a neighbor's son, despite her fairly recent "betrothal." She was heartbroken once she realized that the boy had superficial intentions only. Winters at school left little impression on Polly. She did well enough scholastically, but she formed no meaningful friendships. Her greatest achievement was being named "the original American girl scout." On a tour of Rosemary Hall in the fall of 1910, Lady William Baden-Powell decided that as long as her husband was in Washington trying to organize an American Boys Scouts, she would initiate a girls' unit in Greenwich, Connecticut. Polly was chosen to wear the eagle feather and amulet because of her distinguished record in "self government." Nobody at the time, however, could fathom the depth of Polly's independent spirit.

During her years at Rosemary Hall, Polly was distracted by the suspicion that all was not well at home. She was acutely aware that no matter how much she loved her mother and father, the happy span of time spent with the Barnums had created a psychological distance between her parents and herself. Moreover, her father had moved to San Antonio, Texas, because, in part, he suffered from asthma and could breath more comfortably in the dry southern climate. His lack of business acumen—responsible for a doomed-to-fail housing project in New Rochelle and a community ranching proposal for a Texas town dead set against any kind of socialized structure—was not easily tolerated by his wife. As Caresse recalled, her own idealism came from her father, a perspective that her mother believed was nothing more than "crazy ideas."[5] The elements for a happy marriage did not seem to be present in the Jacob relationship. Perhaps Polly gravitated towards the Barnums to avoid watching her parents quarrel.

Thin and ill, Will Jacob surprised Polly with a visit to Rosemary Hall in the autumn of 1908. She was in her second year. Shocked by his frail appearance, she clutched him around the neck and gave him a "wild uncomprehending kiss."[6] That December, while staying at Windward for the Christmas holiday, she got the news that he had died in Texas. Twenty years later, she found an outlet for her filial emotions in *The Stranger*, her one attempt to write an epic poem.[7] Although he is not specifically named, in her autobiography, Caresse identifies the hero of this poem as her father.

Despite the poem's ambitious scope, and pretentious imagery, Caresse manages to capture her father's sense of romanticism and adventure in her portrayal of him as a god-like figure who, with a "silver bird and a bird of gold / . . . harnessed to [his] Chariot of Hope," urges a pair of lovers to seek their fulfillment, because it is worth any suffering to do so: "We must yield to the rain / Intentional kiss for intentional pain," he says. Following her father's death, Polly repressed in herself such ardent emotions, on some level suspecting that if she gave into them, she certainly would be unable to function in the socialite world that impatiently awaited her departure from Rosemary Hall, the world in which both her mother and the Barnums expected her to succeed.

Flourish she did. She lived with the Barnums at 11 East Forty-fifth Street at the Home Club, her first brush with communal living. (After her husband's death, Polly's mother had moved to Watertown, Connecticut, to be near her sons: at that point, Len was boarding at Westminster School in Simsbury, and Bud was a day student at nearby Taft School.) The residents of this home were Wall Street lawyers and their families, who thought to economize by living together. They could entertain one another by congregating in the evening for supper and conversation. The experiment lasted long enough to provide Polly with a ready-made group of girlfriends in whom she could confide plans and dreams. The young women's schedule of activities was far more glamorous than that of their parents.

The daily routine did not vary much for Polly:

> I danced at from one to three balls every night that season and my usual hours in bed were from four in the morning to noon. Marie's hours were four to ten. [Marie was her personal maid.] At twelve I was called and got ready for the customary debutante luncheon, and then again to and from Sherry's or Delmonico's (which we had quitted only a few hours previously), Marie walking eight paces behind up or down the Avenue. We always stopped at Huyler's for ice cream soda.[8]

Occasional lapses of etiquette occurred in this regimen when young men managed to escort young women home without a chaperone at the end of an evening's festivities. Delinquents were grounded, usually for a week or so.

The young women dressed to appear virginal yet enticing—fresh, beautiful, attractive, and innocent all at once. To this end, they were outfitted in restricting whaleboned corsets and corset covers that flattened their bosoms. Polly, who had a full bosom, especially hated the binding corset cover and one evening cast it off in disgust. She hastily designed a replacement with two handkerchiefs and some pink ribbons. When she showed her invention to the others the next day, they wanted one for themselves, and not long afterwards she realized that she might make a profit on her "backless brassiere."

For five dollars, a lawyer helped her apply for a patent for a "corslette," or "corset cover," an undergarment constructed without whalebone meant to be worn with low-cut, backless, or sheer gowns. The bra was pulled tight over the bust by tapes that crossed at the waist and tied in front. It came in one size only and was adjusted by drawing the tie-strings at the end of the tapes until it fit. The shoulder straps were elastic to prevent binding. According to Polly, the bra was suitable for playing tennis as well.[9] On November 3, 1914, the patent was granted. Several years later, she sold her product and patent for $1,500 (a large sum in those days) with the help of an old boyfriend who worked for Warner Brothers Corset Company in Bridgeport. Warner Brothers got the better end of the deal by far, but under the circumstances, Polly demonstrated the entrepreneurial gumption that Polly's mother had expected from Polly's father. She would later claim that, in part, her penchant for design came from "the loins" of Robert Fulton (1765–1815), from whom she was descended on her mother's side: "I can't say that the brassiere will ever take as great a place in history as the steamboat, but I did invent it."[10]

However, before Polly had displayed such creative business acumen, she was presented to the king and queen of England in the spring of 1914, apparently the only American to be presented that year. Dressed in a white brocade gown with a train eight yards long and with three white ostrich plumes in her hair, she missed not a step in the procession. A string of parties, balls, and hunting trips followed, and at the age of twenty-two, Polly had completed the initiation into her social world. However, in London she grew homesick, not so much for her family as for her longtime beau, Dick Peabody, who was now a Harvard student.

They had seen one another during Polly's frenetic social schedule, their so-called engagement still something spoken of between them alone. They had quarreled prior to Polly's departure for England, but now Polly wanted to know if he was waiting for her. Dick Peabody, it turns out, was also eager for the match, and in August 1914 on Long Island's North Shore, they formally announced their engagement. Their families were moderately pleased, although the Boston Peabodys regarded the New York Jacobs as social intruders. The Jacobs' reservations were of a different nature.

Dick Peabody was a heavy drinker who enjoyed escapades with young women he would meet at roadhouses outside Cambridge. His behavior was not radically different from that of his Harvard friends, but Polly and her family were apprehensive. Despite the hectic social schedule, the ball gowns and country weekends, Polly, like many of her socialite friends, saw herself as the patient Griselda, remaining pure so that she could reclaim her man once he realized he had wallowed too long in the mud. Her courtship with Dick, which resembled so many others in her circle, had a perverse dynamic fueled by the double standard for sexual conduct. Yet the first summer of their betrothal was such a happy one for them that Dick, rather than complete his final year of studies, decided to take a job in New York City so that he and Polly could marry soon thereafter. He secured a position at Johns-Manville, a buildings supply company, and the wedding took place at Windward in January 1915. Polly and Dick occupied the stone cottage hidden in a corner of the Barnum property, the established first home for newlyweds of their family and of their relations, including William and Mary Jacob.

Oddly enough, Caresse makes no mention in her memoirs of her mother or brothers attending or participating in the celebration. She only recalls that she wore a blue cotton dress preferred by her Uncle Will for the simple ceremony, changing into a white velvet-and-lace gown for the reception that followed. We are told that Reverend Endicott Peabody, distinguished headmaster of Groton and Dick's uncle, officiated, but we don't hear a word about Dick's parents (he was an only child) either. Neither family, perhaps, had resolved their trepidations about the union, and those attending did so out of a sense of duty more than a genuine wish to share in the couple's happiness. Caresse's failure to remark on her family's presence—whether they were there or not—suggests they did not provide the emotional support she might have appreciated at such an event.

The first year of marriage went smoothly enough: Dick commuted to Manhattan, and Polly stayed at home in Quaker Ridge, luxuriating in the independence that married life brought. She grew accustomed to heading a household herself, small though it was, and enjoyed the steady and loving attention of her handsome husband, who apparently kept his drinking under control. The good times lasted for about a year. When Polly learned that she was pregnant, the couple moved to town, into a small apartment on Fifty-third Street, because the ice on the steps of the stone cottage became too slippery and dangerous for her to negotiate. Polly gave birth on February 4, 1916, to a boy, William Jacob Peabody. Dick was thrilled to be the first father among his friends but soon resented the noisy infant who diverted his wife's attention.

Dick's own childhood had been circumscribed by his parents' insistence that he be silent and invisible. He knew no better than to expect that his child would be raised with the same constraints. Polly herself seemed to feel peculiar about the onset of motherhood, so embarrassed about her swollen shape that she burst into tears one evening in the New York Belmont Hotel because she had to walk across the length of the lobby before she could retrieve the coat that disguised her condition. As a new mother, she was offended when Dick spent more time celebrating the baby's arrival with his friends than keeping her company at home. He would flee the apartment when the baby fussed and cried, only to return much later four sheets to the wind.

Polly was in a predictable fix. She had led an exemplary life as a debutante. Indeed, she even demonstrated an extra share of spunk and ingenuity, given the fact that she could claim a U.S. patent to her credit. The whirlwind of excitement that marked her life as a budding socialite, the exacting details required of her behavior and deportment in boarding school as well as at the royal court of England and Long Island country clubs did little to prepare her for the postpartum depression into which she sank. She recalled no baby showers or friends' visits after Billy was born. Indeed, Polly was remarkably isolated for a person trained to flourish in public. She appeared to be on more intimate terms with the baby's nurse than with any friend or member of her family.

In April, when the weather warmed up, Polly, Dick, and the baby moved back to the stone cottage at Quaker Ridge. Frustrated by working for other people, Dick decided to start a shipping company of his own using Polly's inheritance from her father. The business, however, soon failed, and to dull his disappointment, Dick precipitously entered active military duty with Battery A, "Boston's crack militia," whose mission was to stop Pancho Villa's raids across the Mexican border. Polly and Billy were forced to move into the North Shore estate where Florence and Jake Peabody ("Florrie and Jake"), Dick's parents, were spending the summer. She chafed at their chilly welcome and regimented schedule, but she was trapped.

Less than a year after Dick returned from Mexico, he signed up to fight in the Great War. Billy was a year and a half old, and Polly was pregnant again. The day daughter Polleen was born, July 21, 1917, Dick was in boot camp in Plattsburgh, New York. He was granted a leave for that afternoon only. A week and a half later, and with her doctor's permission, Polly traveled by herself to New York City so that she could see her husband off to France. The two spent a raucous evening with Dick's fellow officers, certainly not what Polly had expected. Feeling morose, exhausted, and abandoned, she fled to Windward, the home where she had passed much of her youth. Mrs. Jacob was there to look after her daughter this time: Polly did not regain her strength until autumn.

Unfortunately, as a reward for pulling herself together, Polly faced a new exile with Dick's parents. She moved with her two children, one an infant, the other also still a baby, to the grand but dreary Danvers, Massachusetts, home of her in-laws, not far from the commercial town of Peabody. Once a star in society, Dick's mother was now a cranky recluse devoted to curing her various physical ailments. Mr. Peabody, a major in the army soon to be promoted to lieutenant-colonel, was getting ready to go overseas himself. His bellicose spirit permeated the household. The Peabodys provided little solace for their daughter-in-law, seemingly oblivious to the possibility that Dick could easily become a war casualty. To fill her lonely days, Polly joined the Red Cross. Her chief function was to operate the switchboard. She kept her sanity by writing to Dick daily and cherishing his intermittent replies.

None of the Peabodys took much interest in her children except Great Uncle Jack, who was known to the world as J. P. Morgan, and who was Dick's uncle and godfather. (Coincidentally, it was Morgan who bought the East Island estate that belonged to Caresse's grandfather.) Other occasions of meager relief included luncheons with another "war widow" and visits to Dick's grandparents in Salem, which boasted the Peabody Museum, filled with treasures "collected" from around the world. Grandma and Grandpa Mouse, as they were fondly called, doted on the children of their only grandson, showering them with exotic and antique toys and dolls.

By midsummer of 1921, Polly was out of Danvers. Without advance notice, Dick had returned from France and was stationed near Columbia, South Carolina. He summoned his wife—his nickname for her was "Pittans"—to visit him even if he could see her for only an evening. With money borrowed from the children's nurse and Uncle Will Barnum, she managed to meet him twenty-four hours after his call, dressed as a proper captain's wife, the big bow at the back of her navy blue taffeta dress, and the pond lilies in her small Panama bonnet small concessions to her own individual style. The couple spent a passionate but hilarious night sleeping in a slit trench on the maneuver grounds because there was no hotel space for them.

Within the next two days and on her own, Polly found an apartment for the family atop the official residence of Columbia's mayor, a bachelor who did not need the space. She took the train back to Massachusetts, gathered up Billy, Polleen, and their nurse, and brought them south to their new sweet home, swelteringly hot as it was. Polly furnished the attic where she and Dick would sleep "at floor level with Oriental taste and missionary expenditure. That division of the American army might just as well have been stationed in Malaya. I even found a Canton-Carolinian cook."[11]

Although she felt happier than she been for a long time, all was not well. As playful a life as they managed to lead those next few months, the possibility that Dick would return to France loomed in the background. When the war did end that November, they settled in Boston, to a cozy house that they rented on Marlborough Street in exclusive Back Bay. But Dick was no better suited for domestic life after the war than he had been before, and the family started to fall apart.

Once Dick realized that he could no longer escape to the Mexican border or to France, his spirit crashed. It was not a question of whether or not he loved his wife and children, if his eagerness to live with them in South Carolina is any indication. But for Dick, fighting a war had made it more difficult than ever to adjust to the permanency and predictable routine of domestic life. Caresse was sympathetic to his suffering. Unlike her husband, who during the war had tasted again the freedom of bachelorhood, she had reconciled herself while living with her in-laws to the restrictions that accompany motherhood. She was quite aware of the disparity in their sexual activity during this period: "I had lived like a nun while he was away, but in France it was hard to live like a monk."[12] For Dick, the contrast between his life as the brave army captain, a recipient of the Croix de Guerre no less, and as an unemployed father living on a family allowance was devastating.

Dick rejected the life at home by drinking too much. His personality changed the more he drank, and "there were awful moments that had to be weathered" during the winter of 1919.[13] Polly hired a nurse to supervise Dick, but she knew that such an arrangement could be only temporary. Dick's father was still overseas and his mother preoccupied by her own illnesses, so Polly turned to Uncle Jack. Although he was intricately involved in negotiating a private loan to the French government, he carved out a half hour for her at the Morgan Library in New York City. He suggested that Polly find someone to care for the children, round up one of Dick's close friends, and go to the Morgan camp in the Adirondacks so that Dick could dry out and break his depression. Polly got Charlie Codman, a longtime buddy, to help her. He was Billy's godfather and had been a member of the Lafayette Escadrille in France, where he had learned to love French food and wine.

Uncle Jack's plan did not work. Dick and Polly got to camp a few days before Charlie, and feeling sorry for himself because no one would give him a drink, Dick refused to budge from his great easy chair in front of the fire. After Charlie arrived, he was persuaded to venture out into the beautiful winter world. Together, the three took long sleigh rides, went ice-fishing, and generally tried to romp around like carefree youths. But what sounded like a winter paradise—once back indoors there were delicious meals, a superb library, a pool table, and so on—felt like hell for Dick. After he bribed the boy who delivered the mail to sneak in a bottle of whiskey for him, the situation turned nasty. Charlie had to get back to Boston but feared for Polly's safety if he left her alone with Dick. With the assistance of Junius, a son of Uncle Jack, Polly closed up camp, and took her husband home. By the time spring came, Dick had been committed to a sanatorium to cure his alcoholism. Once again, Polly and her children were on their own. She was twenty-seven, Billy was five, and Polleen nearly two. Polly had been an exemplary war widow. Now she would discover a different kind of independence.

2

Polly Meets Harry

To all concerned, Polly appeared to be a solid member of Boston society. Her years at Miss Chapin's and Rosemary Hall were put to good use on Beacon Hill. Even though her modish short haircut and pink nail polish gave away her allegiance to New York City fashion, her etiquette withstood the closest New England scrutiny. She was given the respect and sympathy owed to a proper Boston matron when Dick was sent off to hospital; it was understood that the problems of the Peabodys should not be discussed beyond the walls of this exclusive neighborhood.

So accepted was Polly by her community that Mrs. Henrietta Grew Crosby—the matriarch of one of Boston's most patrician families invited Polly to chaperone a Fourth of July celebration for her son Harry and his friends. A student at Harvard College, Harry had turned twenty-one recently (June 4, 1920). After he was graduated in June 1917 from St. Mark's School in Southborough (where he had distinguished himself by winning the Punctuality Prize),[1] he volunteered for the American Field Service Ambulance Corps in France. In September, after the United States declared war on Germany, he enlisted as a private. He was sent back to the ambulance corps, but he was no longer a member of "The House of Lords," as less well-heeled volunteers of the 71st section referred to Harry and his prep school friends.

Harry was an energetic patriot who believed no self-respecting healthy young man could stay at home once the United States formally entered the war. A good, popular boy, he wrote to his parents faithfully, read his Bible daily, and maintained his chastity. He wondered if any of his girlfriends would be waiting for him when he returned. However, once he experienced the true savagery of war at Verdun, like so many others, he threw away old definitions of heroism. As a volunteer, he was given the gruesome assignment of carrying barrels full of amputated arms and legs from the front. After he enlisted, his unit had reputedly evacuated more than two hundred wounded from the battlefield in a day. The most devastating experience for Harry was a brush with death. His ambulance was decimated by a shell that exploded close to the field dressing station: he survived; his friend Spud Spaulding spent six months in the hospital recovering from the shrapnel that had torn open his chest.

Harry accompanied Spaulding to the hospital room in nearby Beaulieu. When he got back to camp, "he was seen running, more or less in circles, fifty yards in diameter, lap upon lap, without purpose or destination."[2] Confronted by the reality of war's consequences, Harry no longer believed in the ideals he had been once taught to treasure, and the comfortable harness of decorum was broken. He took pride in receiving the Croix de Guerre shortly before the war ended—ironically, he had thought at one point that it was worth being wounded to get one. However, by the time he returned to Boston in April 1919, he was alienated, dissipated, and possibly shell-shocked.

Under pressure from his family, Harry had enrolled at Harvard that very same spring as a "war degree" candidate, which would enable him to be graduated in June 1921. The majority of his coursework was in French and English literature, but he kept away from literary-minded students and such college-sponsored publications as the *Advocate* and the *Lampoon.* A chief interest of Stephen Crosby in sending his son to Harvard was to continue the tradition of Crosby membership in the A.D., one of Harvard's two original "final" clubs for seniors. (The other was the Porcellian.) The exclusive private organization took its name from the first two words of Alpha Delta Phi, the fraternity chapter at Harvard that gave up its charter in 1860 after its members failed to concur on the course of the Civil War. It took three nominations to get Harry elected, because unlike his fellow classmates, who drank and partied as long as no one was watching, Harry carried out his antics and excesses without a shred of self-consciousness. He had learned to drink during the war and saw no reason to curb the habit at home.

Many of his friends began to regard him as a "public nuisance." As Geoffrey Wolff reports, they noted "with no little revulsion that he had painted his fingernails black. Harry's clothes were correctly cut, but uncommonly stark: he had already begun to dress almost entirely in black, double-breasted suits. He quickly won himself a reputation for self-indulgence and carelessness."[3] Some people saw him as charming, but odd (he inserted a black cloth camellia in the lapel of his black suits), nervous; generous, but contemptuous of people who yielded to the restrictions of etiquette and conventional mores.

His parents were painfully aware that he was trying to come to terms with the war experience in his own fashion, and they patiently hoped that he would conform as the other boys had. They gave him an extravagant allowance and sporty cars and made as many social arrangements for him as he would allow. The July Fourth party in 1920 was one of those events.

Polly had not been impressed by Harry Crosby. She had seen him only once, not long after he had returned from France, looking dissolute and seedy, too thin for the unkempt uniform he was still wearing. Alone with her children, bereft and bored—Dick Peabody was still in the hospital—Polly eagerly accepted Mrs. Crosby's invitation to chaperone Harry's Independence Day party. When he called for her on the evening of the party, his demeanor surprised her. Meticulously groomed, he was wearing plus fours, an unflattering garment on anybody in Polly's estimation, but a well-tailored one nevertheless. Harry was fair-haired, small-boned, of medium height. His good looks were the delicate kind; the natural curve of his lips formed a near pout, but his gaze was intense and impossible for Polly to deflect.

Harry had embarked on the evening's activities more with a sense of moody obligation than cheerful anticipation. Polly watched him walk slowly, awkwardly from his shiny Lancia to her doorstep.[4] He was roused when he saw that his chaperone was the pretty stylish woman he had noticed a few weeks earlier pushing a baby carriage at a local charity bazaar. (He later told Polly that he assumed she was too young to be the mother of the child in the pram.) The party was supposed to be informal and fun, starting with supper at a new roadhouse. Oblivious to all decorum, Harry devoted himself to Polly for the entire meal, ignoring the young woman with whom he had been matched for the occasion. Afterward, in a feeble attempt to fulfill her charge as chaperone, Polly rode with some others in the group to the next activity for the evening, a tour of the Ferris wheel, roller coaster, and rifle range at the amusement park on Nantusket Beach. But, as soon as Polly stepped out of the car, Harry dragged her away to the Tunnel of Love. She felt the rush of being desired and gave up the premise of resisting Harry's overtures.

For the present, the fact that Polly was six years Harry's senior and a married woman with two young children seemed not to matter a thread to either of them. While their boat burrowed through its darkly lit course,

Harry told Polly that he loved her, and she let herself believe him. Polly and Harry were two attractive and vivacious people of similar background, neatly primed by circumstance to find one another irresistible: Harry eager to shock and defy a society he no longer trusted, Polly ready, whether she had known it or not, to break the lonely and sterile route that her married life had taken.

Harry had no qualms about pursuing Polly after that heady evening, but Polly was more sensitive to her position. Indeed, she had far more to lose than he if she allowed herself to make a habit of one evening's lapse in propriety, which could have been explained as her way of handling Harry's well-known erratic behavior. Although she insisted that they keep their sexual yearnings for one another in check, she fell under what she called Harry's "spell": to know him was a "devastating experience." They were frequent companions that summer of 1920, arranging dates at the beach and drives along the countryside between Harry's summer classes at Harvard and the nap times of Polly's children.

Just as their affair began in a fantasy playland, it continued under the pretext that there would be no conflict between the purity of their infatuation and the power of society's dictates. For a few brief weeks, they plotted their future believing they could make everyone happy including parents and spouse. That August (1920), Harry sailed for France with his college roommate who had also been an ambulance driver during the war. Together, they had planned a tour of the battle sites, a trip that might help them confirm the legitimacy of their postwar trauma. It was too late for Harry to cancel the trip. Polly accompanied him as far as New York, where they spent the night together at the Belmont Hotel. She saw no point in holding back. Apparently Harry lost his virginity that night. The lovers were reckless, but they felt they were right to be so. "For the first time in my life," Polly recalled, "I knew myself to be a person."[5]

However, once autumn set in, Polly could no longer ignore the reality of their situation. Dick Peabody had recuperated sufficiently to return home and, after a few strings were pulled, landed a job in a Boston bank. With a small allowance from Dick's parents, who were eager to be relieved of living with their grandchildren, the family moved into two floors of a three-story tenement building on River Street. Although it was in a poor section of the Back Bay, it was close behind the Crosby residence on Beacon Street, where Harry was living with his father while he continued his studies in French and English literature at Harvard. (His mother and sister Kitsa were wintering in Switzerland.) Polly tried to give Dick the attention he required without much success.

While Dick established a routine at the bank, Harry dominated the scene, a gallant and appealing devil of a suitor. Every week, he sent to the River Street apartment crates of flowers from Mrs. Crosby's hothouse garden, which helped mask the stench from the fish store on the ground floor of the building. Many afternoons, instead of studying at the library, he dashed over to Polly's, bringing piles of books and toys for Billy and Polleen, who were now seven and four. Polly and Harry would drive to the shore, catching the setting sun as they crossed the Salem Bridge.[6] Polly felt drawn into "his golden orbit, as metal to the magnet by his magic."[7] She was not inclined to end the affair.

Dick retaliated by volunteering for the fire department, which precluded any possibility of sex between them: in order to coordinate his movements with the regulars, he installed a fire gong by their bedside. The fire chief did not permit the overly zealous newcomer to stay on very long. Once again, Dick withdrew into whiskey, afraid to confront his faltering marriage, or to openly acknowledge that he had never relished domestic life with Polly in the first place. Harry was on the offensive, Dick in sulking retreat, and Polly wrenched between real if detached affection for her husband and overwhelming desire for her lover.

That spring of 1921, Polly broached the subject of separation. Although divorces were unheard of in the Peabody family, Dick capitulated without rancor. If a reconciliation could not be reached within six months, the couple would dissolve their marriage. Mrs. Jacob insisted that Polly avoid Harry's company during the trial separation. If Polly pursued her affair with Harry, if she did not at least pretend to drop him, she risked permanent disbarment from society in Boston and in New York. Her sin was adultery, her crime stealing from the cradle, and Polly had only begun to sense the magnitude of her transgressions.

From her mother's home in Watertown, Polly wrote Harry that she could not see him again until December. Thwarted for the time being, Harry responded with a long letter filled with hope, optimism, and declarations of love. He was sure that they could hold out since Polly was "the same as God" to him, and their love was "so deep and pure and true that it is bound to be everlasting."[8] A few years later, he would express such adoration of her in impassioned, earnest (and outmoded) verse:

> Each soul must have its God so I choose thee
> To take the place of sun and moon and stars,
> To be for me the odour of the rose

> To be for me the turquoise of the sea,
> To be for me the nectar in the jars
> Of magic love, in Thee I seek repose.[9]

On a more practical plane, he also allowed that six months apart from him might give Polly a chance to gather strength after a tumultuous year—besides coping with the stew of emotions over Dick and Harry, she had also nursed Billy through a severe case of measles.

Polly decided to spend the half-year's respite determining whether or not she could earn enough money to support herself and the children—although neither her mother nor Dick's parents expected her to. Harry kept reassuring her that they would have all the money they would ever need. But Polly was not yet ready to exchange dependency on one man for dependency on another. Indeed, before legally separating from Dick, she had shamelessly exercised her entrepreneurial skills by running a two-woman sweatshop on Washington Street in Boston. On May 10, 1920, intent on peddling the strapless brassiere she had invented more than seven years earlier, she had filed a legal certificate with the Commonwealth of Massachusetts, which indicated that she was a married woman conducting a business, the Fashion Form Brassiere Company, supported by funds separate from her husband's banking account.[10] Unknown to family and friends, the tiny factory also served as a convenient locale for trysts with Harry.[11] Although Polly wrangled a few orders from several major department stores (she had not yet sold her patent to Warner Brothers), the product did not sell. At Harry's urging, she shut down the operation.

By the summer of 1921, Polly no longer felt at home in Boston. She was ready to leave once she understood that the friendships and family relationships that she had cultivated for seven years were only as solid as her marriage to Dick. She was regarded as more than a nuisance now, deflecting Harry Crosby's attention from the young women of his set. The Crosby and Peabody families were distraught, all too eager to exonerate their sons by placing full blame on Polly. These two fully grown men, recipients both of the Croix de Guerre, were perceived as victims. Harry had threatened to kill himself if he could not eventually marry Polly; and Dick could not stay sober. Yet Boston society—including Harry's friends, who thought they knew what Harry wanted better than Harry himself did—was all too ready to welcome the men back into the fold as soon as they were ready to return. Polly was shut out.

Later, during an account of her family background in *The Passionate Years,* Polly confessed how well she knew what it meant to be part of the family tree that was considered "distaff." She had grasped the full implications of that word when her trial separation was announced in local gossip columns. The position and status she had gained as a young matron in Boston was on a contingency basis only, never to be hers in her own right. Harry and Dick owned their names and family crests forever, whether they wanted them or not, no matter how obviously they defied the dictates of their community. Polly was an object of scorn among her former friends, and an embarrassment to her family for tampering with established modes of conduct.

Polly moved to New York City, where she was able to live rent-free in the empty Park Avenue apartment that belonged to her Uncle Will Barnum. She left Billy with her mother in Watertown and shipped off Polleen to a friend in Topsfield, Massachusetts. To the great consternation of her mother, who made Polly promise not to tell the relatives of her plan, Polly decided to try acting. With all the role-playing she had already engaged in for Boston's Back Bay, she figured that she had probably acquired enough experience for a screen test. It was hardly a respectable choice for a woman of her breeding, but she figured that she might as well see if she could turn a profit with her good looks and feisty disposition.

Harry was appalled that she could aspire to be a movie actress, a vocation he considered degrading. He preferred that she try her hand at writing the short stories and plays she told him she had dreamed about. He saw no reason for her to concern herself with financial matters since he expected them to be married within the year, enjoy a honeymoon in Europe, and proceed to create a life of domestic tranquility near Boston. "Can't you see the pretty Mrs. Harry Crosby driving down to the station with the kids to meet me? God it will be Heaven."[12] Perhaps for him, but not for Polly, at least not for now, and never in Boston.

Through a girlfriend from long-ago days at Rosemary Hall, whose father had been an attorney for David and Myron Selznick in their early days as filmmakers, Polly wrangled her way as an extra into a film. She adopted the stage name Valerie Marno, which to her ear sounded better than any combination of her maiden and married names, and which would help keep the promise she made to mother that her stab at acting would remain a secret. She spent a miserable first day on the set as "a one-girl welcoming committee" kissing by the hour other extras who played World War I soldiers home from the front.[13] She was thrilled when offered the opportunity to stand as double for a leading role that called for the actress to ride horseback. But a family emergency called her to Boston before she could demonstrate a skill she had acquired early during her exclusive education.

Polleen had been rushed from her friend's Topsfield home to Massachusetts General Hospital because her face had swollen up. A local doctor had diagnosed it as mastoiditis, which in those days called for a disfiguring operation. Refusing to believe that Polleen had fallen so terribly ill, and horrified that she would be scarred for life, Polly caught the midnight train from Penn Station hoping to prevent the operation. At her request, the family pediatrician met her at the Boston hospital and, after consulting with other doctors, determined that an alternative course of action should be taken—the injection of an antitoxic serum. It turned out that Polleen had been bitten by a poisonous insect, and within twenty-four hours, she was nearly back to normal.

Polly and Dick, who had rushed to the hospital at the start of the crisis, brought Polleen home to the River Street apartment above the fish market. Polly felt triumphant and credited her "maternal hunch" for canceling the operation. And yet within hours of tucking her daughter safely in bed, she was on the train headed for New York. Dick was behaving like the perfect father, Polleen the dear and suffering child, but Polly cut off any possibility of a family reunion. She did not trust Dick's transformation to last, and Polleen's assured recuperation was left in the hands of the hired housekeeper. Polly's nurturing instinct was put on hold. Back in New York, she learned that she had lost the part she had been offered because the studio could not reach her. The next opportunity came with the condition that she accompany Myron Selznick to Paris.[14] She rejected the proposal.

Fed up, Polly left the city in September, her bid for independence funded by the world of entertainment stymied. She was going to divorce Dick and marry Harry because she wanted to realize the belief that she had harbored all along: "once one had known rapture, security is not enough,"[15] or not worth working for anyway.

The road to ecstasy proved to be a lonely one. In order to obtain a divorce, Polly had to establish residency in New York State. She went to live in tony Millbrook for eight weeks. She stayed at its well-known inn, which was filled with people up for the hunting season. Some of her family and her family's friends were there on and off and did their best to bolster her spirits. To add to the fiasco of her summer, she came down with so severe a case of tonsillitis that she had to undergo a tonsillectomy, then a traumatic procedure for an adult.

Rather than play the tawdry role of an outcast divorcée, she wrote passionate letters to Harry, which totally delighted him. "I love to feel you love me so much and absolutely depend on me and want to be close in my arms all the time," Harry wrote to Polly from the Apple Trees, the Crosby estate in Manchester-on-the-Sea, Massachusetts. Acting like a mother hen deprived of her duties, he hovered over her from afar, exhorting her to rest properly and eat well. He told her how much she needed him. "You never can be terribly independent, (thank the Lord), as you're too feminine and are not strong enough to battle in the world all alone."[16] He also tried to pin her down to a wedding for the following September.

The divorce proceedings went smoothly after Polly's lawyer convinced her that child support was vital even if she did not want alimony for herself. It is not clear whether guilt or a private code of ethics prevented her from claiming a share of assets accrued while she and Dick were married. By the time the divorce was granted, Dick Peabody had forgiven Polly's infidelity. He had made a new friend who happened to work at Shawmut National Bank (where Harry worked after he was graduated from Harvard in June 1921) and assured Polly that he was reconciled to the divorce as long as it helped Polly in her search for genuine happiness and contentment. However, he was concerned about losing Billy and Polleen and missed celebrating Christmas with them because they were with Polly at her mother's house in Watertown.[17] He was still struggling with alcohol, but his gestures on behalf of Polly and the children were generous and well meant, and he promised Polly that the children would inherit the Peabody trust. The divorce was granted in February 1922, two months before Polly turned thirty.

The true nature of her newly granted freedom hit her with full force. For one thing, she had very little money of her own, although it was a condition of the settlement that Dick Peabody would reimburse her for the money she had lent him for his failed shipping business during the second year of their marriage. She chafed over the realization that she had been bred to marry affluence, and could not boast a single marketable skill. She loved Harry and knew that he was determined to support her, but it was essentially with his family's money. She had already experienced what it was like to be a wife and daughter-in-law living under such circumstances. She remained apprehensive about Harry's commitment for the long run and was not persuaded by declarations that he would be a good stepfather to Billy and Polleen. Nor was she convinced when he insisted that he was capable of reforming his ways— especially drinking and gambling— if he had good reason to.[18]

Distraught that Polly refused to marry him immediately, Harry went on a six-day binge in March, after which he quit his job at the bank. His parents grew anxious. At first they hoped that Harry's affair with Polly would blow over, but they soon acknowledged that his devotion was steadfast. For help,

Henrietta Crosby turned to the same person whom Polly had sought out when she was trying to get Dick Peabody to stay sober: J. P. Morgan, Uncle Jack, Harry's godfather, who also happened to be Dick Peabody's godfather.

Like everyone else connected to Boston society, Morgan knew about the affair between Harry and Polly, but he was one of the few people who did not condemn Polly. Indeed, he had maintained a real affection for her ever since he found her languishing in the Peabody home in Danvers while Dick was overseas. Morgan arranged for Harry to fill a position at Morgan, Harjes et Cie in Paris, which suited Harry just fine. Polly would not be far away. Her solution to the impasse they reached had been to take flight, not back to New York City, but to her Aunt and Uncle Elin's estate in Ardleigh Park near London. Mrs. Jacob took over the care of Billy and Polleen.

Desperate for rest, Polly basked in the attention and pampering she received from her English cousins, the Elins. When Harry called May 1, 1922, from Paris to tell her he was coming over to get her, she feigned surprise. Although the Atlantic ocean now separated her from the scrutiny of Boston eyes, she remained sensitive to rumors that she had followed Harry to Europe to keep him in her snare. To the dismay of the Elins, who assumed that Polly was on the verge of repudiating Harry, she and Harry returned to Paris together, where they took up residence at the Regina, a small hotel on the Right Bank.[19]

These few months may have counted among the most fulfilling that Harry and Polly spent together. Certainly they could not have been more carefree. As numerous accounts have made clear, Paris in 1922 was a perfect place for a pair of American lovers with enough money to indulge their passions with abandon. For Polly and Harry there were additional advantages: no gossips, no children, no parents, nor any other reminders that they had left behind a good deal of emotional baggage. In a sense, they had stepped out of time, where the consequences of their actions were suspended, the people who judged them or needed them or wanted to change them turned silent and invisible.

Although Harry assumed his position at the Morgan bank a week after he brought Polly back to Paris, the couple enjoyed all the sights of the city. Harry had little intention of taking his work seriously and would act impulsively, catching a taxi with Polly to the Normandy coast, hopping the Simplon Express to Venice, where the two registered at a small hotel overlooking the Grand Canal as the Count and Countess of Myopia.

Their bubble burst, however, in late July when Polly learned that Harry had been flirting with a young woman from Boston. In Paris, the girl's mother had called on Polly in her hotel room, and shamed her into agreeing that she should leave town so that Harry and her daughter would have the chance to make a proper marriage. Polly left Paris for Ardleigh Park soon after and booked passage home on the Cunard ocean liner *Berengaria* for early August.

Distressed by her precipitous leave taking, Harry promised Polly that he would lead the straight and narrow path, suitable punishment he thought for his infidelity. Instead, he gambled, drank, looked for one-night stands, generally behaving like a souped-up version of an unreformed Charlie Wales in F. Scott Fitzgerald's "Babylon Revisited." Polly's conduct was puzzling. Angry as she was, she wrote a loving letter to Harry from Ardleigh Park: "I have again that terrible ache in my heart and I have lived with loneliness for you all day. I want so to feel your arms about me, kiss your dear mouth and give myself to you completely."[20] From Paris, Harry responded by telling her that he never knew he could be as happy as he had been with Polly in Paris and reminisced about their lovemaking, "the culmination of all bliss . . . absolute perfection."[21] By this time, their term of endearment for one another was "Bunny."

From the *Berengaria,* Polly responded to Harry's missives with happiness and longing. She had achieved a kind of resolution: "I realize you love me. I feel full of courage and very rested and well and the world seems to be with me, almost at my feet so to speak. I don't mean this selfishly, or conceitedly at all, but I do feel that our love has been justified."[22] In certain passages, Polly sounds conspiratorial, pretending that their summer together had remained a secret: "There is a certain satisfaction in getting away with a thing so beautifully," she observed.

Yet in her memoirs, Caresse recalled that she was so furious with Harry that she stayed with her mother in Watertown just long enough to see her children before taking off again, this time to catch the last of the season in Newport. She instructed her mother not to forward any letters from Harry. However, some correspondence between Harry and Polly does exist during the period, mostly about how repentant Harry is feeling, how the two resolved to cut back on their drinking, how much they loved one another, and how Harry could not bear the thought of spending the winter without her. There was also some talk about a business venture that Polly was concocting in which she would sell French toiletries in New York (it never happened).[23] Ever the considerate (and persistent) suitor, Harry sent presents to Billy and Polleen, for which Polly was most appreciative.

In retrospect, Caresse may have wished she had played harder to get. She wrote in several places in her autobiography that from the beginning, Harry exerted a kind of mysterious power that made her yield to his wishes. "My love for Harry blinded me like the sunrise," she conceded, happily enough.[24] She was not concerned with a particular moral issue here, since on numerous occasions she stated that she was proud to be the rebel, the nonconformist. Nor would she allow her family to lay the blame for her divorce from Dick Peabody on his alcoholism. She had left her husband because she was in love with another man, and she allowed no one to badger her into claiming otherwise.

By changing the "facts," by giving her readers the impression that she considered breaking off with Harry permanently, Caresse may have been trying to save face. But she was also creating tension in a section of the memoir that lacked momentum. She had to wait for Harry to make his move. For all her defiance of social convention, once she returned to the United States, there was nothing Polly could do about the impasse she and Harry had reached. She gives her side of the story a keener edge when she alleges that she refused to read six cables and several letters. Her omission that she responded to other, unmentioned cables and letters from Harry suggests that she was eager to bolster an independent image.

Harry's bad habits grew worse after Polly's departure. Determined that Polly alone could rescue him from self-destructing, he intensified his efforts to win her over. On August 30, 1922, he cabled that he was sailing home to get her if she would promise to marry him. Her return reply was a simple "yes" (a word she would later claim to articulate with particular pleasure). Before he left he talked to Lou Norrie, his American roommate at the Metropolitan Hotel, his "official" residence in Paris, usually rotten, as Harry would put it, with Boston tourists. Norrie was sailing for New York on September 1, and Harry, desperate for cash, bet him that he would get stateside first. With a hundred dollar loan from the Morgan bank, he booked passage in steerage on the *Aquitania.*[25] On September 9, Polly met him as he passed through customs. She had been concerned about Harry's health and safety on the hardship crossing. But he was fine, having for part of the voyage sneaked up to first class, where he gambled and dined on caviar.

Harry wanted the wedding arranged without delay, and Polly rounded up her brother Len to serve as witness at the city hall ceremony. That evening, the newlyweds met Norrie as he passed through customs to collect the $100 Harry had won. They took a room at the Belmont after Len stood them to a champagne toast. But the next forty-eight hours of married life turned into an ordeal.

Polly summoned her mother to bring the children from Watertown to New York since they would be sailing for France on the 11th. The officers at

Morgan wanted Harry back, even though it had become quite obvious that his position was a sinecure, a sad joke for all concerned. But for the present, the bank job was not the problem; Harry's family was. Harry wanted his mother's blessing before they sailed and telephoned her at his sister's home in Chevy Chase, Maryland. Kitsa, recently married herself to Robert Choate, a classmate of Harry's at St. Mark's, informed Harry that his mother was too upset to come to the phone. Not one to be refused, Harry announced that he and Polly were coming down on the midnight train in order to make amends.

Breakfast was grim. Robbie Choate was the only person civil to Polly; mother and daughter barely acknowledged her presence. The couple returned to New York that afternoon, Harry dispirited, Polly humiliated. Polly's mood lifted when she found her mother and children waiting for them at the Belmont. Here were allies whose first allegiance was to her. Harry bolted and did not reappear until sailing time the next morning. This was not the first time that Polly had watched a man take flight at the sight of children—Dick Peabody had pulled more than one disappearing act in his weaker days—and she coolly handled the situation. She never asked Harry where he had been and counted on their journey across the ocean to freshen the foul air that hovered over them.

As Caresse herself would later say, her role on board was to be "a spectacular bride and a devoted mamma, a sort of saint and sinner combination."[26] The children had a nursemaid, but she was a queasy sea traveler and passed the major part of the crossing in her cabin. The children turned to their mother for amusement, which she provided at the expense of more regular visits to the beauty salon. She was relieved that Harry refrained from commenting that she did not look her usual chic self, or that he pretended not to notice the difference. Nor did he object to the mounting figure on the children's restaurant bill, the result of their voracious appetite for caviar. Billy and Polleen dined earlier than the adults, and Harry's chief concern was that they behave while he and Polly enjoyed the cocktail hour. Polly went along with the extravagance, grateful that Billy and Polleen could be bribed so easily.

As soon as "the family" arrived in Paris, however, Polly discovered that her juggling act would require more expertise. While Harry made up time at the bank for his unscheduled holiday, Polly searched for suitable quarters. They could not last long in their small, shabby rooms at the Hotel de l'Universite, which offered only a modicum of privacy. It was hardly a setting that Harry would abide. After making some inquiries among Harry's colleagues, they moved to the Right Bank, to a suitable if ordinary apartment on the rue des Belles Feuilles, close enough to Morgan, Harjes and Company so that if he chose, Harry could take luncheon at home. But Harry did not want to see the children at lunch or apparently at any other time.

To please Harry, Polly divided the apartment in two. The door from the front hall to the nursery was permanently closed, and the children used the rear staircase to get outside. When Polly wanted to see her children while Harry was home, she went out the front door, down one flight of stairs, and up another to the back door that opened into the kitchen. Polleen and Billy could count on gaining entry into Polly's boudoir twice a week when the linens were changed and they were permitted to jump up and down on the bed. Other times they stationed themselves in the kitchen near the servants' signal panel waiting for the four rings that meant their mother was expecting them.[27]

On at least one occasion, Polly did not succeed in her mistress/madonna role. Ellery Sedgwick and some other friends from Harvard were in town, and Harry invited them to the races at Longchamps. The day was cold and rainy, and claiming that she was tired, Polly declined to go along. She changed into a dressing gown that her children remembered her wearing at home in the States and called them into the forbidden salon to play. Their cozy pleasant afternoon was abruptly interrupted when Harry and his friends appeared, intent on dragging Polly out to the Cirque Medrano. Harry was embarrassed by the domestic scene before him and shooed his friends away before they could say a word. This time, Polly thought her short-lived marriage was over until Harry appeared three days later bearing toys for the children and an alluring negligee for her. But it was obvious that other living arrangements would have to be made unless Polly was to be left alone with the children, a situation with which she was already too familiar.

3

How Polly Became Caresse

In the spring of 1923, Polly replaced the children's American nursemaid with a French governess, Mme. Doursenaud, and sent them all off to live in a Versailles pension. Billy was seven years old, and Polleen not yet six. Polly and Harry moved out of their bourgeois quarters to a summer sublet: a romantic apartment with a balcony overlooking the Seine on the Île Saint Louis. Here they played out their own version of life as young marrieds against the background of a Paris summer. Every weekday morning, Harry dressed in business attire for his token position at the Morgan bank. Polly slipped on a bathing costume. They climbed into a red canoe tied to a willow tree on the quai d'Orleans just beneath the apartment and paddled down the Seine to the place de la Concorde. From there, Harry could walk to the bank in minutes, while Polly maneuvered back by herself, a sight apparently appreciated by Parisians looking down from the bridges above. During business hours, Polly, fully dressed, would go marketing along the charming back streets of the island, sharpening her French as she made her way through the various shops and stalls. The couple was isolated, as they wished to be, and intense in their love for one another. They pretended that they could behave like newlyweds forever.

At the end of the summer (1923), they took another luxurious sublet for a few months before they found a house on the rue Boulard behind the Cimetière Montparnasse. It was a small, narrow building, one of seven on the block, and Polly went on a small decorating binge that would set their home apart from the others: the creeping vines were cleared from the windows, the exterior whitewashed, yellow striped awnings installed on all windows, and mirrors mounted on the walls. Slipcovers for the furniture were designed in mauve, pink, and yellow, and the doghouse in the garden was "painted like a Chinese pagoda." The place resembled a "giddy toyland house."[1]

For the children, however, it was no paradise. Again Harry would not tolerate their proximity—a thin wall separated Polleen's bedroom from theirs—and Polly looked around anxiously for a solution. It took the form of a six-by-eight-foot tool shed out back for Polleen. With some ingenuity Polly turned it into a nursery, a "fascinating playroom." Heating the shed was problematical; yet Polleen managed to stay in good health that winter. Her sense of well-being was another matter. Once Harry found Polleen sitting outside on the steps taking off her shoes because, she told him, she did not want him to hear her footsteps when she came indoors. Amused by her candor, Harry carried her off to the Ritz bar and got her drunk on champagne.[2]

Billy faced a different kind of exile: a series of exclusive boarding schools. When in 1925 he got to Le Rosay in Gstaad, he was eight years old, the youngest in attendance. Polly feared that the boy might feel abandoned, but she risked his sense of security so that she could relish her life with Harry. She tried to convince herself that pushing Billy out of the nest at so tender an age would toughen him up, do him good in the long run. To this end, she also refrained (with difficulty) from overtly demonstrating much affection for him. In his letters, the child hardly sounded like a cast-off. He wrote that school was nice; he boasted of the two gold stars he received and described the different sports he played. He was a well-bred, amazingly sophisticated eight-year-old, beginning more than one letter with the hope that his mother was having a good time. In one instance, he wanted to make sure that she was not feeling "anxiouse" because one of his letters ended up in the laundry instead of the mailbox.[3]

The domestic scene under control, Polly and Harry were drawn deeper into the richness of Parisian life. Because Harry was still working at the bank, Polly had more time on her hands than she had expected and decided to follow her artistic impulses by taking instruction in sculpting. The first school she tried was Julian's Academy off the Champs-Elysée. She left after two days because no nude models were permitted in classes for women, a firmly established prohibition that had just begun to break down at the turn of the century.

Her second experience provided a greater challenge. The instructor insisted that she come for a private lesson in his Vaugirard studio in Montparnasse.

As soon as he closed the door, Polly recognized his intentions. She knew that Harry would arrive in time to rescue her if she could outmaneuver the wolf beneath the artist's apron. In order to slow down his advances, she suggested that she perform a striptease as a prelude to posing for him in the nude. By the time she had undressed and arranged herself, Harry was ringing the bell outside. She knew her man. Harry had a history of being punctual and had arrived at the arranged hour. She quickly put her clothes back on and fled.

Finally she found the perfect mentor, Antoine Bourdelle, who worked out of the famous studio Atelier de la Grande Chaumiere. Had she wanted to study painting, she would have been instructed by Fernand Léger. It was there that she met artists working in the surrealist mode: the Greek sculptor Apartis, designer and sculptor Isamu Noguchi, painter and sculptor Alberto Giacometti. At the center of the Paris bohemian community, they represented a group far more eclectic than Polly and Harry met at more familiar spots like the Ritz or Fouquet's. Although Bourdelle thought Polly was more of a painter than a sculptor, he regarded her work as "tres fine and tres fraiche." She needed to work more on balancing her proportions.[4] Her bust of Harry demonstrates that she took instruction seriously: its near flawless symmetry is offset by the strength and integrity of his individual features.[5]

The Crosbys were also drawn to the people who were invited to dine in the elegant rue de Varenne home of Walter Van Rensselaer Berry, the cousin of Stephen Crosby, Harry's father. Born in Paris in 1859, Berry, like many in his family, attended St. Mark's and Harvard. An international lawyer, he served as counsel to the French and Italian embassies in Washington, D.C., and sat on the International Tribunal in Cairo between 1908 and 1911, after which he returned to Paris. His friends included such distinguished and talented people as Edith Wharton, Paul Valéry, Jean Cocteau, the Count and Countess of Noailles, Marshal Foch, Marcel Proust, Henry James, and Sinclair Lewis. His house resembled a small museum with magnificent works of art and a vast library. Berry served as mentor to younger writers and artists, a relationship he relished.

Both Harry and Polly were devoted to this elegant patron of the arts, and Harry regarded him as a surrogate father. To the initial puzzlement of Stephen and Henrietta Crosby, Berry encouraged Harry to give up his masquerade as banker after Harry confessed to him that for some time he had dreamed of writing poetry. Polly herself was writing poems already. Harry submitted his resignation at the very end of 1923. Through Berry's influence, Harry immersed himself in Flaubert and Huysman, and the symbolist poets, especially Baudelaire and Rimbaud, whose biography Berry hoped Harry might write.[6] The two men had found much to talk about since Harry had become intrigued by the rituals of sun worship, just as Berry was an expert on Egyptian culture.

Polly got along with Berry and liked to think that she had displaced Edith Wharton as hostess at his dining table.[7] Of course Wharton would never have described her relationship to Berry in such a manner. Polly thoroughly enjoyed the occasional rivalry that erupted among guests at the Berry table: "a puree of wit, beauty and bitchery, for I think Cousin Walter believed as I do that a woman without a touch of bitchery is like milk without Vitamin D."[8] Perhaps Wharton and Polly felt each provided that nutritional supplement. In any case, Polly had a keen sense of the graceful, erudite, and "wicked" impression that Berry made on his guests, his cultivated charm gracefully wrapped in a body that "could have been exhibited as a sculpture by [Lipchitz]." Not everyone was as enraptured with Berry's sangfroid—two of Wharton's close friends, critic Percy Lubbock and art historian Bernard Berenson among them. But Polly held him in such high esteem that she considered him, along with her father and J. P. Morgan ("Uncle Jack") heroes of their generation.[9]

Actually, Polly cultivated a lifelong adversarial relationship with Edith Wharton and recollected her as a thoughtless, greedy, pretentious person. When Walter Berry died in 1927, Polly claimed that Wharton pulled a "Grab Act"[10] because she interpreted Berry's will as stipulating that his library be left to Wharton. Polly also describes in hilarious fashion the events that followed Berry's death. Armored with a bottle of brandy and a volume of Baudelaire, Harry served as the family member required to witness the Berry's cremation. Afterwards, the Crosbys drove the ashes to Versailles, where Wharton had arranged a solemn ceremony, complete with burning incense and huge silver candlesticks ("I supposed then that Mrs. Wharton's church was very high indeed"), that would precede burying the ashes in her garden: Wharton had "determined that the ashes would be happiest reposing at the end of her garden, underneath the rambling roses, where 'dear Walter' used to sit." This was against the law as Paris police made clear to all, having trailed the Crosbys to find out what they planned on doing with the urn of ashes. Berry had told Polly that he wished his ashes to be "chucked away," but nobody could fulfill those last wishes of his. However, Wharton's diary entry for that day makes no reference to a police chase, although she did keep the ashes in a velvet covered box beside a large wreathe and pietà set on a Persian carpet for twelve days while Harry scouted for a final resting place.[11]

Why did Caresse choose to treat Wharton with such contempt during one of the most painful times of Wharton's life? Perhaps from the start, she envied Wharton's literary success. Perhaps she was the loyal wife bristling at Wharton's accusations (as reported by Benstock) that Harry Crosby was inexperienced, unmanageable, and a "half-crazy cad." Caresse's report is the better story, irreverent and as inaccurate as it may be. It gives us some indication of her inner turmoil, and her need to promote a rakish public image of life with Harry.

By 1924, Stephen and Henrietta Crosby had reconciled themselves to their son's marriage and welcomed Polly as a full fledged daughter-in-law. That winter, Henrietta Crosby visited the couple in Paris and treated them to a holiday of skiing at St. Moritz in February. (Billy Peabody wrote a touching note to his mother while she was there, thanking her for his birthday present, apparently not disturbed that she wasn't with him to celebrate it. "I hope you are having a nice time and ski and the coating is good," he added.[12]) This was the first of several trips that the Mrs. Crosby, Harry, and Polly would make together. Polly had better success with her second mother-in-law than she had had with her first, and a lasting friendship was established, bound by genuine warmth and affection. More reserved, but once won over a faithful advocate, Mr. Crosby also visited the couple, and took them on a trip to Vienna.

Disappointed as they may have been by the direction of his career, Harry's parents saw that marriage to Polly provided much needed stability. However, Harry's eccentricities in dress would grow. He solemnly vowed "to the day of his death" to wear only dark blue suits with an artificial black gardenia in the buttonhole and a black knitted tie, and to always go without a hat.[13] He would indulge his appetite in gambling, and his expensive tastes in food, drink, opium, books, gifts, and horses. An obsession with death, dating from his war experiences, dominated his thoughts day and night. But as far as Harry's parents could observe, Polly was in love with him and devoted to his well-being.

How real was Polly's dedication? According to the tone and vibrancy of her recollections of these first years with Harry, she often sounded ecstatic, thrilled to be abroad in Paris with a man she considered brilliant and daring. They had embraced life on their own terms (albeit with Crosby funds) and firmly pledged to art and literature, were latter day decadents sanguine rather than cynical, ready to expand and explore the realms of consciousness.

Polly chose to flaunt society's dictates, in frivolous ways as well—in their apparel and forms of hospitality—that could be shocking but not hurtful (to former husbands and parents, for example). Friends were invited to dine in their bedroom at small tables set up around an enormous bed where they were perched, Harry dressed in an elegant smoking jacket, Polly in a negligee. There was no room for children on their agenda, but they adored dogs, especially show dogs that could place in competitions. Their most beloved was Narcisse Noir, a beautiful black whippet who was their constant companion. He wore a jeweled collar, and the nails on his paws were painted gold. Polly's own precious ornaments were another matter. In the fall of 1924, Polly sold two of her Cartier diamond bracelets so that the couple could buy a Corot. She also shared her husband's contempt for the more philistine aspects of their upbringing.

Sexual fidelity, however, was one convention that Polly might have observed had Harry been willing. His first serious encounter with another woman during their marriage was with Constance Crowninshield Coolidge Atherton. A member of the Boston Coolidge family, Constance was in Paris during the fall of 1923 after living in Peking with her husband, Ray Atherton, from whom she was recently separated. Polly met her first, at a luncheon party in a restaurant near the Madeleine. Polly thought she was dazzling, "an exciting pagan,"[14] and invited her for a day at the races with Harry. Instantly drawn to her beauty and her spirit, Harry proposed that they have an affair. He assigned Constance the name of the Lady of the Golden Horse because she adored horse racing and often wore a bracelet with a gold charm shaped like a horse in homage to her passion. Harry would continue to give special royal titles to his lovers, of which there were many. But Polly alone achieved the rank of Queen, specifically "Cramoisy Queen," his crimson star of noble passion.

Polly's outward acceptance of the liaison was self-effacing. "All that season the Lady of the Golden Horse was tangled in my hair—all through the Paris years she was my most formidable antagonist, but I could not help immensely admiring her."[15] Polly showed an angrier face to Harry. "[She] has revolted against anyone sharing with her the queenship of my heart," he wrote in his diary November 5, 1923, "and she is tragic and unbalanced and I am nervous and erratic."[16] Nevertheless, the Cramoisy Queen willingly identified Constance as the Lady of the Golden Horse when seven years later, she edited Harry's diaries. Jealous she may have been, she did not want to leave the impression that her marriage was ever truly at risk.

Polly herself had a share of love affairs, but her approach seemed more casual than Harry's, at least in the beginning. For Harry, attraction to a woman took on an occult status, as though acting upon it was more a spiritual crusade than a romantic or sexual conquest. He believed that had the right to have sex with anyone he wanted; he neither explained nor apologized. He wrote to his mother about his liaisons (and of Polly's), not to shock her, or seek her approval, but to keep her informed. While dining out with Polly and friends, he was capable of abandoning them all to approach a woman sitting at a table across the room.[17] For Polly, taking on lovers created a sense of comradery with her husband, and she seemed to enjoy the adventure of it. But she played reactor more than initiator. If her husband was going to misbehave, so would she to keep things equal. Above all, she did not want to appear hurt or reveal that she was breaking more rules than she had expected to when she married Harry. She wanted to believe that women who committed adultery did not suffer broken hearts.

Her affair with the Spanish painter Manolo Ortiz, for example, began when she and Harry were invited to tea by the Count and the Countess de Beaumont, friends of Walter Berry and great collectors of ancient and modern art themselves. At this particular gathering, a Picasso hanging over the fireplace stimulated much discussion. Ortiz, who was a friend of Picasso's, was escorting a beautiful Russian aristocrat now exiled in Paris. Harry wasted no time becoming friendly, and Polly surmised that she had lost her husband for the evening; her rival's "domineering and sophisticated charm were too perfect for me to vie with."[18] Polly left the party with Ortiz, and a warm and lively relationship ensued intermittently until 1930.

However different a role lovers played in their lives, and no matter how bitterly they argued, neither Polly nor Harry wanted to dissolve their three-year-old marriage. Clearly they had rejected middle-class morality back home, and in Paris, they discovered all the encouragement (and indifference) they required to carve out their own rules of conduct. They compartmentalized their lives, perhaps suspecting that if they did not, all they had suffered to become an extraordinary couple would have been wasted. Trying to understand his feelings about Polly, Harry wrote in his diary: "Elle est a la fois ma femme et mon enfant."[19] Doubtless he had some sense of the peril a woman with Polly's history would face if he were to abandon her, and if she lost the strong backing of her family.

Nor did Harry and Polly easily adjust themselves to temporary separations. Polly and Polleen spent most of June and July in the States visiting the Jacobs in Nantucket. The contrast between their staid routines and her newly acquired foreign customs proved too much for Polly to handle gracefully. She complained to Harry of endless boredom, and also of her mother's overreaction to Polly's hairy armpits and legs, visible to all sunbathers, who were scornful of the European custom.[20] Harry responded with lovelorn letters. "I worship you," he wrote. "I have just been kneeling before your miniature which I have arranged in a sanctuary in my desk and before which I burn incense while repeating Our Prayer over and over before God."[21] The prayer went like this: "Thank You O God for Pollee. I pray Dear God that our Love shall be immortal. I pray Dear God that we shall have a perfect marriage together. God bless us and take care of us. Grant O God that our two souls shall be together as One in Heaven. Forever. Amen."[22] Harry beseeched Polly to pray for them as well, but there is no indication that she did.

However unorthodox their way of life, they both appreciated bouts of domestic tranquility, and Polly was the one who made them happen. "The house without [Polly] was dirty and desolate, now it is bright and delicate," Harry wrote in an August 9, 1924, diary entry soon after her return. With Polly back from the States, there were no more cold meals and no more "untidiness," as Harry put it. Polly rounded out the comforts of home that summer by painting the bathroom and by gardening. Harry's perverse interest in reading about suicide blossomed. Polly quietly continued to write poetry, as she had done since their early days as a married couple while Harry was still working at the bank.

Polly did not share Harry's fascination with death and suicide, although she agreed to sign a contract with him that they would die together, and have their bodies cremated and the ashes buried in the Cimetière de l'Abbaye, a graveyard in the Bois de Bologne whose maintenance was eventually abandoned by Paris authorities. (Scattering their ashes over New York City was another possibility that they considered.) When thirty-two volumes of the *Encyclopedia Britannica* arrived in November, a gift from Harry's mother, the first entries Harry consulted were the stories of love eternal, as in Hero and Leander, Pyramus and Thisbe, and Tristan and Yseult.[23] He regarded his marriage to Polly in this same tradition, a chilling thought since these lovers were all doomed to die early deaths.

Harry's fervent insistence that their love was immortal sustained Polly even as his bizarre and unpredictable behavior bewildered her. From the medieval city of Carcassonne, where Harry stopped with his mother on their travels through southwestern France and Spain in March 1925, he wrote Polly that he was overcome with passion for her, and that someday they had to make this same trip together.[24] (The two had made a trip to North Africa that past winter.) The freshness with which he expressed his devotion here and at other times concealed his growing morbidity. At times, Polly felt that she was being courted all over again. Indeed, when she alluded to the same legendary but doomed lovers who were so important to Harry in a poem entitled "One

Way Like the Path of a Star," she declared "The death the others chose shall lead us far; / Immortal is the path to Love's Bright Star." The tender if jejune innocence of this perspective is remarkable for a thirty-three-year-old mother of two who had walked miles on the other side of respectability.

For the summer of 1925, Polly and Harry rented a house perched on a cliff in Etretat, on the Normandy coast. It had once served as a tiny fort and from a distance looked "like a cube of Domino sugar on a hill."[25] But it was large enough to accommodate Billy and Polleen without hampering Harry's need for privacy. Polly went with the children to the beach in the morning and spent the afternoon in an elegant gown and jewels at the Etretat Casino, playing "for the house." The children occupied themselves with their new puppy, Corydon, until he was run over by a bus while standing in the road, barking fearlessly to warn his young masters of its approach.

In the evening, Polly wrote poetry. She drew on her observations of the local people, like the French count who shopped daily in the local fish market. For him, "choosing the right fish was like a daily aperitif."[26] Polly wrote a prose poem called "Constance Martel" about a woman she often saw on the beach combing the sand for fish discarded by the fisherman.[27] Polly had no illusions about the kind of life this woman led: "You'd think her back would surely crack to see her bending double; you'd think that thirty francs a year were hardly worth the trouble." Yet she saw in her a certain authenticity of being, an independence that enabled her to find some joy in her meager lot.

Friends and acquaintances in Paris also gave Polly incentive to write. She composed a poem about Walter Berry that revealed the nature of their friendship, how they liked to gently tease one another, mocking the inane conversation that often takes place in formal dining rooms. Another, a sonnet, is a tribute to renowned sculptor Antoine Bourdelle: "strong seeker after elemental truth / High priest of Beauty, striding toward the goal." It is a good if overblown example of how much Polly respected her teacher and a man who devoted himself to art.

Her most ardent compositions were for Harry, expressions of her passion for him and her eagerness to share his romantic quest. She was not always confident that she could follow the convolutions of his private search. In "Harry" she writes:

> Your way lies through the bright mists of morning,
> I fear to lose you in their shining depths;
> So swift, I bathe in moonlight, and hair flying
> I follow you, with winged shoes for my steps![28]

She sounds slightly mad for a sophisticated woman of the twentieth century. Determined to follow his dangerous course, she idealized their union, glossing the unfaithful acts as she tried to keep her spirits up.

Polly labored to maintain the illusion. In retrospect, she chose to blot out the reason why in Etretat Harry was not as much a presence as he might have been. In one account she pushed back Harry's resignation from the Morgan bank three years and said that the responsibilities of his position there kept him in Paris Monday through Friday. In another recollection, she marks Harry's resignation from the bank with this summer in Etretat after he saw how steadily Polly was turning out poems.[29] In actuality, Harry was engaged in a number of affairs. The most unsettling for Polly was a passionate liaison with a fourteen-year-old girl whom Harry referred to in his diary as Nubile, and whom he had met at Etretat. She would be invited to tea and join Harry on the roof of the villa where he sunbathed nude. Polly would take off to the casino or visit Paris without telling Harry when she would return, arousing in him no small degree of anxiety. She allowed future readers of Harry's diary to understand for themselves the events of that summer but chose to present another reality for herself more closely aligned with the fantasy of a relationship that she and Harry presumed to enjoy.

A picture of Harry and Polly taken at Etretat shows a young couple, arms linked as they stand on the lawn of a gracefully landscaped cliff-side garden. Uncharacteristically dressed, Harry is sporting white slacks and sweater, the dark tie adding little formality to the casual appearance he presents. Holding a parasol to protect her from the sun, Polly wears a low waist dress and pointed buckled shoes fashionable for the twenties. Harry stands forward, staring straight at the camera. Polly turns slightly towards Harry, looking up to him with shy adoration, a traditional wife's pose. Except for the one taken on their wedding day in 1922, there were not many other photographs of them like this one. Harry would later say that it was one of his favorite pictures.[30] Ironically, Polly and Harry look like a stylish but rather conventional couple of their day. Despite the peculiar twists and turns their marriage was taking, here they presented an ideal model for posterity.

Steadfast to her inner calling, Polly by now had written enough poems for a book and paid a call to Comtesse de Noailles, the well-known and flamboyant literary figure and member of the Legion of Honor. Polly had met her at Walter Berry's. The visit was wild, interrupted by the constant ringing of the telephone and announcements that still another gentleman was waiting for an audience with the comtesse. She advised Polly to read Victor Hugo and Shakespeare and to write poetry that would be accessible to the average reader.[31] Polly seemed less inclined to take her advice than to enjoy the sight of this popular novelist and poet holding forth from bed, like Proust, cushioned against a phalanx of lace-covered pillows, her hair quite undone.

Polly and Harry arranged to have her poems privately published by Albert Messein in Paris, who had first published Rimbaud, a favorite of Harry's. (Nearly four years later while on a trip through the Middle East with Polly and his mother, Harry would have the uncanny experience of discovering Rimbaud's name carved into the stone of the Temple of Luxor in Egypt.) Although she and Harry had agreed on a title for the volume—*Crosses of Gold*—they were stumped when it came to identifying the author. Polly liked none of her present names: in her estimation, "Polly Crosby" was unpoetic, "Mary Crosby" too bluestocking. Her family name felt as if it belonged to someone else. Harry could not abide "Polly" because it reminded him of the days when she was Mrs. Peabody, and suggested that they think of a new name for her.[32]

One of Harry's latest interests had been the macabre works of Edgar Allan Poe, a logical outcome of his reading Baudelaire and other French symbolists. At this moment in time, Harry was intrigued by Poe's fascination with puzzles and acrostics and decided that Polly's new name should form a cross with his, and that for the sake of alliteration begin with a "C" as in Crosby. After consulting a dictionary and running through all the possibilities, including Constance, which Polly vetoed immediately, they still could not come up with anything. Harry said he wanted the name to sound like a caress, and they suddenly had it, Frenchified with an "e" at the end, a symbol that their true life together had begun in France.

Polly was perversely delighted by the inevitable disapproval that her new name would provoke in both Harry's friends and family and her own. Her mother and brothers were never to address her as Caresse, though Harry's family, after a flutter of derisive reactions, accommodated themselves. What Caresse particularly enjoyed, however, was the knowledge that the friends they would make in Paris from now on would know her first off as Caresse, beloved wife and published poet. She was on her way to feeling that she had her own identity, but oddly enough, she was not disturbed that Harry owned the copyright to her first book. The cross that their names now formed was an emblem of their merged identities, and that cross would appear in all subsequent publications, both Caresse's and Harry's. The frontispiece for this first volume of Caresse's poetry, which appeared opposite the cross of their names, is a pastel watercolor by Daniel-Gerard entitled *Daybreak: Île Saint Louis,* the site of Polly and Harry's fanciful summer of 1923.

4

A Woman of Many Trades

In October 1925, Caresse and Harry rented an apartment that suited them perfectly: three spacious stories in 19 rue de Lille, an elegant eighteenth-century townhouse in the Faubourg St.-Germain. Crystal chandeliers hung from the ceiling, delicate wood paneling lined the walls, and high windows faced two streets and an interior courtyard of small, manicured gardens and statues. At the gate, a plaque marked that the French statesman, lawyer, and activist in favor of the Republic, Charles Floquet died there in 1896. Harry fantasized that someday a plaque would commemorate their passing away together in this house. Less morbid, Caresse felt that she had landed in another scene right out of Proust and preferred to imagine that their distinguished predecessor had been Baron de Charlus.

The muted grandeur of their new home gave the Crosbys a sense of security, especially since for the first time they had signed a long-term lease. With the monetary exchange rate only getting better, they spent a good deal of money furnishing their large home. Their one mistake in decorating took the form of a massive and ghoulish headboard, which they dumped off the Pont Neuf the day after they moved in. Caresse's small family trust was spent on the children. For household expenses, she received a 2,000-franc allowance from Harry, a good part of which she turned over to Louise, their *cordon bleu* cook who had also fathomed the techniques for creaming codfish and baking brown betty. The Crosbys delighted in serving the exotic American cuisine, along with caviar and champagne, to their Parisian friends and to visiting Boston relatives yearning for New England fare.

They made no attempt to live on a budget and patronized the most expensive shops for their elaborate wardrobes. Harry ordered his silk buttonhole gardenia from an exclusive rue de la Paix tailor. Caresse bought her hats at Patou and dresses from Tolstoy's. On formal occasions, she wore a gold cloth evening suit by Vionnet which had a short skirt, an outfit considered chic in Paris but unacceptable by their "various titled cousins and aunts" living in the Faubourg. Caresse and Harry blew their biggest amounts on the races, seeming not to care whether they won or lost. They gave little thought about providing for the future, in part because Caresse had agreed to Harry's wish that together they would put an end to their lives (the method as yet undetermined) on October 31, 1942, a date Harry had chosen because astronomers had calculated that on that day the earth would be in perihelion, closest to his beloved sun.

Occasionally, Harry would register remorse over their contempt for property and, on one occasion, insisted that Caresse's uninsured jewels be placed in a safety deposit box. Over her objections—she was not the type who lost things and wanted her "treasure" at home for the wearing—Harry gathered them up in a bag and set off in a taxi for the bank. On the rue de Rivoli, he stopped the driver so that he could step out and chat with a cousin whom he saw crossing the rue Castiglione. After waiting a short while, the driver took off with the jewels. That was the last Caresse saw of a pearl necklace, three diamond bracelets, three ruby, sapphire, and diamond pins, pear-shaped pearl earrings, and more. She cried briefly over the calamity, but she was too engaged by the general program of life with Harry to mourn the loss for long. He would have been annoyed if she had made a scene. For her next birthday, Harry bought her a sapphire ring.[1]

They seldom deviated from their daily routine: their life "was divided into riotous hours of entertainment and secluded hours of work."[2] Every morning at eight, they were served tea and croissants in bed. They shunned the newspapers, a reminder of the mundane events of the world they fought to forget. After breakfast, Harry would seclude himself in the third-floor library to write poetry. Caresse would visit the children in the nursery and review with the cook and housekeeper what would be required of them for the day—if there would be guests for luncheon or tea or what delicacies were missing from the pantry. Harry would work until noon, and another two hours after lunch.

In her own room directly below his, Caresse composed enough poems to fill six volumes of verse by 1931, one of them, *Graven Images*, for Houghton Mifflin in 1926. Walter Berry had encouraged her to send her poems to the Boston publisher on the grounds that Amy Lowell's death in 1925 had created new room for "a lady poet from Boston."[3] Caresse did not regard herself in the same class as the renowned imagist poet—as she put it, she was quite content to rhyme "dove" and "love." She was more comfortable casting her own literary endeavors in light of Harry's, eager to indicate that she depended on him to provide her with a working schedule. They were both full of praise for one another's work, but Caresse was convinced that Harry was "training for the big race."[4]

Caresse and Harry continued to observe their preference for taking their meals in bed at day's end when they were home for the evening. Harry would read aloud to Caresse until one in the morning. Often she fell asleep under the bright lights that Harry required. Nor did she ask any questions when Harry slipped out of the house in the middle of the night for places unknown. She was content, it seems, that he always returned with the sunrise.

One of her few gestures of protest over these escapades occurred during this period, shortly before they moved to rue de Lille. Harry believed that Constance, his "Lady of the Golden Horse," needed the protection of a police dog and, without her consent, purchased and arranged delivery of a very large one. When she refused to accept the merchandise, the salesman promptly brought the dog to Caresse, who believed at first that Harry had purchased the creature for them, without bothering to inform her. As soon as she discovered that the dog was intended for Constance, she banished it.

One of Caresse and Harry's wildest adventures occurred during their first year at the rue de Lille. They had befriended a group of architecture students taking life-study drawing classes at l'Academie des Beaux Arts, located at the end of the street. After treating the entire thirty-two of them to a glass of wine at an impromptu housewarming party, Caresse and Harry were invited to join them in June at the Quartre Arts Ball, an annual Dionysian costume affair. Fueled by champagne, the Crosbys and students were among the most frenzied participants. Harry sported a red loincloth and a necklace of three dead pigeons and carried a bag of snakes. Caresse wore a flimsy chemise and covered her bobbed hair with a massive turquoise wig. Both she and Harry stained their skin with red ochre. Caresse went topless and, a huge success, was hoisted on the shoulders of ten students who paraded her around the Salle Wagram for all to see. Her outfit won first prize, twenty-five bottles of champagne. Caresse thought the event "harmless," although she knew that her young, upturned bosom was her victory ticket, that here was an event where "a firm breast was worth a thousand lifted faces."[5]

Harry beat her home that evening, after being roused by some friends who found him "ossified . . . sprawled against a pillar."[6] He brought three girls along for the purpose, he subsequently explained, of helping one another scrub off red dye. Caresse was too drunk herself to care but remembered that seven people occupied their bed that night. Caresse cultivated a habit of casually casting off the distress that Harry's escapades may have caused her. Years later, she would allow herself to acknowledge, usually in some subtle fashion, that on occasion she was unhappy. She developed, for example, an aversion to pink bubble bath, a reminder of the scene she encountered upon her return home from the Quartre Arts Ball.

Indeed, the poems Caresse composed during this period emphasize her unqualified devotion to Harry. Lines such as "With you I have known beauty in the night / And watched with you the loveliness of dawn / Come stealing to our window down the lawn" hardly suggest the chaos that often marked the hours they spent together. The couplet that closes this sonnet, printed both in *Crosses of Gold* (1925) and *Graven Images* (1926), tidily wraps up the romantic conceit: "With you I have known all love's radiant hours / And gathered them like fragrant, dewy flowers."[7]

Her idealization of their circumstances can only be matched by the heroic stature she assigns to Harry himself on the first page of *Crosses of Gold.*

> **H**eaven has given thee strength, wit, integrity,
> **A**ngels, Beloved, might envy thy soul,
> **R**ich is thy spirit in fairness and charity,
> **R**are charm is thin and a dearness untold,
> **Y**outhful and passionate, Heart of pure gold.

Caresse had grown up in a family that prided itself on showing the world that, for them, life was working out in the best possible way, that whatever decisions they made were the right ones. Caresse did not rebel against this ethos of her upbringing. She had put her best efforts forth to be Harry Crosby's wife. She was not going to admit to any suffering, or express regret, even in a memoir.

With her children, however, Caresse acknowledged her divided loyalties. She wanted them to act like a family at least occasionally, but Harry could not play the game. She asked Harry to accompany them on summer trips to the United States, but he balked. Boston reminded him of bad times, and visits to the grandparents were oppressive, especially when he saw how much fuss they made over Billy and Polleen. For Harry, life in the United States epitomized vulgarity: the more he stayed abroad, the better. Because Polleen and Billy now attended boarding school a good part of each year, Caresse was determined that they would spend every Christmas together, even if that meant in a hotel. Harry wanted no part of these cozy reunions, even if they were in France or Switzerland, and made it plain to Caresse that he would engage in flirtations during her absence.

Christmas of 1926 was particularly horrible: at the last minute, Harry weakened and appeared unexpectedly on Christmas Eve at the Palace Hotel in Gstaad, where Caresse had managed to secure only cramped accommodations. He found her in bed, her face smothered in cold cream and her hair set in curlers. It was a scene reminiscent of "the family" arrival in Paris, when Harry begrudged Caresse the rainy day she devoted to Billy and Polleen. Rather than disappear immediately for three days as he had in Paris, he dragged Caresse on a walk through the snowy forest. She could not match the pace he kept, but he pretended not to notice. By the time they got back to the hotel, her knees were scratched and bleeding. Then he left. But Harry and Caresse were together again a few days later to celebrate the New Year together as always, this time with a luxurious vacation in and around Florence. Caresse continued to play this balancing act over the next three years, insisting on seeing her circumstances in the best of light, even if she declared that "[her] feet were in the Ritz and [her] heart in the nursery."[8]

There was no conflict, however, about their mutual devotion to literary matters, especially Harry's poetry. Rather than depend upon approval from editors at commercial presses, the Crosbys started a press of their own, Editions Narcisse, named after their beloved whippet. Caresse designed the colophon, a gracefully poised racing dog transfixed by reverie. The enterprise was renamed the Black Sun Press in 1928 in deference to Harry's favorite color and symbol.

They were far from alone in aspiring to be independent American publishers in Paris. By 1925, Sylvia Beach had published James Joyce's *Ulysses* for Shakespeare and Company. In addition to publishing his own prose, Robert McAlmon oversaw Contact Editions works by Mina Loy, Ernest Hemingway, Marsden Hartley, William Carlos Williams, Mary Butts, Emanuel Carnevali, and Gertrude Stein. Bill Bird's Three Mountains Press had published Ezra Pound, Ford Madox Ford, William Carlos Williams, Ernest Hemingway, and Robert McAlmon. (Black Manikin, Plain Editions, Carrefour, and Hours set up shop later.) Caresse and Harry were not close associates of these publishers, but they had a keen sense of what books they wanted to produce. Together they walked the streets of the Left Bank seeking a printer with a handpress capable of producing exquisite books, like the Brussels edition of *Heloise and Abelard,* the *Boussle des Amants,* and the Bodley Head edition of John Donne's poems.[9] Their books were going to be works of art, printed on beautiful paper, in graceful font, with original illustrations—drawings and watercolors—when possible.

They found their printer, Roger Lescaret, in his small and grimy shop on rue Cardinale, not far from their apartment. Although he was far more used to printing business cards and announcements, indeed he had never printed a book before, Caresse and Harry's enthusiasm for their venture was contagious. He accepted their offer, with the warning that they would have to spend a good deal of money. The first book was Harry's *Sonnets for Caresse.* Caresse and Harry chose the paper, designed the outlay, picked out the typeset and binding, and were thrilled with the results. They thought the book had a Shakespearean look.

As they planned future projects, a division of labor developed: Caresse was in charge of copy, format, and traffic, while Harry selected the writers they would publish. Both husband and wife continued to chose the paper and binding. Slipping into a secondary role was an easy arrangement for Caresse. (Would she ever have admitted that it wasn't?) She believed her taste was nearly identical to Harry's. She never imagined that there would ever be a conflict.[10] Caresse was especially happy to discover that by taking some back streets, she could easily reach rue Cardinale, so in the early days of the Press she regularly stopped by two and three times a day to watch the progress of each book. Eventually she had her own tiny office on site.

The Crosbys exhibited considerable acumen in developing their list no matter how random their decisions were about who they would publish. In a sense, they were guided by the same rebellious yet well-heeled spirit that had drawn them to one another. As a result, during the first three years of the Press, they published "new" writers like Ezra Pound, James Joyce, D. H. Lawrence, Archibald MacLeish, Ernest Hemingway, Kay Boyle, and Hart Crane and reprinted current favorites of Harry's, like Oscar Wilde, Edgar Allan Poe, and Laurence Sterne. They were also able to function as a vanity press for special friends with literary aspirations, like the young and future Earl of Portsmouth Gerard Lymington. One of Caresse's lovers and a lifelong friend, he was ready to accompany the Crosbys (and was welcomed by both Caresse and Harry) on whatever fresh escapades beckoned. No matter the author, Caresse and Harry took great care in turning each book into a work of art.

Lescaret had to buy a larger and more efficient press to accommodate the growing Black Sun audience. But he never moved into a more commodious working space, nor did Caresse herself mind the cramped, dingy quarters, flies buzzing around. She seemed to enjoy the adventure of it. As accustomed as she was to luxury, she did not complain if forced to do without—if it was for a good cause. Art and literature were always worth the sacrifice. She was establishing a pattern for the rest of her life.

After founding the Black Sun Press, Caresse and Harry assumed a more professional status in Parisian literary circles. Although they continued to indulge in sex, drugs, and drink, and gave little indication that they wanted to dispel their well-earned rakish reputations, the Press somehow legitimized them. Stimulated by the knowledge that he was assured publication, Harry matured as a writer. Caresse, on the other hand, slowed down as a writer, as the responsibilities of the Press infringed increasingly on her working hours. Between 1926 and 1929, Black Sun (including Editions Narcisse) published seven volumes of Harry's poetry, and three volumes of his diaries. Caresse produced three volumes of verse, and two drawings to accompany Harry's *Mad Queen: Tirades* and *Sleeping Together, A Book of Dreams.*

A certain kind of melancholy pervades Caresse's *Painted Shores.* As modern a woman as she may have been, she persisted in expressing the sentiments of someone whose moments of joy are tempered by weary worldliness. Moreover, she expressed these feelings formally, in sonnets, as though she were oblivious of the new shapes and sounds her contemporaries were exploring. In "North River," she says that her "heart is tuned for holidays sans strife," and the somber watercolor by the French modernist François Quelvée that faces the poem is of a woman, clearly meant to resemble Caresse, standing on the deck of a ship, all the colors muted beige, brown, and gray, the color of the sky, sea, and smokestacks. She seems weighed down by her past and incapable of pursuing the uninhibited life that she and Harry had set out to follow when they moved to Paris. She wonders if she is brave enough to "pull off [her] shoes and stockings in the square / Or shout 'How stupid' through the tea-room doors." She wants to be "allowed to stray," to walk "abroad with heart undone / Mindful alone of seasons and the sun," forlorn but wandering "any way."

By now, Caresse had experienced the rush of defying social convention, and of trying to be true to herself. Why would she write verse with so different a persona, especially when she encouraged her readers to identify her as the speaker of these poems? She may have been trying to describe the price she had paid to become a free spirit. And she insisted on no regrets. In the last poem of the book, "Journey's End," she writes "Though you and I, my heart, are sealed with pain / Would we not turn and seek it all again?"

It is likely that writing poetry provided her with an outlet for emotions whose fluctuations she could not discuss intimately even with a friend. Indeed, one of the striking characteristics of Caresse's memoirs is the absence of occasions spent with close woman friends. Although she would enjoy vital relationships with talented women including writers Kay Boyle and Anaïs Nin, designer Elsa Schiaparelli, and artist Dorothea Tanning, their careers and lives were as complex as Caresse's. None of them had agendas that were flexible enough for sessions of shared confidences, and more to the point, only Kay Boyle was on the scene at this time. A collection like *Painted Shores* offered Caresse a chance to articulate some private conversations she may have had with various sides of her personality, a process of sorting things out by herself.

Among such poems as "North River" and "Journey's End," the poem entitled "Dawn" stands out for the quiet invitation it gives readers to share the way Caresse sometimes felt after staying out with Harry (presumably) until the sunrise. Caresse personifies the dawn, a "wanton jade," a girl wearing a "gown / of mistral sweeps the night-dew from the street / The fading lamplight stains her wayward feet." The poem can easily evoke derision with its predictable rhythms and its "poetic" language ("She runs before us through the slumbering town / To where the harvest carts come with their crown / Of golden pumpkin and bloodred beet"), and yet it evokes the speaker's reflective mood, someone who is acutely sensitive to the changing colors of a slowly awakened city, who appreciates the bountiful richness of the surrounding farm country, and who counts off the inevitable tasks that await the workers who live there. She is aware of the privileged place she enjoys in this setting but does not make much of it. Nor is she is particularly embarrassed that she is "lingering home to bed" when many others are going to work. There are no qualifiers to indicate that she feels sorry for anyone. Her observations stand in place of her commentary. Indeed, she applies the same detached perspective that her contemporaries often did, but she persists in using the tools of an earlier era. Such a style of writing is a commentary on the life she was leading—modern but still governed by old fashioned concepts, especially about love and loyalty.

The poem "Au Louvre" describes some of those concepts. The speaker in the poem has quarreled with her lover. He sends her violets (Harry's flowers of choice for Caresse and his mother),[11] she wipes her tears, and they repair to the museum to find peace in a beautiful and stable setting. Soothed by the larger-than-life paintings and sculpture, they begin to feel better. But the speaker reveals the compromise she has made with herself. Her lover's transgressions will not disturb her as long as they fire his passion for her: she should not doubt that "the bare / Bright breasts of Psyche may not prove / The lovelier for another pair, as fire / Is fed with fuel, or beauty flames desire." If his infidelities assure another round of fidelity, why should she object to them? Such rationalization helped the marriage last longer than perhaps it should have.

In "Heritage," one of the more intriguing poems in *Painted Shores,* the lover in the poem appears to be a painter, not a poet, whose "workman's blouse with all its complex stain / Of brilliant colors" the speaker has saved in a "marriage chest" along with his pipes and pencils. She, herself, has given up the idea of painting, because she sees his profile in each brush stroke of her "ships and birds, and girls and flowers," his "ruthless shadow dwarfs [her] finest towers." The speaker may be packing a marriage chest, but she also declares that it is time for her to "leave this land." If this poem is autobiographical, it suggests at least on one occasion Caresse thought seriously of leaving Harry, no matter how much she wanted her family, friends, and acquaintances to think that his private code of morality matched her own. Caresse may also have harbored the suspicion that her own creative endeavors were being sacrificed for the sake of Harry's.

On the other hand, a model for the male figure in this poem was Frans de Geetere, a painter from Amsterdam who lived with his wife Mai, also an artist, on a barge the "Marie-Jeanne," docked near the place du Vert Gallant, near the rue de Lille. In the early spring of 1927, Frans and Mai stepped into Lescaret's print shop to place an order for business cards: the recently married couple hoped to make names for themselves in Paris art circles. In the meantime, they lived frugally on the money Frans earned from odd jobs he picked up at Les Halles, and from bartering sketches and the Dutch cheese and cabbage stowed aboard. Caresse was working at the shop when they walked in, and she was drawn to their story. About a week later and unannounced, she and Harry brought the ordered cards to the barge. They were immediately charmed by what they saw: a young, loving couple devoted to their art, pure in their intentions but ambitious to succeed, willing to sacrifice everyday comforts to realize their dreams.[12]

A new friendship was formed. Caresse and Harry would visit Frans and Mai on their barge, often toting along friends, food, and wine. Frans and Harry shared an interest in the work of the French Decadent poets, and in the erotica that filled Frans's portfolios. Later that year, Harry wrote an introduction to woodcuts Frans had created to illustrate the outre prose poem *Les Chants of Maldoror* by Comte de Lautreamont.[13] After Caresse and Harry caught sight of Frans and Mai washing themselves in their primitive tin tub, they invited the couple every Saturday morning to the rue de Lille for a more indulgent kind of bath. Afterwards Caresse and Harry would take them to the races.[14] When the barge started to leak, the Crosbys had it towed to the outskirts of the city for repair.

Eventually Frans achieved modest success, the barge was docked once again on the Seine, near the Pont Neuf, conveniently close to rue de Lille. Fast friends, Harry and Caresse stopped by several times a week, and in the warm weather, Harry spent the afternoon sunbathing on the deck. Frans developed an infatuation with Caresse and most days made a point of presenting her with a rose fresh from Les Halles. Caresse savored the attention, which outwardly disturbed neither Harry nor Mai, whose portrait of Caresse appeared in the 1927 edition of Caresse's long poem *The Stranger.*

A figure like Frans could have inspired the image cut by the man in "Heritage." The open workman's shirt "with all its complex stain" in the poem could be the black wool lumberman's shirt Frans wore while making repairs on the barge or the open shirt that Caresse refers to in her memoirs. The pencils that Caresse saves in her "marriage chest" could belong to Frans, including the "good black pencil in the pocket of his open shirt" that Frans carried on the day he first met Caresse.[15] Frans smoked a pipe, but Caresse could have also been alluding to the times that the Crosbys and the de Geeteres smoked opium together in Melun, a Paris suburb.[16] Later, in 1929, Frans painted a rich portrait of Caresse in a modish, gold suit. He was not the first of her admirers to do so.

The focus of *Impossible Melodies,* published in 1928, is similar to that of *Painted Shores.* The speaker is a spirited woman contemptuous of her elite background but nevertheless dependent on her upper-class connections to sustain her romantic and artistic interests. For the frontispiece portrait, Caresse's friend and lover Angeles Ortiz produced a spare, elegant line drawing of Caresse. She gracefully reclines on a sofa. She looks modern, with a flapper's bob, and a diaphanous gown, which she probably purchased at a toga, scarves, and sandals shop on the boulevard St.-Germain owned by Raymond Duncan, brother of Isadora Duncan, and leader of a commune in the Paris suburb of Neuilly. Caresse, however, wears the more "feminine" pumps not sandals. Her gaze is distracted, pensive, and indifferent to her audience despite the seductive quality of her posture. Although the book is more late-nineteenth-century than early-twentieth, the style has loosened up: not every poem is a sonnet; rhyme schemes are occasionally abandoned; there is more room for humor. Personification is still strong, with yet another poem devoted to the dawn, this time in the guise of a man who casts a harsher light on humanity than the dawn of the earlier volume.

"Beauty and Bread" is one of the more skillful poems in the book. It is tempting to identify Harry, Caresse, and another woman with the major actors on the scene. Harry could easily be the unnamed "he" whose confusion about the meaning of life the speaker reduces to an adult's nursery rhyme about the search for a proper tea. Although he never participates in this afternoon ritual himself (Harry did take tea occasionally, but not happily), by the end of the poem, he accepts the offer of bread in order to captivate an attractive woman who is flirting with him about his special tastes and aversions. "I also like beauty," he says, "just beauty and bread." Caresse is mocking Harry's obsession with whatever woman piqued his interest, as though that were the way to uncover life's mystery.

Caresse had few illusions about the company her poems would keep. As the Black Sun Press grew, Harry's reputation as a poet eclipsed hers. He became associated with Eugene Jolas, who in April 1927 founded the influential experimental magazine *transition.* Jolas broached the idea that Harry translate a selection of the strange, cruel prose poems of Comte de Lautreamont. In return, Harry offered Jolas one hundred dollars for the best poet who had appeared in the first twelve issues of *transition.*[17] Caresse could not recall the occasion she and Harry first met Eugene and Marie Jolas, perhaps her way of dealing with their obvious preference for Harry over her.

Marie Jolas was especially unimpressed by Caresse and considered her name an indication of her artifice, conveniently avoiding or perhaps unaware that Harry had played a major role in changing Caresse's name.[18] Caresse made no allusion to any ill will between herself and Marie Jolas. She describes both Jolases as "grand and gifted people, with minds like new brooms, hearts like hearts."[19] She admired Marie, who served as office manager and consulting editor for *transition* and contributed translations as well. Harry eventually became an associate editor of *transition,* and his poems appeared there regularly. Only one of Caresse's poems, "The Stranger," was published by Jolas.

But Caresse appreciated the avant-garde writing that *transition* published even if she herself was still mired in "easeful cliché and well-worn rhyme."[20] She was also happy to sign a manifesto that Harry and Jolas had drafted, "The Revolution of the Word." It feverishly announced that modernist writers had finally found the new language the world so desperately needed. The document addresses many issues that concerned twentieth-century poets, including their right to manipulate grammar and syntax, the importance of the irrational and hallucinatory in the creative process, and the conflict between art and politics. Its bombastic style and pitch to an exclusive audience undercut any possible lasting impact, but neither Harry nor Caresse sensed its shortcomings. Among the cosigners were Kay Boyle and Hart Crane, both of whom would later express embarrassment for having lent their names to this particular revolutionary act. Nevertheless, both cultivated stronger relationships with the Crosbys.

5

Treasures for the Black Sun Press

Eugene Jolas introduced Kay Boyle to the Crosbys on May 19, 1928, at the Bal Nègre, a smokey Montparnasse nightclub famous for black jazz. Frans and Mai de Geetere were part of the Crosby party that evening, as was Armand, Comte de la Rochefoucauld, one of the most eligible bachelors the Crosbys knew, another naughty boy. Howard Hare (nicknamed "Pete") and Gretchen Powel were also in attendance. Like Harry and Caresse, the Powels had fled their monied, respectable lives back in the States. A fighter pilot during World War I, Pete had met Caresse at a party in tony Newport, Rhode Island, his home town. Gretchen was Texas aristocracy, a pretty woman who like Caresse had bobbed her hair and studied sculpting at Antoine Bourdelle's studio. "We luckily never appealed to the same men and so got along beautifully," was how Caresse described the basis for their friendship.[1] The Powels seemed to have no other agenda but self-amusement. Camera in hand, they cruised on sailboats, crashed parties, attended the opera. The couple was known as "the Crouchers" because Pete would squat as he got his pictures into focus while Gretchen inevitably hunched over his shoulder to register her approval.

The Powels and the Crosbys enjoyed many escapades together, including a country trip through Normandy with stops permitted only in towns with names no longer than one syllable, an outing of several days that Caresse describes in much detail, especially meals topped off by rum and Calvados. The Crosbys and the Powels made a nice fit. Actually they were six: the Powels had Zulu, a white Great Pyrenees, who got along well with her counterpart, Narcisse Noir. In the town of Bu, there were no accommodations for the night except for a downstairs room usually occupied by the owners' father and daughter. The four adults and two dogs tumbled into the huge featherbed together. The next day they tore into a hearty breakfast.

Kay Boyle's first image of Caresse and Harry that evening—an ultramodern, raffish couple with an entourage, sipping champagne, poised against the railing of a balcony that appeared ready to collapse momentarily—remained with Boyle forever in a "white blaze of the nightclub's lights that have never dimmed."[2] Jolas led her up the stairs, and their meeting at the Bal Nègre marked the beginning of a mutually devoted friendship.

Kay Boyle was twenty-six when she befriended Caresse and Harry. Before her arrival in France five years earlier, she had made small but significant contributions to the avant-garde literary scene in the United States: she had published book reviews in the *Dial* and a poem in *Poetry* and worked as editorial assistant to Lola Ridge for *Broom.*[3] By 1928, she had made a reputation for herself in *This Quarter* and *transition.* Despite her emerging literary success, she was in dire financial circumstances. Her great love, Ernest Walsh, poet and cofounder with Ethel Moorhead in 1925 of *This Quarter,* had died of tuberculosis, leaving her as a single mother of a daughter, Sharon. (Boyle was still technically married to Richard Brault, a French engineer.)

For a while, Boyle lived comfortably as the secretary to Gladys Palmer, heir to the Palmer biscuit company fortune and currently the Princess or Dayang Muda of Sarawak. Boyle, however, was drawn to a commune outside Paris in Neuilly organized by Raymond Duncan, brother of Isadora Duncan. Sharon would be cared for at the commune (she was not permitted to live with her mother in Palmer's home) in exchange for Boyle's managing the shop on the boulevard St.-Germain where the togas, sandals, and scarves presumably produced by Duncan's colony were sold. Harry often visited Kay at the shop, episodes that provided Boyle with material for a number of scenes in her fourth novel, *My Next Bride* (1934). Caresse apparently suspected that Harry's frequent visits to the boulevard St.-Germain were not merely shopping expeditions. And there was gossip that a ménage à trois or a lesbian relationship between Caresse and Kay existed. None of these speculations was ever confirmed,[4] although Boyle dedicated *My Next Bride* to Caresse partly to dispel suspicion. While not strictly autobiographical, the book sheds light on the early relationship between the Crosbys and Boyle.

The plot revolves around Victoria, the Kay Boyle figure, who is living in a colony like Duncan's—Duncan is called Sorrel—and who sells batiks in a

Paris shop. Like Kay Boyle, Victoria gets pregnant at the time and cannot be absolutely sure of the father's identity because she has been bedding down with many men. Fontana and Anthony Lister—the Crosbys—give her the money so that she can have an abortion. While Boyle would claim that the book is about women's friendships and "material inequality,"[5] critics preferred to see it as yet another book about the 1920s that glorified people of little consequence. If the book fails to mask Boyle's romantic perspective on this period, it can be appreciated for its lively portrayal of Caresse as Fontana.

Like Harry in one of his possessed moods, Anthony describes Fontana in fantastic terms, as someone who appears like a bride, in white satin slippers and a lace veil, "but otherwise she forgets to dress. I never remind her because it is not necessary to wear clothes if you carry a bouquet. Fontana carries five or six bouquets because she always stops and gives one away to anyone who asks."[6] He extols her beauty, fidelity, and innocence, yet he regards her as a maternal figure also, someone to whom he can confess his peccadilloes and affairs, as Harry did to his own mother Henrietta, and to Caresse. During one hot fantasy scene on a boat that resembles the de Geeteres' barge, Fontana comes looking for Anthony, who is trying to seduce Victoria. Fontana reminds him to come back after he runs away with Victoria because they have a trip scheduled to the United States that cannot be changed. She is the all-forgiving earth mother: supportive, understanding, and appropriately tolerant. He is pleased that she never carries a handbag, wears gloves, or gets her hair curled, and that neither of them is attached to material objects: "we eliminate everything we might forget or leave behind."[7]

Fontana appears in a sharper, less idealized light when she is alone with Victoria. At first she pretends that she does not suspect that an affair is brewing between Anthony and Victoria. She is dressed in a chic black-and-white outfit, looking youthful and boyish. "Fontana was talking, as well-bred women talk, of everything else but of what was before them," Victoria reports.[8] She sounds buoyant and tolerates Anthony's eccentricities to a point. She finally confides to Victoria that she is determined to maintain her sense of well-being no matter how outrageously Anthony behaves. She will remain impervious to anything that would cause her pain: "I wouldn't let them get me, I mean none of the things that put their arms around you and get you down . . . I would be very cunning from absolutely the crack of dawn until going to bed at night. I made up my mind to outwit things as fast as they come up, one after another. But I would do it incredibly as Rimbaud did it. Not a niche left open in the armor."[9] Here is a vision of an embattled Caresse who understands the consequences of preserving her marriage: self-imposed inner isolation.

Boyle's perspective, however, as accurate as it may have been, was not easily shared by Caresse. Once in a while, she recalls in bald terms the nature of her predicament. She admits, for example, that during the latter part of 1928, she was growing distraught over Harry's infidelities, his "search for clandestine fires" as she puts it. "He made me believe," she continues, "that our children balanced our account. Though beleaguered, I felt safe, still centered in the widening circle of his interests, and I knew it would be treason to even wish for a simpler love."[10] A suit of mail does not get any thicker.

When they first made acquaintance, Boyle and the Crosbys were reserved. In her initial correspondence, Boyle addressed them as Mr. and Mrs. Crosby despite their raucous introduction and the Crosbys' immediate concern with Boyle's welfare. In several letters from this period, Boyle expresses great yearning to see the Crosbys and deep regrets for missing dates with them. She also confides that she has found a new love, poet and aircraft pilot Laurence Vail, known as the "king of Bohemia," and who at the time was married to Peggy Guggenheim. "I am as happy as Harry looks when he is so—every atom of him radiant—for I've never known anyone who could shine with it as he does so absolutely."[11] An intimacy soon developed among these three.

From the start, then, a kindred feeling existed between the Crosbys and Boyle, and their emotional involvement intertwined with their interest in mutual literary, artistic endeavors. The Black Sun Press would publish Boyle's first collection of short stories and publish her translation of René Crevel's *Mr. Knife, Miss Fork.* (Later, in 1932, Caresse published Boyle's translation of Raymond Radiguet's *The Devil in the Flesh* and her novel *Year Before Last* under her own imprint, Crosby Continental Editions.) When the Crosbys traveled to the States in the fall of 1928, Boyle would provide the Crosbys with letters of introduction to William Carlos Williams, painter Charles Sheeler, and Alfred Stieglitz. Whenever they visited various relatives in New York and Boston, the Crosbys extended to Boyle the use of their chauffeured car, complete with sable seat blanket. The Crosbys also provided the first, albeit brief, stopping place for Boyle after she rescued her daughter from the Duncan colony, a plot of several stages.

First, Boyle smuggled her belongings out of her quarters in Neuilly and into the apartment of the Princess of Sarawak. Then on December 30, 1928, nine of the children from the colony were invited there to lunch. They arrived in two taxis, but after eight of the children disembarked, one of the cabs drove away with Boyle and daughter Sharon. They stopped at the hotel room of writer Robert McAlmon, a great friend of Boyle. With William Carlos Williams, he had started *Contact* magazine and published on his own writers such as H.D., Mina Loy, Ernest Hemingway, and Gertrude Stein. McAlmon knew that the Crosbys had returned from the States and were about an hour's drive away in Ermenonville, at a country home they had purchased in 1928. He suggested that they go there for New Year's Eve. Caresse's children, Polleen and Bobby, would be home for the holidays.[12] Boyle couldn't think of a better destination. Although it turned out to be a safe place at the moment, the scene there was hardly tranquil.

Caresse and Harry had been longing to escape from the daily intensity of Paris life. An adventurous voyage they took with Mrs. Crosby to the Middle East in the winter of 1928 and a romantic sojourn in Italy during the spring of 1928 had left them hungry for a nearby retreat. There were advantages, they realized, in controlling the boundaries of their escapades. In Egypt, for example, Harry appreciated neither the heat, the food, nor fellow English tourists. Caresse felt oppressed by the sickness and poverty that she saw on the streets: "children born into blindness and filth, the shame of our century."[13] Caresse and Harry had also put their lives in jeopardy when Harry insisted that he wanted a six-inch image of the sun tattooed on his back. Little did the Crosbys anticipate the daring of such a desire. Harry ended up bound and gagged on a boat floating down the Nile in the middle of the night. A tattoo artist performed the illegal and painful operation while the captain of the ship molested Caresse.[14] Sensing the great danger they were in, Caresse did not resist her attacker's advances: "I decided to cajole instead of anger our captors."[15] When Harry was set free, Caresse tried to persuade him that they should make light of the experience, to write it off as a joke. She believed, though, that he suffered more from watching the captain paw over her than from the hot pinch of the needles. She wanted her readers to believe that, indeed as she told Harry, she had remained "intact."

That June (1928), Caresse and Harry located the pastoral setting they were searching for, quite unexpectedly, after they attended a house-warming party for Armand de la Rochefoucauld. He had recently inherited with his brother a chateau from their uncle, Prince Leon Radziwill in Ermenonville, thirty miles from Paris. It had once belonged to the Marquis Girardin, a captain of the Royal Dragoons in the Seven Years War in the 1700s. He was a great fan of Jean Jacques Rousseau and built for him a chalet facing the chateau where he "received queens and revolutionaries."[16] Rousseau died there, and Girardin buried him in a sarcophagus on the Île des Peupliers, as Rousseau had requested. During the French Revolution, Girardin was imprisoned and, after his release, impoverished, was forced to give up his property.

During a tour of the estate, Caresse and Harry were captivated by its untamed beauty, which Caresse eloquently describes:

> Honeysuckle choked the entrance. Four-leaf clovers pushed their way through the cobbles in the paved courtyard, doves circled about the tower eaves and the soft thunder of the waterfall made the lovely enclosure seem distantly removed from the outer world across the castle moat.[17]

Harry and Caresse wanted to buy the place on the spot. Although surprised at their impetuosity, Armand agreed to sell it to them for $220 in gold pieces. Caresse wanted her readers to believe that Harry dared Armand to accept as payment the balance of his checking account, an amount known only to the Morgan bank. But Harry's correspondence with his mother suggests that he was appropriately businesslike and exact figures were negotiated.[18] Was Caresse misremembering or deliberately creating this charming fantasy? Was she trying to impress upon her audience that far from being seduced by Harry's wealth, she was drawn to Harry for his daring, for his contempt of mundane matters, for his romantic, quixotic nature?

The property was theirs, until Armand's mother discovered the imminent deal. Adamant that the land remain in the family, she offered Caresse and Harry a twenty-year lease instead, which they readily accepted. As it turned out, the house that Harry and Caresse inhabited, which they named Le Moulin du Soleil, was not the building in which Rousseau had resided. But that did not matter to the Crosbys either. Le Moulin was still magical for them. Caresse and Harry believed that the Mill was haunted, that when he was in retreat there, the alchemist Count Cagliostro had brought a pillar from the Abbey de Chalis, which cast a local spell. They believed, among other things, that a flock of sheep had walked right through the three-barred gate of the house, and that little fish leaped twenty feet from the millstream to reach a pool above.[19] Paradise on earth for the Crosbys would necessarily be surreal.

Le Moulin was actually three buildings built around a courtyard. Caresse and Harry lost little time moving in. The walls of the main building were whitewashed, the ten little bedrooms were painted in the colors of the rainbow, and a swimming pool was "scooped out" so that it could be fed by a nearby waterfall. No one bothered to get rid of the bugs and fish that turned the water dark and scummy.[20] Caresse and Harry also built a bathroom for their bedroom on the first floor. The cobblestones on the ground floor were left bare, and a long trestle table turned the space into a dining room. A terrace off the attic, a haven for bats, served as Harry's sunroof, and the cellar and washroom was converted to a large kitchen. A regular menagerie was installed: burros, whippets, schnauzers, Afghans, cockatoos, pigeons, a parrot, and a cheetah. Caresse furnished the rooms to resemble the Adirondack camp where she had spent summers with her Aunt and Uncle Barnum. At the front gate, signs indicated the various trails that visitors could follow through the forest. Guests were asked to leave their signatures in colored paint on the whitewashed wall under the staircase near the entrance to the main building. There was also a cannon in the hayloft that was hauled down and fired in honor of distinguished guests.[21]

By the time Boyle and her daughter and McAlmon arrived at the Mill, New Year's Eve festivities were in full swing. Boyle was far less shocked by the situation than McAlmon. She understood that Harry and Caresse's frivolous antics concealed a more serious agenda to forge a personal ethic and to create a quality small press. (They added twelve books to their list in 1928, including a French and an English edition of Oscar Wilde's *The Birthday of the Infanta.*) Nevertheless, their parties attracted a significant number of people more interested in rejecting propriety, respectability, and sobriety than in realizing any kind of artistic or moral integrity.

Sophisticated as their tastes were—they gravitated toward classical art, literature, and history along with Dada and jazz and Eastern cultures—Caresse and Harry were remarkably naive about the tantalizing image they presented to the Parisian world. Although they constantly urged friends and acquaintances to visit Le Moulin, they were surprised by the chaos that resulted. Undoubtedly, they sought pleasure, but occasionally they were so exhausted by their guests that Paris appeared to be a better retreat than Ermenonville.

McAlmon beat a hasty exit on New Year's Day, too early to bid good-bye to Boyle or his hosts.[22] Despite the possibility that the Black Sun Press might publish some of his work, McAlmon never warmed to the Crosbys: Harry's intensity was too fixed; Caresse was no more and no less than "an attractive, smartly dressed woman."[23] Boyle would continue to visit Le Moulin with Laurence Vail. The first book published in 1929 by the Black Sun Press was Boyle's *Short Stories.* Indifferent to McAlmon's opinions, Caresse published McAlmon's *Indefinite Huntress and Other Stories* in 1932.

Shortly after New Year's Day (1929), Hart Crane arrived in Paris and, like Boyle, was introduced to the Crosbys by Eugene Jolas. Again there was an immediate attraction, especially after Crane showed Harry and Caresse sections of his long poem "The Bridge," a work in progress. Although it was under contract with Horace Liveright of New York, the Crosbys wanted to publish it in a deluxe edition. Delighted with the proposal, Crane thought it would provide the stimulus that he needed to complete the poem. He was not working efficiently at all, spending too many raucous days and nights in Paris and at the Mill, drinking excessively, carousing, and getting into arguments, including one with Boyle, who had made the mistake of criticizing him in front of other Moulin guests and who had written a mean-spirited review of his *White Buildings* for *transition*—no reflection of her good feelings for him or her generally high estimation of his work.[24]

A temporary solution to Crane's writer's block was devised. At Harry and Caresse's insistence, he moved out to the Mill. Supplied with a case of Cutty Sark, his favorite whiskey, he holed up in the tower and got to work. He did not finish the poem, but he had broken the impasse. Grateful to the Crosbys for their hospitality and indulgence—everything and everyone at the Mill were at his disposal—Crane took off to the south of France for the spring, corresponding with Caresse and Harry to apprise them of his progress. In April, Caresse suggested that perhaps "The Bridge" in its present state was publishable. As she noted in an April 23 letter, she regarded the work "already to be one poem. Why do you think it must be added to? It is eternal and alive and beautiful."[25] Crane was pleased with the idea, if only because it relieved the pressure on him. Now, perhaps he would write at a faster pace. "At least I'm becoming weary of the burden," he wrote to Caresse from the Pyrenees-Orientales on April 25, 1929, "and am ready for almost any compromise."[26]

Back in Paris, Crane continued to be "dynamite to handle."[27] He remained in the Crosbys' good graces and fared better than Caresse's children. That winter, while Caresse was in London, shopping for such items as rose-scented bath oil and a mate worthy of their favorite whippet, Narcisse Noir, she made sure to stock up on a supply of Cutty Sark. During a drunken tryst with a chimney sweep whom he had picked up in the middle of the night, Crane trashed the guest room of the Crosby's Paris apartment, recently redecorated to welcome Polleen home for her spring vacation.

While Caresse spent most of July in Cannes, Harry remained in Paris, where he rescued Crane from jail. Unable to pay his bill at the Café Select, a very drunk and obstreperous Crane got into a brawl with the police, who had been summoned to arrest him.[28] When he heard from Kay Boyle that Crane had been incarcerated in La Santé, Harry quickly arranged Crane's legal representation. He covered all legal expenses, attended the trial, and took Crane for eggs and toast the evening he was released from prison. He also bought Crane a ticket back to New York on the U.S.S. *Homeric.*

Settled in Brooklyn Heights, Crane wrote in a September 6, 1929, letter to Caresse that he looked forward to seeing them both in New York that coming winter, and he promised to complete "The Bridge" in time for their arrival. Crane felt closer to Caresse than to Harry, whom he regarded as a "drinking partner and hale fellow who [could] be trusted to pick up the bill."[29] As the correspondence between them indicates, Caresse was more involved in propping Crane's morale, and in tracking his progress towards completing "The Bridge." When Crane wrote specifically to Caresse, he often included declarations of love and loyalty.

Caresse and Harry were eager to accommodate Crane, whom they considered a genius, and by now a dear friend. When Crane quit the Mill that spring, he left behind a mess of books, pictures of sailors, and victrola records and had moved chairs, tables, and bureaus into the yellow room where he'd stayed (guest rooms were painted in primary colors). Caresse left everything as it was, perhaps to curb her sadness over his departure. One day not long after Crane left, Caresse searched the room for a mirror that was missing. She rummaged through the chaos but stopped midway. She sensed Crane's aura surrounding her and reflected on how extraordinarily talented she thought he was: "I like his voice best—it is a fog-horn far at sea, and "The Bridge" is a masterpiece. I am so glad we're to edit it."[30]

The attention that Caresse directed towards Crane contrasts startlingly with that she gave her children. Caresse understood that Harry had little interest in listening to her domestic concerns. The trip she made to London in the winter of 1928 (when Crane trashed Polleen's bedroom) included a visit with Billy at Cheams, a boarding school popular with English nobility. Billy was not getting enough to eat, and his room was so cold that ice filled the water jug that he used for his bath.[31] Caresse arrived with a good supply of cookies and chocolate and paid an extra fee so that Billy would enjoy eggs with his tea, not just the standard ration of bread, butter, and milk. She left without staying for lunch since Billy had warned her about how awful the food would be. Presumably she found it impossible to take him out for a meal. The strict regime at Cheams, Caresse let herself believe, would do Billy good in the long run, and she barely mentioned his predicament to Harry. Her visit to Billy was a "mission [she] dared not stress."[32]

It was far easier for Caresse to forgive Hart Crane his barbaric indiscretions, and to act the gracious hostess and sensible publisher, than to be a caring mother.[33] Caresse took pride in herself for understanding Crane but did not permit herself to express the compromises she was making as a mother. She admitted some measure of regret, but pleasing Harry and developing the Press were her chief priorities.

Caresse and Harry kept open house at the Mill, except when people like Frieda and D. H. Lawrence stopped in Ermenonville for a weekend. An admirer of Lawrence's early fiction, Harry had read *The Plumed Serpent* while in Egypt the year before and wanted Lawrence all to himself and Caresse. He had written to Lawrence, who was living in Italy at the time, about his own interest in the sun god and offered him five twenty-dollar gold pieces if he would give a "sun" manuscript to the Black Sun Press.[34] He also sent Lawrence some of the poems that he would be publishing in *Chariot of the Sun* and asked him if he would write an introduction. Lawrence complied with both requests, sending separately a mixed review of Harry's poetry (which later served as an introduction to the first volume of Harry's *Chariot of the Sun*) and a manuscript copy for the short novel *Sun*. The story of an American woman whose sexuality is awakened in lush Italian surroundings, *Sun* had been published twice before, but the Black Sun edition would mark its first appearance in unexpurgated form, with the frontispiece—an Aztec sun-worshiper—drawn by Lawrence himself. (The closing sentences of the censored edition read: "Nevertheless, her next child would be Maurice's. The fatal chain of continuity would cause it." The Black Sun Press edition read: "She would feel her husband's futile penis inside her once again.")[35] It was limited to 165 copies and was widely pirated in the Unites States.

In the spring of 1929, Lawrence had come to Paris seeking a commercial publisher for *Lady Chatterley's Lover.* He and Frieda called upon the Crosbys. As was often the pattern at meetings with writers published by Black Sun, Caresse served first as host, then gradually asserted herself as general liaison between author and publisher, as managing editor, and as art director. Caresse handled this difficult balancing act of mixing business with pleasure on her own.

Despite a shared literary sensibility, the Lawrences and the Crosbys did not make a good fit. Lawrence had been generous enough to praise Harry's poems for demonstrating a powerful naivete and vibrancy, but he may have been cultivating the good will of a future publisher when he did so. Harry and Lawrence did not agree on writers—for example, Lawrence despised and Harry adored James Joyce. Harry was unimpressed with *Lady Chatterley's Lover.*

Frieda and Caresse also made a poor match. Not surprisingly an aggressive advocate of her husband's work, Frieda envied the success of other writers. Caresse, on the other hand, was an ambassador of good will, eager to please most writers she met. Caresse of course also enjoyed the distinct advantage of having the resources to publish her own work. By the time she met the Lawrences, she had three volumes of her poetry to her credit in addition to *Graven Images*, the volume published by Houghton Mifflin in 1926. She could afford to be gracious.

Actually the more compatible pairings were between Lawrence and Caresse and Frieda and Harry. Although Caresse thought that Lawrence was strange and frightened, she was impressed with his "tennacuous [sic] and complex" mind and believed that his red beard was a symbol of "his fortress and his strength," especially since she could plainly see how poor his health was.[36] During a visit to the Mill in March, Caresse and Lawrence tooled around the grounds in a donkey cart while Harry and Frieda stayed inside—he writing, she, exasperated with Lawrence, listening to jazz on the gramophone, enduring a visit that she assumed would advance her husband's career. Unable to engage her attention, Caresse believed that Frieda was arrogant. (Caresse refers to Frieda as "Freda" in her published memoirs, a small retaliation, perhaps, for Frieda's comportment.[37]) Nevertheless, Caresse and Frieda would remember that a genuinely warm if fleeting friendship had been established that spring weekend.[38]

Caresse and Harry were determined to publish another work by Lawrence, this time a twentieth-century resurrection story, *The Escaped Cock*. Correspondence between Caresse and Lawrence reveals that Caresse was the one in charge of overseeing art work (once again Lawrence's), printing, and distribution. *Forum* magazine had published an excerpt of *The Escaped Cock* in 1928, but the Black Sun edition would serve as the definitive source for all subsequent editions when it would appear under the title *The Man Who Died*. And while Lawrence was annoyed with the arrangements that Black Sun made with their New York bookseller, Harry Marks—Lawrence felt that Marks was making too great a profit—he did not prevent the book from going to press.[39] Money matters aside, the tone of the correspondence between Caresse and Lawrence was congenial. Lawrence graciously thanked her for the gramophone that Harry had sent Frieda, even though he hated the machine and the music that Frieda had played on it at Le Moulin. He shared some details of his travels with Frieda to Germany, Mallorca, and France, and the pleasant little villa they had found in Bandol on the Riviera. Caresse was the model of diplomacy, sensitive to the daily risks of Lawrence and Frieda's nomadic life. Confident of the trust she had established with Lawrence, she addressed him as Lorenzo and signed off "with love."

Harry Marks was not the hard businessman that Lawrence took him for, although he obviously enjoyed turning a profit. During the spring of 1927, while browsing in a bookshop on the Right Bank, he came across a Black Sun Press book and was immediately drawn to its elegant design.[40] He decided at once to search out the headquarters of the Press and, upon reaching the rue Cardinale offices, learned that Caresse and Harry were in consultation with Baron Hans Henning von Voight, who under the pseudonym Alastair had illustrated their English and French editions of Wilde's *The Birthday of the Infanta*. He was captivated by Black Sun before he reached the Crosbys' inner offices:

> It was tiny beyond belief and yet it contained an unbelievable amount of large objects. Here stood a massive hand-press; there another one; by that wall a case of type; here a stack of paper; here bottles of ink. In short—all the delightful confusion of an old-fashioned printery. In the mellow light the scene seemed like an etching by Rembrandt. . . . In this absorbing atmosphere, time seemed of little importance. Everything was done leisurely, with infinite care. The papers used were hand-woven, the ink of special composition. On proofs that lay around the shop I noticed the beautiful clarity of the type, the perfect spacing, the wide, elegant margins.

His enthusiasm grew stronger once he saw the Crosbys themselves, surrounded by a "glorious disarray of proofs, manuscripts, pictures and bindings," exuding what he could only describe as "radiance." Marks made no distinction between the duties performed by Harry and Caresse, although Harry tended to choose the bindings, boxes, and ribbons while Caresse did the editorial work and typographical design. Unlike Harry, Caresse did not mind dirtying her hands with printer's ink.[41] Without signing a contract, the Crosbys and Marks agreed that Marks would be their distributor in the United States.

Perhaps the relationship established between James Joyce and the Black Sun Press best epitomizes the Crosbys' commitment to their authors. With the first edition of *Ulysses* published by Sylvia Beach and excerpts from *Work in Progress* that appeared in *transition*, Joyce had become the leading writer in Paris's English-speaking community of writers. The Crosbys were eager to sign him up; Harry was a devoted fan of *Ulysses*,[42] and Caresse shared his excitement. Caresse does not allude to anything that Joyce wrote, and it is possible that she was acting more the weather vane than sensitive reader when she and Harry decided to pursue Joyce. That she makes no mention of reading Joyce (nor many of her other authors for that matter) could suggest that the text itself was not what primarily engaged her. "We yearned," she wrote in her autobiography, "for a piece of the rich Irish cake then baking on the Paris fire."[43]

However, something else could explain Caresse's silence on her authors' writing: an assumption on her part that her readers would take for granted that she read the work of her authors; or a reluctance to pretend that she was a literary critic when in reality she was an appreciative yet modest reader. It is interesting that she felt more self-assured when it came to decisions concerning artists and illustrations, or to appropriate tactics for soothing idiosyncratic writers.

At this juncture, an appointment with Joyce was as difficult to arrange as an audience with Gertrude Stein.[44] Many small presses wanted to publish a piece of *Works in Progress,* and it is conceivable that if their efforts had not been supported by the Jolases and by Stuart Gilbert, who was working on the French translation of *Ulysses* at the time, the Crosbys might never have established a lasting acquaintance with Joyce. (Ernest Hemingway had introduced them briefly to Joyce in 1928 at a concert by a mutual friend, Ada MacLeish, who was married to poet Archibald MacLeish.) In March of 1929, they accompanied the Jolases to the Joyce apartment near the boulevard des Invalides, behind the Gare Montparnasse. Caresse was disappointed in the dullness of the place—no art on the walls, a bowl of goldfish set atop an upright piano, guests seated around the dining room table even though no meal was served, Nora hovering off to the side. Joyce barely uttered a word until the subject of Irish tenors came up, and then Caresse saw another side of Joyce: the eccentric artist sharing his warehouse of clippings on John Sullivan stored in a dilapidated suitcase (his desk) under his bed. The Crosbys were invited back to the apartment for a party in honor of a concert of tenors the following week. It was a far livelier occasion complete with Dublin dinner prepared by Nora.

After a few weeks had passed, the Crosbys asked Joyce if he would be interested in publishing a special edition of his work with the Black Sun Press. Assured that he would see page proofs and have the right to make changes that he thought necessary, Joyce chose three pieces that had already appeared in *transition:* "The Ondt and Gracehoper," "Mookse and Gripes," and "The Triangle." Stuart Gilbert delivered the copy to the Crosbys the day after they made their request, and on April 3, a formal contract was signed. Sylvia Beach had telephoned Caresse before the terms were completed to make sure that Joyce was paid a fair sum for his work. Agitated by the call, Caresse promised herself that Beach would be accommodated, that Joyce was "too important to lose."[45] Among other conditions, the final contract stipulated that Joyce would receive $1000 upon signing the contract, and another $1000 upon publication, a figure agreeable to all concerned.

Caresse and Harry immediately got started on the project. Joyce liked the idea of an introduction and proposed that the scientist Julian Huxley write it. Caresse herself presented the idea to Huxley but he declined, very much to Joyce's disappointment.[46] The musician John Sullivan also passed by the opportunity. Joyce went on to suggest that C. K. Ogden, the mathematician, inventor of Basic English (the "international" language of 850 words into which everything was supposed to be able to be said) and coauthor of *The Meaning of Meaning*. This time, Caresse had better luck: Ogden agreed immediately to get started on the essay.

The legwork involved in securing an artist for a frontispiece also fell upon Caresse. Joyce, Harry, and Caresse all thought that Picasso would be perfect. Although there were rumors that Picasso was going through a difficult emotional period,[47] Caresse took it upon herself to visit him and make her request face to face. Picasso refused outright but was fascinated by Narcisse Noir who often accompanied Caresse on her missions. So much did he like the dog that he asked Caresse if he might have one of his offspring for his son Phillipe. Caresse masked her disappointment, a habit she had cultivated through the years, and assured Picasso that she would remember his request—she would recall it well enough but did not comply. In the meantime, she took full advantage of the visit. Picasso was eager to show her his work: "I was dizzy with new forms and new colours. My education in modern art was progressing at a gallop."[48]

She did not seem to realize that she had inadvertently asked Picasso to compromise his allegiance to Gertrude Stein, whose portrait he had recently completed on the condition that he would not paint portraits of other famous people.[49] He had no intention of alienating this powerful figure nor of establishing a reputation as a portrait painter. Caresse's relationship with Stein was distant. She and Harry had been invited to rue de Fleurus only once, although Caresse on her own would see Stein again, the last time in 1945 when Stein attended an art gallery opening on the rue Furstemberg for American artists, organized by Caresse.

Brancusi was the next artist whom Caresse approached. Pleased to be asked, he suggested a representational drawing. But the Crosbys believed that an abstract design would be more appropriate to the text and its introduction, and Brancusi obliged with "three vertical lines and an elongated curlicue,"[50] which satisfied all concerned except Sylvia Beach. Joyce thought the design might attract customers but confided to Harriet Weaver that he doubted many readers would understand it.[51] Caresse later regretted their preference for an avant-garde drawing, but whatever reservations Caresse expressed in retrospect, she retained fond memories of the visits she made to Brancusi's bright, high-raftered studio in the rue de Vaugirard, where he graciously served her lunch amid his sculpting tools and stacked sketch books.

Several years later, in 1936, on her own in New York City, Caresse published eight hundred copies of a hand-set edition of Joyce's *Collected Poems.* The volume included the *Chamber Music; Pomes Penyeach,* which had never been published in the United States; and *Ecce Puer,* which had never appeared in any edition. A crayon portrait of Joyce by Augustus John was reproduced for the frontispiece. Joyce had suggested that Caresse use this portrait after the plan fell through to have his daughter, Lucia, illustrate each poem with decorative initial letters, some of which had already been reproduced nine years ago for *Pomes Penyeach.*[52] Although Caresse did not like Lucia's designs, she'd agreed to use them because she knew how devoted Joyce was to his daughter, who had been diagnosed with a form of schizophrenia.[53] When it became evident that Lucia would not be able to complete all the drawings, Joyce suggested the portrait John had done, over which Joyce claimed ownership. Caresse went to London for permission reprint, and John gave it to her on the condition that she return the original to him, not to Joyce.[54]

But now, in the spring of 1929, Caresse and Harry together contended with Joyce's precise instructions for revisions, which he gave them during long visits to their rue de Lille apartment. Caresse purchased a special large lightbulb for Joyce's weak eyes and locked away Narcisse Noir in the bathroom to accommodate Joyce's fear of dogs. Joyce elaborated on the various reasons for the changes he initiated, seemingly oblivious to the difficulties that Harry and Caresse might have in following such intricacies. Yet he expressed a fondness for his conscientious publishers at the close of an editing session that took place at the Joyce apartment. He inscribed a first edition of *Ulysses* (no. 34), which the Crosbys had purchased for $100 on Bloomsday 1928 in Paris.[55] In his diary, Harry recalled that after signing the copy, he insisted on making a pretty package of it with pink wrapping paper. Never mind that Joyce misspelled Caresse's name by omitting the second *s.*

Once all additions and deletions were recorded, Lescaret took over. To his horror, when he set the manuscript in type, the final page contained two lines only, a format unacceptable to printer and publisher alike. After the long editorial sessions with Joyce, Caresse was afraid to offend him with any request to lengthen or shorten the work. Without consulting Caresse or Harry, Lescaret went to Joyce and explained their plight. Joyce easily provided him with the extra copy he needed, much to the surprise and delight of Caresse. In any event, *Tales Told of Shem and Shawn* was a plume in the Crosbys' cap. Despite her disapproval of the frontispiece, Sylvia Beach thought the Crosbys had done a splendid job.[56] She also engaged Lescaret to print two hundred leaflets advertising her bookshop Shakespeare and Company.

When the Crosbys attended the supper party at the Joyce apartment after the Irish tenor concert, they ran into their friends Archibald and Ada MacLeish. Like the Crosbys, the MacLeishes had abandoned their secure lives in the United States—MacLeish had left his Boston law practice and teaching position at Harvard Law School to write poetry in Paris. The four had met during Christmas 1926 in Gstaad, where the MacLeishes were vacationing with Ernest Hemingway. They saw a good deal of one another at the rue de Lille apartment. The MacLeishes lived there when Harry and Caresse traveled to Persia—a trip that they undertook at the MacLeishes' urging.[57]

Although the relationship was harmonious, the MacLeishes and the Crosbys were operating on different planes: the MacLeishes, the older couple, believed that they had sacrificed a good deal more than the Crosbys in order to lead the literary life, and the Crosbys thought the MacLeishes would be better off if they took themselves a little less seriously. Neither Harry nor MacLeish cared for the other's early poetry; MacLeish had nothing to say about Caresse's writing. And yet a warm friendship grew between these couples that turned to MacLeish's advantage. In 1929, the Black Sun Press gave MacLeish $200 for permission to publish a deluxe edition of his long poem *Einstein* with a portrait of the author by Paul Emile Becat, best known for his erotic illustrations and for portraits of Sylvia Beach, Robert McAlmon, James Joyce, and others associated with literary life in Paris during the 1920s and 1930s. All 150 copies were sold out, and Harry and Caresse set the wheels going for a first edition of *New Found Land*, fourteen new poems. In addition to the 135 copies printed exclusively for the Black Sun Press in 1930, Houghton Mifflin arranged for another edition of five hundred that same year. MacLeish was understandably pleased with their support in general and thrilled that the edition of *Einstein* turned out to be such an attractive production, the result, MacLeish strongly suspected, of Caresse's efforts and judgement. Caresse would call in her chips on MacLeish, and on his reservoir of understanding and tact, in the not too distant future, during one of the greatest trials of her life.

6

The Death of Harry Crosby

The Crosbys may have worked well and played well together, but their marriage was troubled. Despite Harry's impassioned declarations of love and commitment to Caresse, he carried on love affairs and casual sexual liaisons from the beginning of their days in Paris. Caresse took on lovers of her own perhaps to absorb some of the turmoil that Harry's behavior stirred in her. Outwardly, these affairs with Ortiz Manolo, Lord Lymington, Count Armand de la Rochefoucauld, Cord Meier (a dashing pilot who had been wounded in the war and was known as "the Aviator") appeared to be a declaration on Caresse's part that, like Harry, she was liberated from the constraints of a middle-class conscience and that their open marriage satisfied them both. But behind the closed doors of their bedroom, Harry would instigate "violent fights" concerning Caresse's affairs.[1] It was a classic example of the double standard at work.

Both Caresse and Harry had risked a great deal so that they could marry, but, in spite of what they had been willing to sacrifice, their commitment to one another could be construed as artificial. Harry was able to make nearly identical pronouncements of passion to Caresse and to other women. His demands on his lovers' fealty were so intense that his very existence seemed to hinge on whether or not these demands were met. Caresse projected a different image, that of a modern 1920s woman whose romantic liaisons had a reckless, rakish edge. She was able to articulate her emotional conflicts only in an unpublished journal, which differed decidedly from her published autobiography. Harry's infidelities emerge in an occasional passage in *The Passionate Years*, but in the privacy of her journal, Caresse permitted herself to voice the full force of her distress. Yet even in her solitary ruminations, she demonstrated the same depth of inner reserves that enabled her to put up a good front. She could not prevent Harry from taking on lovers, but she was not going to denigrate herself—or Harry—trying to figure out why she and Harry had not remained faithful to one another. She was worried, even anxious, but would not concede the possibility that she had agreed to live by Harry's private code of conduct without considering its consequences.

Among the multitude of Harry's liaisons in 1929—one with a former lover, Constance, now Comtesse de Jumilhac, and another with a new lover, Josephine Rotch Bigelow—presented dramatic challenges to Caresses's equanimity. The Lady of the Golden Horse (as Harry was fond of calling her), Constance had broken off the affair earlier, partly in acknowledgment of a strong friendship between Caresse and Constance—Caresse had introduced Constance to Harry. However, Constance found adventure at the racetrack, the opium den, or in the arms of another's husband, even a friend's. She resumed what was for her a languid affair with Harry, nothing more. She had no interest in taking Harry away from Caresse since she had already experienced what she regarded as the limited advantages of matrimony. Harry's relationship with Josephine was more volatile because Josephine thrived on the perils of winning Harry at any cost.

Caresse could not avoid conceding if only to herself that Harry had been close to leaving her from the outset of their relationship. Correspondence between Harry and Constance that Caresse read while she was gathering material for *The Passionate Years* (first published in 1953) reveals that Harry began courting Constance not long after he and Caresse were married.[2] In letters to Constance, Harry declares that he cannot go on with Polly any longer, that he cannot meet Polly's demand that he "love her more than anyone else in the world." From the beginning, Constance resisted Harry's pleas to run away with him, but she remained a presence throughout Caresse and Harry's life together, sometimes Harry's lover, and, apparently, a frequent friend. "Let's see one another often when you get back," she wrote to Harry in a June 30, 1926, letter while he was in the States. In France, Constance was staying close by the bedside of her husband, who was gravely ill. Harry had sent her orchids, which she carried from her husband's room to her own, or to whatever room she happened to be in, because their presence made her happy.[3]

Keeping her jealousy under wraps, Caresse beseeched Constance to work things out so that they could keep their friendship intact: "together we ought to be able to find an answer to this." Harry believed they had all "played our cards damn poorly."[4] Harry would tell Constance that she had "awakened everything that's beautiful" in him, that "no one else means anything more" to him, the latter remark written aboard the *Berengaria*Berengaria headed for New York in November 1928.[5]

In that same letter, Harry mentions that he did not care whether or not he would see "the girl I liked last summer." More than two decades later, Caresse pencilled the name "Josephine" in the margin next to this remark. The "girl" was Josephine Rotch who, like Harry, was from Boston aristocracy. The two had met in Venice at the Lido in the summer of 1928, packing in as many assignations as they could manage during the eight days that their vacations coincided. There was no pretext that Caresse would tolerate this affair, as there was in the liaison between Harry and Constance. Yet Caresse's presence at the Lido during this same period did not deter Harry.

Sixteen years younger than Caresse, Josephine had dark hair that contrasted sharply with her pale skin; her gaze was intense. Harry called her his "Fire Princess." Painfully aware that she was not Harry's exclusive paramour, Josephine pursued him with fierce determination. She bombarded him with semicoherent letters and telegrams obsessed with setting dates for future trysts. Nearly a year after she started her affair with Harry, Josephine dropped out of Bryn Mawr College to marry Albert Bigelow, a former hockey star at Harvard and now a graduate student of architecture. Josephine's married state had little discernible effect on her devotion to Harry. Indeed, when she met Harry at the Lido, she had been on a shopping tour for her trousseau. Harry and Josephine saw each other again in the fall of 1928, and the fall of 1929, when Harry and Caresse were visiting their families in New York and Boston. In December 1929, Harry and Josephine traveled to Detroit, battening down for three days of champagne, caviar, and sex in the Hotel Book-Cadillac while Caresse was in New York City. Apparently violence was part of their routine in bed: in a letter to Harry, Josephine complains of bruises on her arm and one on her leg severe enough to require a doctor's attention.[6]

What matters for Caresse is that while she agonized over Harry's infidelities (there is no record of her tolerating physical abuse), the modern image that she and Harry presented to the world required her to bear her suffering in silence. She did not register any public complaint when Harry dedicated to Josephine his latest Black Sun Press book, a collection of poetry entitled *Transit of Venus.* Caresse did, however, demonstrate her wrath while editing Harry's diaries the following year. Among a group of out-of-sequence fragments in Harry's notebooks was the following:

> Transit of Venus (for Josephine)
> Sleeping Together (for Caresse)
> (these are the two books I have written which are damn good the others can go to hell)

With a thick, heavy pencil, Caresse crossed out the words "for Josephine" on her typescript of these entries.[7]

Harry's diaries were published in three "series": (1) 1922–1926, (2) 1927–1928, and (3) 1929. The first editions were published by the Black Sun Press, and then by Black Sparrow Press edited by Edward Germain in 1977. Caresse did not permit the doubts and concerns that surface in Harry's diaries to infiltrate the public memory of *The Passionate Years.* Indeed, her editorial judgement concerning the diaries was guided by a wish to hide some aspects of Harry's affairs of the heart. Germain, on the other hand, maintains the integrity of Harry's entries. From his edition, we learn that Caresse eliminated a number of references to Josephine in order to reduce the significance of the growing intimacy between Josephine and Harry. In one instance, Caresse struck out Harry's statement that he and Caresse were "no longer in love." The entry that followed this deleted declaration reads "now we are in love again." Caresse added the word "wholly" to the entry.[8] She also deleted Harry's broken account of his Detroit holiday with Josephine, which exists in typescript. In the 1930 edition of the *Shadows of the Sun,* the December 5, 1929, entry substitutes "Thank the Sun for Harry and Caresse" for Harry's "J and I each other's arms visions security happiness."[9] Caresse comes closest to confessing that she censored the diaries when she states in *The Passionate Years* that she was going to be faithful to the memory that she preferred to preserve of her life with Harry: "I found my lesson in the pages of the *Needlewoman:* 'If a garment is burnt, it may be possible to embroider the edges to hide the damage.'"[10]

Privately, however, Caresse gave way to her fears and frustration. In "One Spring," she worried that Constance and Josephine were "pursuing" Harry. Harry had told her after all that both women had wanted to marry him. Indignant, she wondered if these women cared about how she felt. She asked herself if she should be fighting harder to keep her husband home:

> I don't know how to attack. I must learn. Take Constance. Take Josephine. They attack again and again and take terrific punishment too—but will they get what they want? I think not—and yet they have had so much of him already—of my Harry—*Mine.* Can I say that any longer? . . . I can't remember ever having launched a campaign to win anyone.

In *The Passionate Years,* she tempered her jealousy by referring to the assignation between Harry and Josephine (that occurred in the Boston home of Robert "Beany" Choate, the divorced husband of Harry's sister Kitsa) as no more than a "foolish secret rendezvous."[11] Yet she was haunted by the stare of Josephine's "small white face" in the crowd at the 1929 Harvard-Yale game that she attended with Harry and his parents. She likened the image to an "impervious ticking clock:" the nature of her marriage to Harry rendered her powerless to prevent such compromising situations. She channeled her venom against the people who made her miserable into the game she was watching: "I have hated football ever since."[12]

The year 1928–1929 was sheer hell for Caresse. Yet she was fully immersed in editing responsibilities for the Black Sun Press. A selected list of titles published during this period includes: *The Birthday of the Infanta* by Oscar Wilde; *The Fall of the House of Usher* by Edgar Allan Poe; *Letters of Henry James to Walter Berry, Sun,* and *The Escaped Cock* by D. H. Lawrence; *Short Stories* by Kay Boyle; *Tales Told of Shem and Shawn, Three Fragments from Work in Progress* by James Joyce; *Secession in Astropolis* by Eugene Jolas; and *Einstein* by Archibald MacLeish. There were eight titles of works by Harry and Caresse; for several of these volumes, Caresse serving as illustrator as well. The joy of seeing a job well done—the volumes are exquisite and now collectors' items—was not enough.

A March 17, 1929, journal entry shows Caresse in trouble.

> There have been so many bad days I have not had the courage to write. . . . I find editing six books at a time hard work and at night I am exhausted, and Spring in the air makes me long for the simplicity and wonder of hand in hand love.[13]

Harry had not been able to gratify her yearnings: he had been "moody and secretive." Caresse adds that she "has not seen A at all." "A" is Armand de la Rochefoucauld, the Crosbys' friend who was so instrumental in their leasing Le Moulin du Soleil in Ermenonville. Fourteen years her junior, "short, sandy haired, full of love and the devil,"[14] he was among Caresse's lovers—quite a coup for her since he was enormously wealthy and one of the most sought-after bachelors in Paris. But no matter how hard she tried to live the life she had enthusiastically embraced, Caresse reached inconsolable lows.

Harry was the one obsessed with death, but Caresse nearly killed herself trying to jump out the window of their Paris home at the end of September in 1929.[15] Although she and Harry had been quarreling over Armand, Caresse never permitted herself to consider the possibility that she should leave

Harry. Over and over, she assured herself that she and Harry had created the most wonderful marriage, an illusion that Harry encouraged her to entertain. "Being together," he would say, "one sometimes loses the true sense of values but the moment we are apart my compass needle points strong and steady penetrating straight into your heart . . . There have been magnetic storms but always the needle has returned seeking its target in your centre."[16]

Caresse attributed her depression to a general despondency that was exacerbated by smoking opium. She felt both agitated and "helpless like the fairy tale Princess chained to the rock while the tide creeps higher and higher" she wrote to one lover.[17] Her melancholy over Harry's mounting infatuation with Josephine and his steady devotion to Constance was transformed into dreamy verse about the mystery of love, as in "Prologue for A":

> Dim castles miming the sublime
> Will glimmer in the memory where
> A castle once upon a time
> Was as a cup of silver air
> To hold the curious wine of wondering
>
> No fuller cup had ever trembled there
> No moon had ever struck so deep a light
> On casement corridor or stair
> And just as love is sometimes still,
> So still the night was.
>
> (And she to know that queens had
> shared this secret
> To know as queens had known
> their castles built of air.)[18]

Caresse's lovers, like Armand de la Rochefoucauld, for whom this poem is written, or Cord Meier ("the Aviator"), could not replace Harry's hold on her heart and soul.

Caresse often locked Harry out of their bedroom after frantic arguments, but tears and talk the next day invariably brought reconciliation. Caresse would confess to herself that "once the first small treachery is fulfilled or even conceived, how the whole aspect of love changes. We rebel, we accept, we hope, we doubt, we love more fanatically than before, but it is less free less simple less natural."[19] No matter how far each of them strayed from one another, they would always, eventually, come home. Such a compromise brought her peace: "Now I feel better than I have for ages,"[20] she wrote at the end of one particularly stormy episode. Such harmony was illusory and temporary. As a peace offering, Harry gave her an exquisite diamond necklace. The dazzling gift was "at once a caresse and a goad, and a blow to the pride" that she would wear as a "badge for invulnerability and for attack."[21] In that capacity, it was worthless.

Consider the scenario for the final weeks of their life together. It was hardly intimate. There was their transatlantic crossing in November 1929: Constance was on board the *Mauritania* with them, and Josephine sent Harry a radiogram four days before the ship docked in New York on November 22. Constance traveled with Caresse and Harry to Boston, where Harry and Josephine set off after the Harvard-Yale game for their woozy sojourn to Detroit, already described. For the moment, Harry's other romantic liaisons had been tamped down.

Back in New York City, Caresse and Harry took a room on the 27th floor at the Savoy Plaza. Harry's mother moved into the room opposite theirs a few days later. Constance was also in the city. Gazing out the window on a sunny December 10 morning, Harry proposed that he and Caresse jump. Although Caresse had already agreed to end her life with Harry, she preferred to wait for the date they had set, October 4, 1944. She persuaded Harry that the next best thing to suicide would be to return quickly to Paris where Black Sun Press activities could deflect his attention from morbid thoughts, and from Josephine. Caresse and Harry booked passage for December 13.

The trip to the States had its rewarding moments. On December 7, Hart Crane hosted a raucous party in his apartment near the Brooklyn Navy Yard. Present were Flossie and William Carlos Williams, E. E. Cummings, Walker Evans, Peggy and Malcolm Cowley, and a number of sailors whose names no one seemed to know. There were elegant luncheons and suppers, theater, and shopping in the busy, festive stores along Madison and Fifth Avenues, already decorated for Christmas. December 10 should have been a pleasant memory to take back to Paris.

Harry and Caresse had mapped out a busy schedule for that day. They attended an exhibition at a Fifty-seventh Street gallery that featured a sculpture of their beloved whippet Narcisse Noir. They parted for lunch with the understanding that they would meet Harry's mother for tea at Uncle Jack's, where Harry would present his uncle with an exclusive copy of *Sleeping Together.* At seven o'clock, they were to dine with Hart Crane, his friend Margaret Robson, and Mrs. Crosby at the Caviar Restaurant, and then proceed to the Broadway production of John Balderston's *Berkeley Square* as guests of Mrs. Crosby.

Harry did not show up for tea or dinner. By 8:15, Caresse was in full panic. She telephoned their friend the portrait painter Stanley Mortimer, who had made available his studio at the Hotel des Artistes for assignations between Harry and Josephine, who had followed Harry back to New York after their Detroit tryst. Mortimer promised to go to the studio at once. Fifteen minutes later, Mortimer called the Caviar with the news that his studio was locked from the inside and that the hotel superintendent had been summoned. Against their better judgement or perhaps in desperate hope, Caresse, Mrs. Crosby, Margaret Robson, and Hart Crane proceeded to the Lyceum Theater.

It became Hart Crane's duty to answer Mortimer's telephone call to the theater.[22] The door to the studio had been broken down with an axe. Harry and Josephine were inside, dead, in bed together. They each had a single bullet hole in their head, and Harry clutched a pistol in his right hand. The coroner's report indicated that Harry had died at least two hours after Josephine, leading to speculation that while the grisly scene appeared to be a double suicide—the couple was in an affectionate embrace—Harry may have committed murder.

Caresse was too shocked to approach the scene of the crime but begged Archibald MacLeish to act on her behalf by identifying Harry's body, arranging for its removal, and handling formal inquiries from the police. Down from his Massachusetts farm to visit the Crosbys while they were in New York, MacLeish had been with Caresse and Harry in their room at the Savoy Plaza on the evening of December 9 and had witnessed the mounting tension between Harry and Caresse. Although Josephine was supposed to have left New York that day, she had gotten off the Boston-bound train at 125th Street and called Harry from the Savoy Plaza lobby.[23] She left Harry an envelope that contained a long poem, a record of what she believed kept the flame of their love burning. (Caresse duly acknowledged this missive in a handwritten note scribbled on the back of the envelope.[24]) MacLeish complied with Caresse's wish that he preside over Harry's body until it could be removed from the hotel to the morgue at Bellevue Hospital.

Caresse was determined to reinforce her perception that Josephine had relentlessly pursued Harry until he lost grip on his thoughts and emotions. She deleted from Harry's journal a December 9 entry that indicates one of his deepest beliefs, that the ultimate declaration of love between two people is their willingness to die together: "One is not in love unless one desires to / die with one's beloved. / There is only happiness / it is to love and to be loved."[25] She would not admit that she lost her contest with Josephine even if it had been a battle whose ultimate reward was death.

Indeed, Caresse demonstrated an overpowering need to dispel the suspicion that the sanctity of her marriage had ever been compromised. In 1925, she had given a gold sun ring to Harry during their trip to North Africa, which he wore as a wedding band. At the same time, Harry had given Caresse a sun necklace, and his notebooks and his will indicate that he intended to bequeath the ring to Caresse, and expected her to leave him the sun necklace.[26] In *The Passionate Years,* she states that the ring was on Harry's finger when he died, and that she planned to wear it forever, that it would be on her finger when she was buried: "It was in Tutankhamen's tomb for thousands of years before us. Unless fission unfuses gold, it will endure forever. The eternal circle, the letter 'O.'"[27] In fact the ring was found by the police, crushed on the floor of Mortimer's studio.[28] Caresse had been desperate about retrieving the ring, and begged Archibald MacLeish to look for it during his death watch over Harry's corpse. He sent a wire: "Absolutely certain police removed ring believe me. Archie."[29] Rather than acknowledge that the ring had been removed and destroyed, that Harry had cast her off, she altered its destiny, and reclaimed it as a golden symbol of the love she thought would last forever.

New York City newspapers covered the story for three days, not always accurately but with a good share of sensationalism. The Boston papers played down the more lurid aspects, reluctant to speculate about motivation. According to the *New York Times,* Caresse, Harry's parents, and Stanley Mortimer were among the few people who attended the funeral service for Harry on December 12 at the Protestant Episcopal Church of the Heavenly Rest on Fifth Avenue and Ninetieth Street.[30] (Albert Bigelow brought his wife's body to Old Lyme, Connecticut, for burial.) But the literary community took note. Transatlantic telegrams of condolence arrived from James Joyce ("Deeply shocked by dreadful news. Please accept my sincere sympathy"), Sylvia Beach ("Love and deepest sympathy"), and Kay Boyle ("Here is my devotion and my love and my homage forever and ever)."[31] Boyle's support of Caresse remained lifelong, although her assessment of Harry underwent so marked a change that by the end of her life, Boyle had transformed him from a saint into a tyrant.[32]

From Santa Barbara, California, where she was visiting her ailing father, Constance sent a frantic cable asking if she should return to New York immediately. Closer to home, Hart Crane used Western Union to reiterate his devotion to Caresse: "YOU KNOW WISH TO BE OF HELP CARESSE YOU ARE CARESSE YOU ARE MY FAVORITE FRIEND POLLY CARESSE I SAY CARESSE YOU ARE NOT ONLY ALL BUT YOU UNDERSTAND ALL."[33] On a more restrained but no less eloquent level, Ezra Pound wrote from Venice: "Perhaps I am not too much of a stranger to say that have felt the tragedy of this mornings news. Whether for having lived through something not unlike it, one is any better able to steady those younger than oneself in a crisis, I don't know—but at any rate I would rather write this to you than leave it unwritten."[34]

It is important to recognize here that Caresse was not in a state of total self-delusion. Although Harry had tested their marriage beyond endurance, despite his private and public ruminations about his romantic attachments to other women, up to his last moments, he fiercely held on to his lifelong commitment to Caresse. In a 1928 entry in his notebook, he wrote:

> When Caresse dies Harry dies
> When Harry dies Caresse dies
>
> We desire to be cremated together
> We desire that our ashes be mingled together
> We desire that our ashes be taken up
> In an aeroplane at sunrise
> And scattered to the four winds.[35]

Caresse read these notebooks and made them available for public consumption, perhaps more in self-defense than the determination to preserve Harry's place in literary history.

Geoffrey Wolff believes that Harry committed suicide on principle, that "he killed himself on behalf of killing himself."[36] A man of his word, he had declared many times that he was going to end his life. Harry's friends wanted him innocent and sidestepped the murder question with comments about whether or not Harry had actually loved Josephine, or how serious he had always been about doing away with himself. On the other hand, Edith Wharton, Harry's rival over the Walter Berry estate, would henceforth refer to him as an outright murderer.[37] Caresse herself received a generous amount of compassion from her first husband, Dick Peabody, Polleen and Billy's father. In a brief but emotionally charged letter, he writes: "To think that one whom I have so loved and for that matter shall always, should have to undergo such a misfortune is almost more than I can bear."[38]

Caresse was silent, although years later, she allowed herself to communicate some of the details of Harry's death. The chief justice of Geneva, Switzerland, wrote to her April 9, 1955, because he was overseeing a murder trial in which the defendant had modeled a double suicide after Harry and Josephine's. The judge wondered if Caresse could help him unravel the case. Caresse responded with concern. There were still "mysterious circumstances" surrounding the death of her husband, she wrote, and she was not sure what she could contribute to solving this present case. She did report, however, that Harry had "received a bullet in the thigh evidently shot by [Josephine]," and that Josephine had been in an asylum two years before her death, and was an "exaltee." She acknowledged that Harry had planned to commit suicide, but had set a date fifteen years later than the time of his demise. She suggested that Harry had yielded to the wishes of Josephine, who insisted that they could be married only by death.[39] Twenty-six years after the event, Caresse still wished the world to regard Harry as blameless.

Caresse asked herself what Harry would have wanted her to do next. What did he expect of her now that she was truly alone for the first time in her life? The $100,000 bequeathed to her in Harry's will would not arrive in one sum. The will had also designated generous sums to Josephine, Constance, and others, and Stephen and Henrietta Crosby brought it before a Massachusetts judge who declared the document invalid.[40] Henrietta allayed Caresse's fears that she would not have the funds to live comfortably and maintain the Black Sun Press. In a January 9, 1930, letter, Henrietta wrote: "Steve and I are each going to give you $2000 a year until you get Walter's [Walter Berry's] money & I will send $500 by April first. The $5000 advanced now should come out of the Estate when things get settled up." For the time being, money was not to be an issue of concern.

On December 12, the day after Harry was cremated, Caresse sailed for France, the thought of staying any longer in New York intolerable. Henrietta Crosby accompanied her on the mournful journey. Caresse refused whatever solace her mother-in-law and friends offered. Although she could have spent the transatlantic journey in a luxurious suite, she preferred bedding down midship, below deck, in a small cabin that resembled a coffin. But Caresse did not maintain her solitude for long.

Disembarking in Cherbourg, she was met by Armand and by Nina de Polignac, Harry's cousin. Bill Sykes (the young friend who had smuggled the gold pieces Harry had promised to D. H. Lawrence) brought eleven-year-old Polleen home from Chamonix, and Gerard Lymington flew to Corydon to bring home Billy, who was thirteen years old. Caresse wanted to spend Christmas at the Mill, and family and friends followed her there, among them Cord Meier, whose offer of fox furs and marriage she refused (the proposal more immediately turned down than the coat). Calling upon an enormous reserve of strength, Caresse decided that for the moment she would maintain a superficially social life, but on a deeper level devote herself to the Black Sun Press, specifically to preserving her union with Harry by publishing four volumes of his poetry and one of her own. In general, Caresse's relationship with her children did not alter much. She did not seem to be drawn towards the routines of domestic life in order to fill the huge gap created by Harry's absence.

Billy was back at Cheam School in Surrey in time for the new term. He wrote his mother cheerful letters: he was proud to be prefect in charge of three dormitories, a position that carried with it the right to wear long trousers and write with a fountain pen. He made the usual requests of thirteen year old boys of his class: a pair of roller skates and "sum money as my finances are very low."[41] Sensitive and accommodating, he would also express concern about his mother's state of health and ask for news about the Black Sun Press. He did not appear disturbed by the idea that next year he would be attending Lenox, a Boston prep school, and did not balk at the summer reading list he was to follow as an entering student. Three of the items on the list were of special interest to Caresse: *A Tale of Two Cities,* because she believed that her home with Harry—no. 19, rue de Lille—appeared in the novel; *The Rime of the Ancient Mariner,* a favorite poem of Harry's; and *As You Like It,* because she had played the part of Rosalind to critical acclaim while she was a student at Rosemary Hall.[42] Caresse was not the mother typical of the era, who would have been reluctant to appear this self-absorbed, but she was probably more fun to be with. Before Billy was packed off to the States, he would spend two weeks in Cannes with Caresse and two more weeks at the Mill.

The correspondence between Billy and Caresse suggests that Caresse was slowly adjusting to Harry's death. She managed to keep up a brave front. She even handled the untimely death of her beloved Narcisse Noir gracefully. The whippet had been run over in June 1930 near the Mill. Caresse had kept one of his puppies, Fleur, who looked just like him, and whom she thought would be a great comfort to Billy. "Just think if he [Narcisse Noir] had died without leaving any children," she observed, not catching the irony that Harry had done precisely that.[43]

Caresses's relationship with Polleen was far more problematical. Polleen had spent some time at home with Harry in the rue de Lille apartment, and her own recollections of this period imply that her attachment to Harry was ambiguous. When she learned of Harry's death, she apparently felt more like a woman who had lost her lover than a girl who had lost her stepfather.[44] Polleen's emotions during this period suggest that an unhealthy state of affairs could have been developing between Harry and Polleen. Harry never made a secret of his attraction to young girls. Polleen spent the first night she returned to Paris after Harry's death sleeping in a chaise lounge not far from her mother's bed. Mother and daughter had been grieving together, but Caresse, perhaps in an attempt to comfort her daughter, observed that Polleen was better off with Harry dead. Polleen did not know what to make of this observation, but she felt keenly that her mother was jealous of Harry's affection for her. She believed that her mother stole the letters that Harry wrote to her and the jewelry, books, and paintings that he had given to her. Jealous or not, Caresse knew that such a relationship, between stepfather and stepdaughter, could not be tolerated, no matter how many rules Harry had wanted to break. Polleen stayed with Caresse that winter and spring of 1930 and refused to attend school. Instead, she accompanied her mother on shopping sprees around town, and on trips to London and the English and French countryside.

Of course the literary world took note of Harry's death. Eugene Jolas ran a special Harry Crosby issue of *transition* with accolades from Kay Boyle, Stuart Gilbert, Hart Crane, Jolas, and Archibald MacLeish, who years later would recall that Harry was "frightening because it was perfectly apparent that he didn't exist—he didn't live in the real world at all. But if you could forget that, he was a charming person."[45] Caresse received numerous telegrams and letters, among them an odd tribute from Hugh Henle, treasurer of Rebel Poets, a left-wing association, that included a request that Caresse send poems to Jack Conroy, editor of *Morada.*[46] The winter 1930 issue of the journal was devoted to Harry.

In *Exile's Return,* a study of the 1920s American expatriate scene in Paris, Malcolm Cowley devoted an entire chapter, "Echoes of a Suicide," to Harry. He believed that Harry's life could serve as a paradigm for the decade, and that his suicide was the "last debauch, the final extravagance, the boldest act of sex, the supreme gesture of defiance to a world he despised."[47] Caresse would later describe Cowley's chapter in *Exile's Return* as myth. More interested in preserving Harry's character than in appreciating Cowley's observations about Harry's place in cultural history, she declared that she and Harry "did not know [Cowley] in those days; nor he us."[48] But indeed, Cowley had met the Crosbys at Hart Crane's party for them the same week that Harry died. In the prologue of the 1936 revised edition, Cowley confessed that he would have used Hart Crane instead of Harry as his model, but that his close friendship with Crane made it too painful to write about him.[49]

In a letter to his Italian publisher and friend Pino Orioli, Lawrence was not kind to the memory of Harry Crosby. He wrote that Harry "had always been *too* rich and spoilt: nothing to do but commit suicide. It depressed me very much."[50] But the letter he wrote to Caresse was very supportive, and perhaps it was Lawrence's words that Caresse took most to heart. Not long before Lawrence's own death, he advised Caresse that she should gird herself against the pain that inevitably awaited her:

> Don't try to recover yourself too soon—it is much better to be a little blind and stunned for a time longer, and not make efforts to see or feel. Work is the best, and a certain numbness, a merciful numbness. It was too dreadful a blow—and it was wrong.[51]

Caresse took his advice. She managed to persuade four literary stars to provide introductions to each of the four volumes of Harry's poetry: D. H. Lawrence for *Chariot of the Sun;* T. S. Eliot for *Transit of Venus;* Stuart Gilbert for *Sleeping Together;* and Ezra Pound for *Torchbearer.* (It had been Pound, in the short but moving letter to Caresse, who had speculated about the ability of an older person to console a younger one in crisis, but thought that he was "not too much a stranger" to offer his condolences.)[52] The Black Sun Press published all four volumes in 1931 as well as Kay Boyle's translation of *Mr. Knife, Miss Fork,* by the French surrealist René Crevel. The volume, a favorite of Caresse's, was illustrated by Max Ernst, with a Victorian design, black on white.[53]

Caresse was also busy completing and putting together *Poems for Harry Crosby,* a collection of twenty-eight poems published by Black Sun in 1931. Like all Black Sun books, this one was exquisitely produced. The lettering on the cover was black and red, the red reserved for the title, author, year of publication, the black for publisher and place of publication. The frontispiece was a photograph of the bronze bust of Harry sculpted in classical style by Caresse. Involved as ever with the press, Lescaret hand-set the book in Caslon type. Forty-four lettered copies were printed on Hollande Van Gelder paper together with the sheets of five hundred numbered copies on uncut Latuma paper. The dedication is a slightly revised version of the acrostic "For Harry" that had appeared in *Crosses of Gold* nine years earlier.[54]

At Caresse's request, Stuart Gilbert wrote a seven-page preface, which compares the Crosbys' life together to the "ecstasies" shared by Elizabeth Barrett and Robert Browning:

> Not only in their poems, but also from such glimpses of the Crosbys' home life as one could gather amid the hurried confusion of post-war Paris, it seemed that the capacity of these two young poets, husband and wife, for being thrown into ecstasies about each other's work, their mutual attitudes and aspirations, was the mainspring of their zest for living. The silver cord is loosed, but its glamour survives in these lyrics.

Gilbert continues in this heady style, praising Caresse's poems with words that Mrs. Meynell used to describe Barrett Browning's. Caresse wrote with a "fervent heart" and "an exceedingly active intellect." He appreciated Caresse's ability to recreate Harry's presence, to treat her dead husband as inspiration and companion, ephemeral yet somehow real.

As the speaker in these poems, Caresse has the unsettling habit of being direct and evasive at the same time. She takes for granted her readers' familiarity with the details surrounding Harry's death and with the general circumstances of her marriage. Without using names, she alludes in several places to Harry's relationship with Josephine. While she struggles to control her hostility, which adds some healthy tension to the poems, she often floats into amorphous declarations of devotion to an ideal or concept that she does not fully articulate. "Symbol," the first poem in the volume, for example, could be viewed as a writer's disdain for the weight readers attach to symbols, in this case, the image of one person's hand in another's. Here, whose hands are embraced—the speaker's and her lover's, or her lover's and another woman's—is the clear image that sits in murky waters. "It cannot matter" whose hands are clasped, that is "Only one symbol / For a final matter." However, there is no way to understand the import of the poem, what that "final matter is." Caresse's disdain for someone or something is apparent, but she is unwilling or unable to finger the enemy. Doing so would be contemptible, uncivilized.

In "Ghost," Caresse is quite definite about Harry's ever-present hold on her heart and psyche. He is no ghost "As though the cracking brilliance / of [his] fire / Could fade to ghost." Harry is alive, "curved round the column of [her] mind," she writes in "Sun upon the Glass." A realist on one level, a dreamer on another, she rejects in "Essor" any hope of meeting Harry in an afterlife, but she expects him to accompany her "To the limitless place of hour from hour / . . . To the ampler space of some dreamlost power." Still on her own in "Pinnacle," however, she will be "A pinnacle from which to fly / The flags you flew," sure that in her work and devotion she will be near enough to wave to her beloved.

There are instances where Caresse openly grieves. In "Invited to Die," Caresse specifically refers to the dreadful day in New York when she refused Harry's proposal that they jump from their hotel window and acknowledges her ignorance of the possibility that someone, the unnamed Josephine, would be more obliging.

> I did not guess
> I did not guess

> That madder beauty waited unawares
> To take your hand upon the evening stairs.

Hart Crane, who read the poems in manuscript, thought that "Invited to Die" was "one of the most perfect things" Caresse had ever written: "You are meant to heart-break people—love-ways, poem-ways, courage-ways. I love you."[55] One of Caresse's companions on the evening of Harry's death, Crane felt especially drawn to this work. In general, he believed that Caresse had "written a beautiful and true and tender book."

In "My Heart," she gives an abbreviated but dramatic synopsis of her Paris years with Harry.

> I have hung my heart
>   from a smoky rafter
> I have tied my heart
>   to a chandelier
> I have danced my heart
>   down a street of laughter
> I have flung my heart
>   from a crowded pier

The Quartre Arts balls, the dinners in bed on rue de Lille, the druggy nights on the de Geeteres' barge lurk behind this poem, adding a resonance for readers familiar with Caresse's life. The poem ends with the romantic declaration that her heart will always belong to Harry because it "never misses / The changing of a mood." But as in "You Out of All the World," the poem that immediately follows this one, Caresse bravely if obliquely confronts a private truth: that she would continue to love Harry no matter how deeply she had been hurt and humiliated, that keeping her love alive not only diminished the pain, but released her from whatever guilt she felt over Harry's (and Josephine's) demise. Her friend and formal part-time rival Constance thought as much. She believed that Harry "never suffered, he never was unhappy because of you. You have never the slightest thing to reproach yourself with in your life with him and think what a glorious thing that is to know."[56] Caresse held on to that perspective no matter how many new roads she traveled over the next forty years.

7

Business or Pleasure

There was something manic about Caresse's determination to conduct business as usual in the months that followed Harry's death. She kept her despair at bay by carefully supervising the publication of Harry's oeuvre, and her own poetry, testaments to her life with Harry and her enduring devotion to his memory. She would prove once and for all that she was more than Harry's helpmate. She would continue the Black Sun imprint, deluxe letterpress editions distributed through subscription, and she would launch another kind of operation altogether, a new line of inexpensive editions of contemporary and avant-garde literature in English, a good proportion of it translated from the French. Its nearest competitor was Tauchnitz, the series of paper editions of classic literary works in English established by Christian Bernhard Tauchnitz in 1841 in Leipzig, Germany. When it ceased operations in 1943, nearly six thousand titles by British and American authors had been published.[1]

For the time being, Caresse could count on funds for both ventures. She was recently named an heir to her grandmother's estate, which included substantial holdings in oil fields sixty miles outside of San Antonio, Texas.[2] Although Harry's will was still in probate, Henrietta ("Belle-Mere" to Caresse) and Stephen Crosby continued to reassure Caresse that she could maintain the lifestyle to which she had become accustomed—and that included running the press. "Don't worry about finances," Henrietta wrote on January 14, 1930,"you will be looked after & Steve says he will help with Bill's schooling

& if necessary we will advance you money for the press. If you should need an advance now on the press just cable amount & I'll forward a check as I am better placed than I thought & can & will most willingly."

Despite their support, the Crosbys assumed that Caresse paid little heed to budgetary matters and did not hesitate to offer minor suggestions. Soon after she returned to Boston after accompanying Caresse back to Paris, Henrietta hinted that Caresse might be more prudent about expenses: Did she really need a third servant in addition to her maid and Polleen's governess? Could she allocate less money in her budget for summer expenses, for the coal and wood needed for firing the range and supplying hot water at the Mill? Nevertheless, the Crosbys maintained a steady, rich flow of money across the Atlantic and offered whatever emotional support they could provide long-distance.

Caresse had refused to accept that, in the most basic sense, her life had become undone, and that her identity had been intricately linked to Harry. She was determined not only to run Black Sun on her own but also to expand the list. She would be the devoted if not always dutiful mother and would resume a social life in order to keep bad memories at bay. She could not pull it off. During Easter week of 1930, Caresse took Polleen and Marcelle, her maid, to pick up Billy at Cheam School for a country vacation at Gerard and Mary Lymington's estate in Fairleigh-Wallop near Portsmouth. Caresse, herself, headed for London in search of more sophisticated entertainment. She wanted some cheering up, but she needed more than elegant suppers and plays by Noël Coward. For the first time since Harry's death, the strong public facade that she had cultivated over the past several months cracked.

One occasion she especially looked forward to was a private showing of the art collection of poet and autobiographer Siegfried Sassoon, whose *Memoirs of an Infantry Officer* had been recently published. Although dressed in mourning, she was elegantly turned out from top to bottom, a fragile but beguiling figure with "hair piled high in auburn curls under a swirl of crepe from the rue de la Paix."[3] But Caresse collapsed while climbing the grand staircase to the exhibit at the Sassoon mansion, overwhelmed by the very kind of event she had been so carefully trained to enjoy since her childhood, when she had first set foot in Miss Chapin's on New York City's Upper East Side. She became unnerved: "Before me was a crowded gallery, a mob of celebrities, a floor like glass that reflected the scene as in a mirror, then suddenly the mirror shattered and burst. The din in my ears became intensified. The stairwell whirled like a spinning top and I quietly wilted down beneath the toes of spangled slippers and the heels of polished boots."[4] She did not regain consciousness until she was back in the luxurious confines of the Claridge Hotel. Edward Crowninshield, older brother of Frank Crowninshield, the editor of *Vanity Fair*, was a frequent bedside visitor. Gerard Lymington and Constance (Edward and Frank were her uncles) would soon appear, both loyal to their memories of wild days with the Crosbys and to their complicated friendships with Caresse and Harry.

Anguished and overwrought, Caresse was delivered by her friends to a nursing home, her state of mind in turmoil. For one of the few times in her life, Caresse lost her desire to live: "All the pent-up agony of months surged through me as I lay inert, awake or asleep, the tears flowed on."[5] Doctors feared that she would not recover. It appeared that at the age of thirty-seven, Caresse had suffered a heart attack.

Yet the optimism that girded her soul from the start reasserted itself, and she decided to return to the living soon after her children came to visit. Released from the nursing home, Caresse did not return to stuffy Claridge's, but to the Cavendish, the legendary Mayfair hotel owned by Rosa Lewis, host to royalty, society, and secrets. Caresse was on excellent terms with Rosa, having first been a guest at the Cavendish in 1910 when she was traveling with her Aunt and Uncle Barnum. She had also stayed there with Harry, quaffing vintage champagne from Rosa's famous wine cellar. Harry's image loomed without setting her back, and after a brief stay with the Lymingtons, she, Billy, and Polleen went home to Paris.

Back at the rue de Lille, Caresse behaved like a china doll and hired a valet exclusively for the purpose of carrying her everywhere she wanted to go. Henrietta and Stephen Crosby came from Boston to take her to Rheims for a holiday and gave up the notion that she should emulate a more moderate lifestyle. Instead, the Crosbys bought their daughter-in-law a bright yellow Hotchkiss sedan and engaged Lucien, Harry and Caresse's former chauffeur, to drive it.

Caresse and Polleen enjoyed a lazy, luxurious July in Cannes, guests of long-standing friends Ellen and Philip Barry, whose *The Animal Kingdom* was the current Broadway hit. Billy had already left for the States in order to prepare himself for his first year at Lenox School, his father's alma mater. Florence Peabody, Billy's paternal grandmother, had overseen the purchase of Billy's uniform. August was spent in Ermenonville. Caresse wrote to her mother in New York that she had been "leading a very quiet month here at the Mill. I have been riding a little gently in the Forest, lying around in the sun when it is sun, taking life very easily and everyone says I look much better and fatter in consequence."[6] By summer's end, Caresse and Polleen were back in Paris. Plenty of rest was still on the agenda. Caresse wanted to be in New York with her mother for Christmas and underwent "a series of hypodermic injections" which the doctor told her would make her strong enough to stand the trip.[7]

Finally standing on her own feet again, Caresse began to implement her plans for the press. She did not start her operation alone. Indeed, her first serious love affair since Harry's death coincided with the birth of Crosby Continental Editions. Her ally was Jacques Porel, the son of French actress Gabrielle Charlotte Réjane. Recently separated from his wife, Porel was eager to renew his acquaintance with Caresse, whom he had met in earlier days when Harry was alive. Ever romantic, Caresse described the beginnings of their relationship at the same pitch that she often employed to relate her adventures with Harry, transforming into melodrama a coincidental meeting at a bank in the place Vendôme, followed by a shared meal at the nearby fashionable La Crémaillière: "I realized the die was cast—all eyes turned upon us, most of the lunchers knew Jacques by sight, he was the Beau Brummell of his day, and not a few recognized me—tongues began to wag at once."[8] Drawn to Jacques' charm, wit, and good looks, she decided that her public mourning days were over. If she was going to be criticized for taking up with this popular Parisian, she might as well have a good time. Once again, she was enjoying all that the City of Light and environs had to offer. She reveled in Jacques' passionate nature, and in the delight he took in going to bed with her.

Porel had no particular expertise in the publishing world, and his eye for working within a budget was not any sharper than Caresse's. Unlike Harry, Jacques did not aspire to be a writer or an artist himself, but Caresse was impressed by the ease with which he moved among the cultural elite of Paris. He would help her arrange intimate luncheons with guests such as George Auric, Salvador Dalí, René Crevel, Cole Porter, and Elsa Schiaparelli. He was savvy in his recommendations for titles the Crosby Continental Editions should acquire—*Big Meaulnes* by Alain-Fournier, *The Devil in the Flesh* by Raymond Radiguet, and *Night Flight* by Antoine de Saint-Exupéry. All of them appeared in 1932.

Crosby Continental Editions was owned solely by Caresse, however. While some of the Press's letterhead listed both Jacques and Caresse as directors, there was no joint colophon, no intimation that their working together was an inspirational venture, as Caresse and Harry had imagined Black Sun to be. Eventually, their relationship disintegrated once Porel understood that Caresse could not be sweet-talked into accommodating his peccadilloes.

In her memoirs, Caresse seemed saddened but not devastated by the unraveling of her romantic relationship with Jacques. Although they were both in New York City during the 1932 Christmas season, Caresse spent most of the time visiting her old friends while Jacques cultivated new ones. When Caresse returned to Paris, Jacques stayed on in New York, pulled by fresh romantic interests. Not to appear undone, Caresse convinced herself that Jacques still "possessed a key to the Press, but it no longer fit my heart."[9] As far as she was concerned, they could remain friends. There would be no messy recriminations, no tearful soul-searching. Caresse had reached the point in her life where a transition such as this one did not have to signal upheaval.

For Jacques, apparently, it was not that simple. He had not expected that fidelity would be a condition of their romance. He feared their "partnership" would be threatened, that Caresse's withdrawal of affection was an "act of business disloyalty."[10] His burgeoning career in publishing, which, by the way, had been his first attempt at earning an income, would be crushed. Without Caresse, he was broke, as he made plain when he asked her for a loan of six thousand francs to tide him over until April. In another letter, he writes that soon he won't have any money at all and accuses Caresse of not putting him in the appropriate frame of mind for meeting people and making money. "I have often been told that is the way American women treat their men—but I thought [that for] you and I it wasn't the same." Both anxious and angry, Jacques continued his invective in another letter: "all you American women are . . . born spoiled, living spoiled, dying spoiled, even when miserable."

Such pronouncements continued. Porel challenged Caresse to "find somebody better as a driver, as a lover, as friend." Despite Jacques' vehemence, there were periodical reprises in the romance. Ultimately, a friendship did evolve between Porel and the "little woman," his term of endearment for Caresse. Both Caresse and Jacques cultivated new relationships and revived old ones.[11] Jacques' "estranged" wife became pregnant during this period. Caresse found new lovers, whom Jacques regarded with mild contempt and some jealousy. He would scold Caresse about her escapades, intimating that she was a push-over: "You lose your head, your heart too easily with people you don't know at all. You tell yourself about them, beautiful, poetical stories that are very far from the truth. Look back at those affairs of yours—Men that were very flat, most of the time and of whom you made heroes."

Caresse did not let such outrageous criticism interfere with her business agenda. In fact, contrary to his misgivings, Jacques continued to work with Caresse at the Press but with the understanding that he would mute all challenges to her publisher's authority. Caresse left the Press in Jacques' hands when she visited her family in the United States, and again when she and Polleen sailed to Greece in 1932, the spring cruise Caresse's birthday present from Henrietta Crosby.

Porel had hardly been Caresse's sole consultant. She sought the approval and recommendations of prominent literary figures. She invited herself to a meeting with T. S. Eliot at Faber's editorial offices in London. He had agreed to prepare an introduction for the Crosby Continental Edition of Charles-Louis Phillipe's *Bubu de Montparnasse,* perhaps to make up for the brevity of his introduction to Harry's *Transit of Venus,* an essay which he admitted was superficial.[12] Although Eliot was not satisfied with Laurence Vail's translation of *Bubu,* particularly his rendition of French slang, he was pleased to help make better known the novel that for him had epitomized Paris low life in 1910.[13]

Caresse was proud to have Eliot's cooperation, to know that he was enthusiastic about her list of projects—he also endorsed her decision to publish Raymond Radiguet's *The Devil in the Flesh,* translated by Kay Boyle with an introduction by Aldous Huxley. She enjoyed a transitory familiarity with Eliot over these works, a mix of serious literary talk and more mundane topics such as Eliot's difficulty in securing a dog sitter for Vivien Eliot's Sealyhams.

Caresse started to resemble her old spunky self. She was adamant about expanding her list of writers, both for deluxe subscription-only Black Sun Press books and for inexpensive paperback Crosby Continental Editions. As before, she was drawing on her own private resources—Crosby estate money at this juncture—to pay writer, translator and printer, and for any publicity. The lure of motherhood continued to elude her as rewards grew for being a woman out in the world of art and business.

For her deluxe books, she traveled to Berlin for the green and brown inks that were essential for creating vibrant and enduring texts. Caresse's doctor advised her to moderate her activities. Porel cautioned her that such a trip would tax her energies: "you know the amount of activity you display for anything and going around everywhere is going to exhaust you." But she paid no heed to his warning that her "spontaneous and childish" behavior would land her in trouble (perhaps because, in part, at the same time, Jacques admitted his admiration for such behavior).

Hart Crane's *The Bridge* was finally published with three photographs by Walker Evans. (To Caresse's dismay, however, reviewers would refuse to touch the book until Liveright's commercial edition appeared on April 1.)[14] Among the twenty-eight other titles that appeared between 1930 and 1936, several are outstanding letterpress specimens: Lewis Carroll's *Alice in Wonderland,* with six lithographs by Marie Laurencin; *New Found Land,* poems by Archibald MacLeish; *New York: 1929,* photographs by Harry and Caresse's faithful friends Gretchen and Pete Powel ("the Crouchers"); *Collected Poems* by James Joyce with a crayon portrait by Augustus John; *Surrealism* by Julien Levy, with sixty-four illustrations; and *Interregnum* by George Grosz (whose studio Caresse visited in Berlin), with an introductory comment by John Dos Passos, sixty-four drawings, and a hand-painted lithograph by George C. Miller. Kay Boyle's translation of René Crevel's *Mr. Knife, Miss Fork* finally appeared with an illustration by Max Ernst. Without Harry, Caresse had established bona fide credentials as a publisher of fine books. Too bad that Porel admonished her: "You go here and there, and fuss alot. All that is terribly bad for your heart."

From his home in Rapallo, Ezra Pound took notice of Caresse's ambition. Hardly one to be fooled by dilettantes and forever on the lookout for publishers, Pound perceived Caresse as a valuable source for helping worthy new writers. He wholeheartedly endorsed her new venture in paperbacks. Like Eliot, Pound had written an introduction to a collection of Harry's posthumously published poems,[15] the fourth volume, entitled *Torchbearer,* in which Pound attributed Harry's suicide to "excess vitality" and praised him for not listening to his elders who would have preferred that he become a banker. Black Sun had also published in 1930 a deluxe edition of Pound's *Imaginary Letters,* the letters he and Wyndham Lewis had published earlier, in 1917, for the *Little Review.* He was pleased with the volume even though he suspected that major publishing firms such as "Random Louse" eventually placed a stranglehold on such editions. Pound also saw an opportunity to complete his edition of the works of Guido Cavalcanti, originally taken on by Aquila Press, now defunct. That wish did not materialize.

A steady correspondence between Pound and Caresse was struck up after Caresse sought out Pound's advice about which writers Crosby Continental Editions should publish and also concerning the financial decisions she needed to make if the Press was going to survive. Pound was eager to compete with Tauchnitz, the only European publisher reprinting classic and modern English texts, but he also made it plain to Caresse that he regarded his role in her enterprise as that of a publisher's reader, someone who gets "a fee for advice, and that ends it. It is either taken or dropped. He is not expected to use the arts of persuasion."[16] Pound wanted nothing to do with negotiating fees for translators or being "held even indirectly responsible for having authors insulted."[17]

That said, Pound composed a list of writers whom he thought Caresse should approach and proposed to help publicize her efforts in his bimonthly literary column for the Rapallo newspaper *Il Mare.* A list of these writers includes Wyndham Lewis, James Joyce, Robert McAlmon, James Farrell, E. E. Cummings, Ernest Hemingway, Mike Gold, and Jean Cocteau. Although he thought it a "dog's job," Pound himself offered to edit an anthology of American poets ("to beat the damn Tauchnitz mortuary").[18] He also suggested that Caresse publish "any damn french or american best sellers that haven't been nabbed by Tauchnitz."[19] When Caresse suggested publishing some of the writers who had appeared in *transition,* Pound was not enthusiastic but conceded that he had no right to object to them. Pound encouraged Caresse to work through her ideas with him. "If you want any more yawp from me; go ahead and ax questions."[20] A long-distance friendship ensued; their face-to-face encounters were numbered yet memorable in very different ways.

Although they had corresponded with each other for some time, Caresse and Pound met for the first time during early spring of 1930 in Paris. Too soon after Harry's death, Caresse was in no mood for an adventure on the town. But after a quiet supper at the rue de Lille, Pound wanted a little excitement. Caresse took him to the Boule Blanche, a club on rue Raspail in Montparnasse, featuring a band from Martinique. Caresse resisted the vibrant rhythms of the music, but Pound could not sit still. Impatient with the tepid, self-conscious movements of the Europeans and North Americans on the dance floor, Pound grabbed the young woman selling cigarettes and led her through a furious pace of numbers in a fit of "Anglo-savage ecstasy."[21] Earlier that evening, Pound had appeared to be the epitome of the laid back expatriate, "bronzed and negligé . . . a becoming saltiness to his beard."[22] Now though he was full of abandon: "head back, eyes closed, chin out, he began a sort of voodoo prance, his tiny partner held glued against his piston-pumping knees."[23]

After Pound let down his guard, he and Caresse became, beyond colleagues in publishing, friends as well. Writing from Rapallo sometime later, Pound alluded to the good time that he had at the Boule Blanche: "Rapallo is not so multiplus with jassbanz as Montparno, but there are enough for our modest wants. My system is, as you possibly observed, to dance it and find out what it was afterward." What the cigarette girl from Martinique thought of Pound's technique remains a mystery.

Although many of the projects that Pound recommended to Caresse were never realized, she periodically approached him with ideas for new ones. She would not always accept what he offered: "I love good advice, I always have, and I court it. But I am as stubborn as a mule about advice that I don't aim to swallow."[24] Although it never got off the ground, one venture that she and

Pound supported with equal enthusiasm was a collection of drawings by Henri Gaudier-Brzeska, the early abstract sculptor and exponent of the Vorticist movement. After he moved to London in 1911, Pound had become Gaudier-Brzeska's patron and promoter. Caresse had discovered the artist at the Tate Gallery. In 1934, she was working on the Gaudier-Brzeska collection, which would include an introduction by Pound, "but the book never did get going and then the war came." Caresse was disappointed by her failure to publish the book. Such a collaboration would have reflected a true meeting of minds.

Later, during the 1950s and 1960s, Pound and Caresse would be connected by at least two other aborted projects. In the fall of 1956, Caresse was introduced to William Watt by her cousin, Boylston Adams Hinds, related to her through his mother Elizabeth Beale, a descendant of the New England Adamses. Caresse was still living in her home near Dupont Circle. Watt was impressed by both home and host.

> [The house] was obviously the abode of someone of taste and means. It was rather heavily furnished, mostly in heirlooms. . . . Caresse was an extremely gracious host, and was moreover that rare combination of *grand'dame* and, reflecting her earlier years, a bit of a *coquette.* She was elegantly if exotically dressed, and well-coiffed, and, though warmly welcoming, indeed vivacious, also duly reserved.[25]

Along with Hinds and another friend, Richard Melville, Watt sought advice from Caresse and Ezra Pound for starting a new journal to be called *Agora.* Full of encouragement, Caresse offered to revive *Portfolio* as an insert to *Agora.* In order to help Watt build support for the magazine, she lent him her list of *Portfolio's* subscribers. But plans for the magazine fizzled. Financial support remained a problem. And the more Ezra Pound heard about the project, the less interested he became. Apparently, Caresse's backing the of journal did not convince Pound of its merits.

The other unrealized publication was conceived later, in 1961. Caresse wrote to Pound in Merano about publishing his letters to her, along with those of D. H. Lawrence, James Joyce, Eugene Jolas, Hart Crane, and Ernest Hemingway, in a volume to be titled *Letters to the Editor.* Pound showed little interest in this enterprise as well. Nevertheless, Caresse would remain solicitous of Pound's friendship and guidance. She had helped Pound during his most difficult times when he was arrested for treason after World War II.[26] Her loyalty to him lasted to the end of her life despite her apprehension about his political perspective.

Caresse had known all along that if Crosby Continental Editions were going to get off the ground, she needed a big name for its first title. She approached Ernest Hemingway. While Harry was still alive, they had asked Hemingway for a story for Black Sun. After her return to Paris in the winter of 1930, she wrote to Hemingway again. She reminded him of the dinner they had shared during which he agreed to send a story as soon as he found a break in his busy schedule.[27] From Piggott, Arkansas, Hemingway replied that he would indeed send a story. Thrilled by his quick, positive response, Caresse made plans to ask Dunoyer de Segonzac to make lithographs for it.

The story under consideration—recommended by their mutual friend Archibald MacLeish—was "A Natural History of the Dead," which Hemingway was to later integrate into *Death in the Afternoon.* Hemingway had doubts about publishing the story separately and eventually withdrew it from Caresse's consideration after Caresse made the mistake of speculating whether or not she could really afford to pay Hemingway $700 for the 150 copies of the story Black Sun would print. Caresse had also expressed reservations about the manuscript, which she assumed Hemingway had hastily submitted for the advance he needed in order to book passage back to the United States: "it seemed to be mostly one-word lines of four-letter words. The whole thing amounted to about one thousand words and had nothing to do with toreadors. It looked to me like a discarded passage from *A Farewell to Arms.*"[28] In actuality, Hemingway had worked on the story throughout 1930 and 1931. It was very much in the experimental mode, a mixture of narrative and exposition that was chastised by book reviewers, who had also attacked Hemingway for his indecorous language.[29]

Any hard feelings between Caresse and Hemingway, however, soon evaporated. Hemingway was ready to return the advance in full. He had not closed all doors to Caresse and relayed the best of wishes for her press. In response to Caresse's request for a book to launch Crosby Continental Editions, he offered the rights to reprint *The Torrents of Spring* in Europe only. Caresse sprang at his offer and, eager to get the best deal possible, asked him if she could also have *In Our Time,* her favorite Hemingway book. He complied. *Torrents of Spring* was published in December 1931, and *In Our Time* in June 1932, the sixth title in the CCE series. Between these two volumes appeared *The Devil in the Flesh,* William Faulkner's *Sanctuary; Bubu of Montparnasse;* and Dorothy Parker's *Laments for the Living,* a collection of short stories that included well known "Big Blonde," published two years earlier by Viking Press. Four more titles would follow between July 1932 and November 1932: *Night Flight* by Antoine de Saint-Exupéry, translated by Stuart Gilbert, and with a preface by André Gide; *Year Before Last* by Kay Boyle; *Big Meaulnes* by Alain-Fournier, translated by Françoise Delisle, and with an introduction by Havelock Ellis; and *The Indefinite Huntress and Other Stories* by Robert McAlmon, edited with much tug and pull by Kay Boyle.

Caresse had ambitious plans to capture attention for Crosby Continental Editions beyond opening the series with a Hemingway title. As a preface to *Torrents of Spring,* she published an open letter to Hemingway, thanking him for his generosity but also explaining to readers the general philosophy of the editor. The letter is a strange combination of publishing hype, good will, and an introduction to the global perspective that Caresse would develop over the next three decades. She wanted to create a line of books that she could sell cheaply, and she wanted those books to serve as opportunities for people to understand cultures other than their own. Although the language that Caresse used to express her mission is bombastic and patronizing, by the end of the letter, she makes clear a genuine interest in creating a list of titles accessible to both sophisticated and general readers. Yes, she wanted to make a profit by selling in volume. Nor would she reject any fame that might go along with the success. But she also wanted to provide a source for people who were not affluent but wanted to read "modern masterpieces in English."

Still on good terms with Hemingway, Caresse and Jacques Porel attended a bullfight with him and his wife Pauline Pfeiffer. Charlie Chaplin was also there, sitting in the box reserved for honored visitors. Caresse longed for the adulation that she saw the crowd bestow upon Chaplin and Hemingway: "There are, they say, a hundred gateways to the Temple of Fame and, woman-like, I fondly hoped to wedge my way in by one of them!" The innocence, or lack of guile, with which she expressed her ambition, was harmless enough. But as yet she had no idea of how to articulate the global perspective of CCE without sounding foolish. She boasted that her list of books would offer "something more than local colour, rather the racial consciousness that makes and mixes the colour, as the painter mixes the paint on his palette." Hyperbole and crude vocabulary aside, Caresse's publishing venture was noble, in the best sense of that word. Her list of new titles and translations would enable readers to appreciate more thoroughly and completely unfamiliar worlds. She would provide easy-to-read books (for fellow passengers crossing the Atlantic on the Île-de-France), and more difficult books that challenged the intellect in new ways.

Caresse worked enthusiastically to get CCE off the ground, but by 1932, she realized that she could not afford the drain on her personal income. She set off for New York in search of an American publisher that would put its weight behind her list. She made the rounds—Random House, Simon and Schuster, Doubleday, and others—without success. No one believed that the American public would buy paperbacks. She was offered, however, two proposals that would create an international Black Sun Press. Random House suggested that she continue to publish Black Sun Press books in Paris, and that Random House distribute them in the States, with Random House and Black Sun sharing the imprint. Caresse was ready neither to share an imprint nor part with her American distributor, Harry Marks, even if he was better known for selling erotica than high-toned literary works.

Recognizing her spirited publisher's instinct, Clifton Fadiman at Simon and Schuster offered Caresse her own Black Sun imprint for a series of modern novels. She would be responsible for acquiring titles and editing manuscripts. Caresse liked this proposal well enough but objected to Fadiman's option to veto her selections if he thought they would not sell—a judgement call that Caresse hesitated to place exclusively in someone else's hands. Her list of authors hardly included household names: Kay Boyle, René Crevel, and Emmanuel Carnevali, the writer and critic to whom Boyle's great love Ernest Walsh had been especially devoted, and who was now suffering from encephalitis and at death's door.[30] (Boyle had been quite insistent that Caresse give Carnevali an advance for his novel *The First God.*) Even if he had written from "The Inner Sanctum" of Simon and Schuster a confidential editorial report in which he stated that at this stage in her career, Boyle was "too esoteric, too subtle, too extreme, too mysterious" to attract a wide readership, Fadiman supported Caresse's interest in Boyle. He predicted that in ten years time, Boyle's "tremulously sensitive, poetic, vivid" prose would probably build a "large *cult* audience, exactly similar to Virginia Woolf's."[31] However, Fadiman rejected outright Crevel and Carnevali. He suggested they go after Katherine Ann Porter and Willa Cather, two authors that left Caresse cold. Frustrated by Fadiman's mainstream taste, at one of their meetings, Caresse broke down in tears and stormed out of Simon and Schuster's offices, terminating any possibility of a collaboration.

Although Boyle and Caresse were dearest friends, Boyle was not about to let friendship stand in the way of getting a contract for herself or for others. Ann Watkins, Kay Boyle's agent, who was privy to Caresse's negotiations with Simon and Schuster, and who bore allegiance to neither Crevel nor Carnevali,[32] was instructed by Boyle to sign a contract for *My Next Bride* only if Carnevali and Ernest Walsh (but not Crevel) would also be provided for. Watkins managed to land a contract for Boyle, Carnevali, and Walsh (who was dead), not with Simon and Schuster but with Harcourt.

Ironically, Boyle had drawn on early years of friendship with the Crosbys in order to write *My Next Bride.* Indeed, in a passionate letter to Caresse (September 30, 1933), Boyle insisted that she had written the novel for Caresse, that it was "in every way" Caresse's book, and that she was "absolutely heartbroken" over the possibility that her decision to go with Harcourt might jeopardize her friendship with Caresse. Caresse had to agree that Boyle should go with the highest bidder—that is, cut her ties to Black Sun and Simon and Schuster, and go to another publisher—if she wanted to protect her career.[33] She also knew that Boyle was desperate for income. The friendship between the two was, after all, strong enough to sustain Boyle's defection to Harcourt. And Caresse did reprint Boyle's *Year Before Last* in 1932, first published by Harrison Smith and Robert Haas. In the end, Harcourt defaulted on its contract with Carnevali.[34]

In the account of her meeting with Clifton Fadiman, Caresse omitted a major detail that helps to explain why she lost her self-control when Fadiman rejected her list. She and Fadiman met in the office of Richard L. Simon, who was present during the negotiations. Caresse acknowledged that she had great faith in Simon's expertise as editor but made no mention of the fact that she and Simon were intimate, that he was the mysterious "D," the "visiting publisher" with whom she had traveled to the Riviera in May 1933. In her biography of Kay Boyle, Joan Mellen reports that at the end of Caresse's meeting with Fadiman, she threw a bottle of ink in Simon's face, which "ended not only any chance" of Simon and Schuster's publishing Emmanuel Carnevali but also Caresse's love affair with Dick Simon.[35] A closer look at Crosby and Simon's relationship, which had begun a year before, provides some insight into the kind of influence Caresse exerted as a woman who courted romance and business at the same time.

Caresse and Dick Simon had met in August 1932 in Sconset. Caresse was visiting her in-laws, who stilled summered at the Apple Trees in Manchester, not far from her own family in Sconset. Although they had little opportunity to spend much time together alone, they had registered their attraction to one another so strongly that they agreed to a rendezvous in New York City, where Dick had bachelor's digs in Murray Hill, at 108 East Thirty-eighth Street. Although Caresse had intended to stay at the Pierre, she was at Dick's apartment for almost two weeks of September.

Dick Simon seemed smitten by Caresse—by her sophistication, glamorous image, and strong spirit, and sense of adventure. Caresse was seven years older than Dick, who was thirty-three when they met, a difference in age that mattered little to Dick and was not atypical of Caresse's relationships—after all Harry, Jacques Porel, and the Count de la Rochefoucauld were all younger than she. At this time in his life, Dick was conflicted about his responsibilities as publisher. He easily got involved in concocting different schemes for advertising Simon and Schuster books and took pride in such successes as Leonard Ehrlich's *God's Angry Man,* Henrik von Loon's *Geography,* and new books about bridge and jigsaw puzzles. But he was also a serious musician who yearned to work full time at composing for the piano. He hoped that someday he might have the chance to take a long leave of absence from Simon and Schuster so that he could pursue his own creative talent instead of encouraging authors to develop theirs. And that side of him, the part that rebelled against toeing the line, pushed him toward Caresse.

At the start, Caresse and Dick could barely contain their passion for one another, even if that passion could be expressed only in letters and cables. They greatly anticipated their rendezvous in the city. On September 14, 1932, soon after his return to New York, Dick wrote to Caresse, who was still in Manchester, that "It's rather astonishing and thrilling to think how much I look forward to seeing you. Scarcely knowing one another makes it all the more exciting."[36] While they were in Sconset, they had watched an eclipse together, an event that became symbolic for them of their eagerness to be with one another as much as their "cosmic destiny allow[ed]," in the words of Caresse. They approached their burgeoning affair with the eagerness of a couple far less experienced than they, acknowledging all the while that the pattern of their established lives would, in all likelihood, preclude a permanent commitment. For now they enjoyed the in-between drama of the situation.

The ten days in New York passed swiftly, filled with all the romance they had expected. Dick had given Caresse a key to his apartment, and sometimes she would be waiting in bed for him when he returned from work. They ate early morning breakfast together, dined at a favorite restaurant (Robert's on Fifty-fifth Street), petted in the back seat of taxis on the way to the theater or a gala at the Waldorf (when Dick was especially dazzled by Caresse in an elegant blue evening gown), strolled through Tiffany's (where Dick bought Caresse a ring), and sipped gin rickeys at cocktail hour. When other friends claimed their time, they silently enjoyed their chance meetings: at a production of *Maedchen in Uniform,* Caresse sat one row forward and two seats to the left of Dick.[37] Dick would play Mozart and Beethoven sonatas for Caresse on the piano in his living room. He thought that he had never played as well before. In lighter moments, Caresse and Dick danced to popular music on the phonograph as a prelude to their lovemaking. They were on leave from ordinary life, as Harry and Caresse had been in the early days of their romance—

keeping it clandestine, believing that they were tapped into a great current of passion too strong for most people to endure.

In early October, Caresse sailed back to Europe on the *Lafayette,* and a rich correspondence developed. Dick apologized for typing his letters to Caresse: faithful to his proper upbringing, which required personal letters to be handwritten, he felt it was "sacriligious" to mention all their "talks and kisses and caresses . . . and the way you say Yesssss" on a business machine.[38] But pen and pencils slowed him down, made him too self-conscious, and he needed to get his thoughts down as directly as he could. Caresse cared little about the medium and wrote a thick packet of letters on her voyage across the Atlantic—it added up to one letter for each day of her trip.[39]

Before Caresse left New York City, she and Dick made a pact about how they would conduct their affair long distance. They agreed that it would be unrealistic to assume that they had entered into a monogamous relationship. Each would be free to pursue other affairs. All that they would ask of one another was an update. If either of them found the love of their lifetime, they would place an "X" at the end of their letter, their romance would be over, and correspondence and any future meetings would be on the level of a warm but casual friendship. However, Caresse and Dick agreed that a sexual liaison with others would not jeopardize the stability of their relationship; indeed, they thought it would be interesting to learn about one another's relationships, each of which they would refer to as a "Y." Jealous thoughts were forbidden.

Much to their surprise, the plan backfired. As the weeks went by, they longed to see one another urgently. In an October 17, 1932, letter, Dick confessed that he was attached to Caresse more than he had imagined he would be, but was trying to keep his emotions in check:

> Listen, Darling, I have found myself thinking of you far more—you are far dearer in my heart, far oftener in it—than I would have thought possible. The first week or two I did think of you often. I smelled those rose petals in the drawer of my dresser and the one next to my bed, I remembered your things in the bath room, and I intimately and closely . . . cherished a thousand little things about you. And all the while it seemed lovely and perfect. I didn't miss them terrifically. And now I do. Not all the time, but often.

He had demurred when Caresse proposed that she send him a silver comb and brush set from Paris, but now he told her he was eagerly waiting its arrival. He wanted another memento besides the photograph of her that he had placed on the bookshelf in his living room. More than that, he wanted Caresse to return to New York immediately. As he neatly put it in an October 31, 1932, letter, "the piano [was] running out of tune." Caresse, for her part, wanted him to drop everything and come to Paris. She had said as much in New York when she proposed that he lead a more reckless life. What better place to do that than Paris?

Unlike Harry Crosby, Dick felt committed to the institution that supported him. If he could arrange a few publishing successes, he would take off for a while. He resigned himself to living with his frustration over Caresse, to seeing the humor in his predicament—that the aloof cad he presented to the world—in his own words, the "cold-blooded bastard"—had fallen in love, had remained in love "so completely with a girl almost four thousand miles away." He was bored with anyone else. Caresse apparently took some pleasure in Dick's suffering; she wanted Dick to be unhappy and lonely without her.[40]

Caresse stood firm in her position that for now, her publishing activities would keep her in Europe. Dick, still amazed that he stayed smitten, did not lose sight of his circumstances or reputation. He decided to honor the arrangement he and Caresse made about "X" and "Y." Indeed, in a November 14, 1932, letter, he felt compelled to report to Caresse that a "Y" had recently entered his life. He was not trying to excuse himself or apologize: "I tell you now because I said I would, and because we're too good friends for either of us to use deception in this sort of thing unless it were at least tacitly agreed that way." On the surface, Caresse was not thrown by the information. Correspondence reached a temporary hiatus, but that was a result of delays in boat mail and winter flu. Caresse revealed that she too had a "Y" during an early winter visit to London. Dick brushed it off in a December 23 letter—"Let's not write each other news of this sort and then comment on it"—and urged Caresse to take the first boat she could to New York. Certainly she had some time to spare, especially since Polleen was in boarding school—an allusion to Caresse's parental responsibilities in addition to her professional ones.

The declarations of love and the taunting and teasing continued. In one letter, Caresse asked Dick whether he would hate it if she were to be a married woman the next time she visited the States. He admitted that he would, but that he would "be a dog to mind," and that he hoped Caresse's reaction would be the same if he were to marry. Dick finally gave in and booked passage to France to visit his "darling," as he usually addressed her, "the Caresse with the blue and gray eyes and the high color and the laughing mouth." He and Caresse were going to drive from Paris to the Riviera. They took off after a few exciting days in Paris, dining at the elegant La Perouse, sleeping together in the Hotel Bristol, and taking long walks with Caresse's black whippet, Fleur—the only daughter of beloved Narcisse Noir.[41] Caresse and Dick spent nearly four weeks together.[42]

Caresse planned the itinerary since the route was familiar to her—she said her chauffeur could drive the road blindfolded. The couple relished the landscape, the culture, and the "sole and truffles with a Chablis sauce fit for angels."[43] They drove through Vienne (where they dined at the famed Pyramid), Saulieu, Macon, Arles, and Cannes before detouring to Villa Coustille in Col-de-Villefranche outside of Nice so that they could visit Kay Boyle, Laurence Vail, and family. As Caresse put it, "the house vibrated with work and fun and that garden supper was the pot of gold at the end of our trail."[44]

Dick was glad to meet Boyle—he would say later that she was "the grandest person" (March 4, 1933) among Caresse's friends—but the busy household turned out to be an inappropriate place for Caresse and Dick to stay. Instead, they found charming rooms with a balcony in a hotel on the Mediterranean for the week. Combining business with pleasure, Dick met with one of his authors who was living near Nice,[45] while Caresse drove back to Cannes to discuss with Jimmy Walker, the popular and debonair former mayor of New York City, the prospect of publishing his memoirs. Walker, known as much for his aversion to enforcing the Volstead Act as for preserving the five-cent subway fare, was living in Europe in order to avoid facing charges of corruption. Several times, Caresse and Dick dropped by Monte Carlo to gamble and had some good luck playing number 36 at the roulette wheel. Back in Villefranche, they dined at Caramello's, sometimes with Kay Boyle. Calvados was their favorite *pousse-café.*

Caresse did not seem to mind when the time came for Dick to leave. It had something to do with his "executive presence," something that made it awkward for her to be with him and the Kay Boyle ménage at the same time for very long. But she may not have been totally honest in marking the time when her affection began to wane, which appears to have been tied in with what would happen in September in Simon and Schuster's offices. Dick wanted her to return to the United States with him, and she encouraged him to think that they would be with one another again. In any event, her reasons for staying in Europe, she thought, were legitimate. She was as loyal to Crosby Continental Editions as he was to Simon and Schuster. They were adults, cool as cucumbers when they needed to take care of business.

Dick retained strong, fond memories of their holiday together and on the voyage home, imagined how grand it would be if Caresse were on board with him, how they could extend their leisurely, hedonistic month, what triumph he would feel when late for supper, they'd enter the dining room, and everyone would stop eating to gaze at Caresse, in a shimmering gold dress, the epitome of glamour.[46] By the spring, however, their correspondence had slackened. Dick was enmeshed in publishing projects once again, very much aware that books were hardly an essential commodity as the Depression asserted itself over the decade. Caresse was as adamant as ever that her press should prosper, and it is within this context that she made her trip to New York City in September 1933 in search of an American partner.

If she expected special consideration from Simon and Schuster, she was not going to get it because Kay Boyle, Carnevali or Crevel were on her list. She chose to ignore the weight of Fadiman's reader's report on Kay Boyle—Dick had sent her a confidential copy. But she had been crossed. Although Dick had told her that he thought Kay Boyle would be the next Pulitzer Prize of Nobel prize winner,[47] he did nothing to help Caresse persuade Fadiman to sign on her authors, short of disagreeing with Fadiman on one or two minor points about Boyle's talent and marketability.

Caresse got a measure of revenge by reserving only a small spot for Dick in her memory. Indeed, in recounting her trip to the Riviera with Dick, she makes a point of saying that "at every turn of the road I remembered that Harry was not with me."[48] In a September 23, 1933, letter, Dick acknowledged that after Caresse's emotional outburst at Simon and Schuster headquarters, their romance was over, and that it had been a mistake to think that Simon and Schuster could have ever served Crosby Continental Editions of the Black Sun Press. (Simon and Schuster published five books by Boyle during the 1940s.) Caresse was still a "darling," still "swell," and Simon would always think of her as "a thrilling and adorable woman," and would "never do, or say or think anything to make the idea of Caresse Crosby other than glamorous and gallant." Caresse took her disaffection one step further. Unless someone was truly interested, Dick Simon would not be apparent on the list of the loves of her life. And in November 1933, Caresse took another romantic journey, this time with "the most glamourous man in the world," through Beaune, Macon, Chablis, Anjou, Yquem, Saumur, Calvados—which she summed up as "Ecstasy upon Ecstasy."[49]

Caresse maintained her enthusiasm for Crevel's work, but *Mr. Knife, Miss Fork*, the first chapter of Crevel's novel *Babylon* (translated by Boyle and illustrated by Max Ernst), remained the only Crevel that the Black Sun Press ever published.[50] Over the next few years, she and Crevel kept up a friendship and exchanged confidences about work and pleasure in their correspondence. Caresse feared that she would have to suspend the Press, which had yet to show a profit. In poor health and consumed by his conflicts with fellow surrealists André Breton and Louis Aragon, Crevel struggled to earn a living between visits to costly Swiss sanitariums, where he tried to slow down the inevitable progression of his tuberculosis. Such concerns, however, did not prevent either of them from pursuing trysts and affairs. Crevel suggested that they might coauthor a best-seller entitled *Between the Legs.*[51]

Crevel often teased Caresse, chiding her for playing the elusive female. In one letter illustrated with a sketch of his tearful face, he accused her of breaking his heart. Caresse recalled a few occasions when she and Crevel had "kissed for comfort," but it was common knowledge that Crevel was in love with a woman much younger than he. And it is likely that Crevel's infatuation was with Caresse's daughter seventeen-year-old daughter Polleen, a secret known only to Caresse and Paul Eluard.[52] By Caresse's account, Crevel did not gas himself to death on June 18, 1935, because of unrequited love. Rather, he was driven to suicide by his disillusionment with André Breton and fellow surrealists, the result of unresolved conflicts between surrealism and Marxism. He was obsessed with reaching a reconciliation, even though Breton had publically humiliated him at a gathering that marked poet Louis Aragon's departure for Moscow by refusing to shake his hand.[53] In failing health, Crevel committed suicide in Paris on the eve of the Congress of the Association of Revolutionary Writers and Artists, convinced that surrealists and communists would remain forever divided.[54]

Crevel had understood Caresse's ambition to be a patron of artists and writers and introduced Caresse to his best friend in need, Salvador Dalí. The association with him turned out to be one of the greater coups of her career. Caresse first met Dalí at a luncheon she gave in her Paris apartment for composer George Auric and his wife Nora, the dramatist Edouard Bourdet, and Crevel. Caresse was surprised when Dalí later recalled that she had served an exclusively white meal that started with cream-of-celery soup and ended with marshmallows and white mint.[55] Dalí described Caresse as dressed in white from head to toe. Although she herself did not remember the menu she had planned, Caresse knew without a doubt that she would never have tried to match white shoes with white stockings. Surprised that Dalí would cast her in such unfashionable light, Caresse accepted the distortion as a small price to pay to gain Dalí's favor.

Caresse Crosby, 1900: "The same winter I went to dancing school."
Special Collections Research Center, Morris Library, Southern Illinois University Carbondale.

Richard Rogers Peabody, Crosby's first husband and father of her children, 1915.
Special Collections Research Center, Morris Library, Southern Illinois University Carbondale.

Harry and Caresse on their wedding day, 1922. Special Collections Research Center, Morris Library, Southern Illinois University Carbondale.

Caresse and Narcisse Noir, Deauville, 1925. Special Collections Research Center, Morris Library, Southern Illinois University Carbondale.

Caresse and Harry, Etretat, 1925. Special Collections Research Center, Morris Library, Southern Illinois University Carbondale.

Clytoris (mate of Narcisse Noir), Harry, Caresse, and Auguste, Le Bourget, 1928.
Special Collections Research Center, Morris Library, Southern Illinois University Carbondale.

Gretchen and Pete Powel, "the Crouchers," 1928.
Special Collections Research Center, Morris Library, Southern Illinois University Carbondale.

Kay Boyle and Harry, Le Moulin, 1928. Special Collections Research Center, Morris Library, Southern Illinois University Carbondale.

Constance Crowninshield Coolidge, Laurence Vail, Kay Boyle, Hart Crane, and Caresse, Le Moulin on the Sun Tower, 1928. Special Collections Research Center, Morris Library, Southern Illinois University Carbondale.

Harry, D. H. Lawrence, and Frieda Lawrence, Le Moulin, April 1929. Special Collections Research Center, Morris Library, Southern Illinois University Carbondale.

Richard Leo Simon and Caresse, St. Anton, 1931. Special Collections Research Center, Morris Library, Southern Illinois University Carbondale.

Caresse peering down at her guests, swimming pool, Le Moulin, 1932. Polleen is second on the left. Special Collections Research Center, Morris Library, Southern Illinois University Carbondale.

Caresse, Billy, and Polleen with Nina de Polignac and her son. Special Collections Research Center, Morris Library, Southern Illinois University Carbondale.

Jacques Porel.
Special Collections Research Center, Morris Library, Southern Illinois University Carbondale.

Kay Boyle and Caresse skiing at Beuil above Nice, spring 1935. Special Collections Research Center, Morris Library, Southern Illinois University Carbondale.

Caresse with Maître Imprimeur Roger Lescaret at the Black Sun Press, 1936.
Yale Joel/Time and Life Pictures/Getty Images.

Caresse and Lescaret outside the Black Sun Press, No. 2, rue Cardinale, Paris.
Yale Joel/Time and Life Pictures/Getty Images.

Blair Clarke, Bert Young, Caresse, Stuart Kaiser, and Billy, Hampton Manor, spring 1938.
Special Collections Research Center, Morris Library, Southern Illinois University Carbondale.

Hampton Manor, 1938. Special Collections Research Center, Morris Library, Southern Illinois University Carbondale.

Salvador Dalí, Hampton Manor, 1940. Special Collections Research Center, Morris Library, Southern Illinois University Carbondale.

Gala Dalí and Salar, Hampton Manor, 1940. Special Collections Research Center, Morris Library, Southern Illinois University Carbondale.

Bert Young, Hampton Manor, 1938. Special Collections Research Center, Morris Library, Southern Illinois University Carbondale.

Canada Lee and Bill Barker, Rome. Special Collections Research Center, Morris Library, Southern Illinois University Carbondale.

Caresse Crosby, "Cittadina del Mondo," with students from Pisa on the steps of the Duomo, Sienna, summer 1948. Special Collections Research Center, Morris Library, Southern Illinois University Carbondale.

Caresse at Rocca, summer 1949. Special Collections Research Center, Morris Library, Southern Illinois University Carbondale.

Caresse opposite Mai and Frans de Geetere, Amsterdam. Special Collections Research Center, Morris Library, Southern Illinois University Carbondale.

Anaïs Nin. Photograph by Robert A. Fitzgerald Jr. Masters and Masterworks Productions, Inc.

Caresse and Peggy Guggenheim, photographed in Venice by Roloff Beny, 1953.
Library and Archives Canada/PRSL 0021.

Caresse with her lawyers on way to trial, *Caresse Crosby vs. Minister of Defense,* Athens, December 1953. Special Collections Research Center, Morris Library, Southern Illinois University Carbondale.

Caresse arriving in Rome from Greece. Special Collections Research Center, Morris Library, Southern Illinois University Carbondale.

Caresse and an unidentified woman beneath the One World Flag at Rocca.
Special Collections Research Center, Morris Library, Southern Illinois University Carbondale.

Caresse at Rocca. Special Collections Research Center, Morris Library, Southern Illinois University Carbondale.

8

Atlantic Crossings

Over the next few years, Caresse cultivated the friendships of many remarkable artists, writers, and musicians. She collected adventures with Max Ernst, Paul Eluard, and Elsa Schiaparelli, who would be the first designer to open a boutique, below her fashion house, on place Vendôme in 1935, as well as with film director Preston Sturges, and with Cole Porter, Philip Barry, and George Grosz. Perhaps one of the best escapades concerned the trip she made from Le Havre to Southampton with Max Ernst in the summer of 1933. In the middle of the night, after a party at Le Moulin, Ernst drove the seventy-five miles to Le Havre at breakneck speed so that Caresse would not miss the boat. At the last minute, he decided to accompany her across the sea. Caresse was delighted: "I was as pleased as I could be, for Max was as wise and amusing a companion as one could hope for, and to arrive in London with the prize Surrealist would mean marks to my credit."[1]

Crossing the channel took on a surrealist edge after Caresse was tapped for a favor by Mildred Dilling, the well-known harpist who was traveling on the same boat. She had exceeded the baggage limitation. Her harp ended up in the bunk-bed berth that Caresse was sharing with Ernst: "We were imprisoned behind bars, as chaste a set-up as ever was. I caught sight of Max's birdlike head between the aeolian strings and laughed until the tears ran into my ears."[2] Max and Caresse's friendship survived the crossing and remained steady over the next thirty years.

In France, Caresse divided her time between Paris, where she continued to hold sedate luncheons at the rue de Lille apartment, and Ermenonville. She preferred the Mill, with its ten bedrooms, a tower, and swimming pool, for less-inhibited parties. She regarded these occasions as theater pieces, public scenes created by surrealist friends on her permanent guest list. They were spinoffs of her soirees with Harry, early versions of 1960s "happenings" and today's performance art without the political edge. One that she held shortly before her cramped Channel crossing with Max Ernst took the form of a costume ball. She put Ernst in charge of the menu, appointed her old lover Armand de la Rochefoucauld as master of ceremonies, and relied on the generosity of her cousin Nina for Polignac estate champagne. First prize for costumes went to Elsa Schiaparelli and André Durst—the photographer for *Vogue* who captured Caresse in a mock-siren pose, dress unbuttoned on top, half her bosom exposed. Caresse's Boston friends were also invited, but the women from this group declined to attend. Apparently they did not begrudge Caresse for moving on with her life, but they felt that their reputations would suffer if news of the party reached local society pages. In their estimation, the presence of daughter Polleen provided no guarantee that a scandal could not be reported. As far as Caresse was concerned, that attitude gave extra cache to her party, and she made sure to include a photograph from it in her memoir.

During the early and mid-1930s, Caresse traveled to Germany and to the south of France, scouting for Crosby Continental Editions, but also visiting friends, especially Kay Boyle when she was on the Riviera or in Kitzbuhl with Laurence Vail and her children. At Boyle's prompting, Caresse became briefly involved with helping Alexander Berkman obtain the documents he needed to remain in France, and eventually to return to the United States. The Russian American anarchist had been deported with Emma Goldman from the United States for the attempted assassination of industrialist Henry Clay Frick in 1919. Taking advantage of her well-placed connections, Caresse had been able to meet with Michel Hauser, an attache at the Ministere des Affaires Etrangeres, where she was allowed to read Berkman's dossier and speak on his behalf. She learned that although the French considered Berkman potentially dangerous, they rated his conduct in France as exemplary. If Berkman would remain in Nice, he would automatically be granted permission to stay every three months. After five years in France, Caresse ascertained that the "embargo" as she described it to Boyle, would be lifted.[3] When Kay Boyle showed Berkman the letter Caresse had written detailing her efforts to help him, his eyes teared up with gratitude. "How can you be such a great-hearted woman and such a beautiful one besides?" Boyle asked her loyal friend.[4] Of course, Sasha (as he was called) Berkman's troubles were hardly over. Caresse would intervene again when he applied for a residency visa half a year later. She also recommended to Simon and Schuster Berkman's proposal for translating and editing a collection of Russian short stories. Despite outward appearances (which sometimes bordered on the frivolous), Caresse was not indifferent to political and social issues and backed up her words with action. As time passed, this part of her personality would assert itself more forcefully.

Caresse made several trips to the States during the mid-1930s. The crossing she made with Salvador and Gala Dalí in November 1934 created one or two headlines. The Dalís' first transatlantic voyage, it also marked the time when Dalí started to achieve commercial success. Julien Levy, a great supporter of contemporary art, had recently opened a gallery on Madison Avenue. He had been urging Dalí for more than a year to come to the United States. But Dalí feared the perils of crossing the ocean to a country where he did not speak the language. When Caresse booked her thirtieth passage on the *Champlain,* she urged the Dalís to accompany her. The promise of Caresse's presence on board gave them the sense of security they needed. Although they were nearly destitute, they scraped together the fare (with the help of Pablo Picasso) for a third-class berth.[5]

Caresse's description of the journey is amusing. It was one of those incidents in her life that she seemed to especially enjoy, since its outcome was a great success. Strapped as she was, financing Black Sun Press projects, Caresse nevertheless managed to travel first-class, with corresponding wardrobe and jewels, a newsworthy member of society who expected to be treated accordingly. On this trip she used her privileged position to push Dalí's career.

From the start of the voyage, Dalí made a spectacle of himself, amusing to Caresse even if, or perhaps because, guests, staff, and crew were not prepared for such engaging eccentricity. Although he may not yet have achieved the success he yearned for, Dalí was convinced of the value of his work. When Caresse looked for him on the boat train platform where they had arranged to meet, she found him in his cabin "like a hunter in covert, peering out from behind the canvases that were stacked around, above, below and in front of him. To each picture he had attached a string. These strings were tied either to his clothing or his fingers."[6]

When the Dalís finally boarded the *Champlain,* Caresse persuaded them that no one would steal the paintings, that Gala needed to eat, and that they should join her in the first-class dining room for supper. As Caresse's guests, they overcame their fears and climbed to the upper deck, covered from head to foot in thick overcoats and mittens to ward off any chill from the night ocean air. Caresse discovered that she was the only one at her dining table who was not scandalized by the Dalís' odd behavior. As the voyage progressed, they added cork life jackets to their ensembles for occasional afternoon walks on deck. The Dalís were snubbed by nearly everyone but Caresse for the duration of the trip.

When the *Champlain* docked in New York harbor, Caresse knew the newspapers would meet it as usual for photographs and a few lines for the society page. Upon disembarking, Caresse pushed Dalí center stage and announced to the press in waiting that they were in the presence of a great surrealist painter. Dalí began to unravel the paintings that he had tied again to his buttons and fingers. Caresse proceeded with "a brief lecture" about surrealism while Dalí tore off the paper from his *The Portrait of My Wife,* a painting of a woman with broiled lamb chops on her shoulders. The reporters' cameras started flashing. Caresse accomplished her mission, or as she put it: "Gala and the lamb chops took the place of cheesecake" for the morning newspapers.[7] Relishing her introduction of Dalí to the press, she nevertheless remained humble about her role in furthering Dalí's career. It was Julien Levy who was his great sponsor from the start. In fact, Levy had helped Dalí prepare "New York Salutes Me," a broadsheet about surrealism distributed to the press at the dock, which may have served as Caresse's crib sheet for her "lecture."[8]

In 1936, the Black Sun Press would publish *Surrealism,* edited by Julien Levy, a cross-disciplinary anthology that included a bibliography of exhibitions of surrealism in the United States; photographs of work by such artists as Eluard, Ernst, Arp, Man Ray, Miró, Chirico, Klee, Dalí, Picasso, and Calder; passages from Rimbaud, Breton (a piece from Eugene Jolas's translation of *Nadja*), Tzara, and a section of Kay Boyle's translation of Crevel's *Mr. Knife, Miss Fork.* Harry Crosby was represented by two brief excerpts from *Sleeping Together.* Joseph Cornell designed the cover. Caresse continued to assert her position in the world of avant-garde artists and writers the best way she could, by creating a public space and acceptance for them.

The next joint caper of Dalí and Caresse's had a name, the "Dream Ball." On January 18, 1935, Dalí and Caresse turned the Coq Rouge, Dalí's favorite restaurant in New York, into a surrealist set. Guests were instructed to wear costumes that evoked their most recurrent dream; the person with the best costume would be rewarded with a Dalí print. Waiters and doorman were outfitted with accessories that Dalí and Caresse picked out in Woolworth's: rhinestone tiaras, hairpieces, wreathes of artificial roses. The more outrageous props included a hundred-pound block of ice tied with a red ribbon and a carcass of a cow with a white veil on its head and in its belly a gramophone that played French songs.

The party, also known as the "Bal Onirique," was covered most extensively in the *Sunday Mirror*. Dalí appeared as a corpse in a tuxedo with a bandage wrapped around his head. Even though Caresse had dressed as "the white horse of dream desire," she was reported to have come as a white rabbit. Gala's outfit, however, actually aroused a good deal of anger. In the middle of her headdress was placed a doll with a wound in its forehead that was filled with painted ants. A lobster clutched its skull, and a glove on each side served as wings.[9] Although Gala's outfit contained some of Dalí's favorite symbols, the public perceived it as a mockery of a recent tragedy, the kidnaping of the Lindbergh baby. Oddly enough, Caresse chose to ignore the public's anger over Gala's costume in her version of the event. She did not mind that a Russian publication described the party as an example of the excess of American decadence; it just added to her sense of its success. She omitted any suggestion that the event had been marred, how Dalí had been forced to make amends with the public and with his "fellow" surrealists who believed he had trivialized their cause.

Caresse's connections to the avant-garde were not confined to writers and artists. She was good friends with Emlen Etting, the painter and illustrator whose works would be represented at the Whitney Museum and the Philadelphia Academy of Art, and who also made experimental films. She and Etting were "always contriving outlets for our surreal response to life."[10] He was a regular among the guests at Le Moulin and easily recalled in a May 11, 1932, letter the pleasures he found there.

> Spring au Moulin du Soleil and the old phonograph churning rudy vallee to the shhh of the waterfall, and the whippets, and the bell ringing . . . and Clito [Clytoris the whippet and wife of Narcisse] making for the woods. . . . champagne and roses. . . . how i should like to see you in your fire cracker dress—all explosions and flames and flashing . . .[11]

Etting and Caresse may have been short-term lovers, since on January 26, 1933, he writes of a "great bond" between them, that they "will always be willing to make mistakes for the ardent desire to transcend." Yet when he learned earlier that Jacques Porel and Caresse had broken up, he did not suggest that a steady, romantic relationship between them was any more likely to occur. Nevertheless, the two remained lifelong friends.

In 1933, Etting produced *Poem 8*, which has been described as a forerunner by fifteen years of the mystery thriller *Lady in the Lake* with Robert

Montgomery.[12] The action of *Poem 8,* a fourteen-minute movie, is seen through the eyes of an invisible observer who "conveys the rush and fervor of love or kindred emotions." Caresse played one of three women and was supposed to represent "passion plus."[13] Etting filmed Caresse during the summer of 1933 (Caresse is off by one year in her memoir) when she was visiting her in-laws at the Apple Trees and he was on his way to visit his mother in Bar Harbour. Mrs. Crosby and a friend had planned a lady's afternoon in town, and when they were gone, Caresse and Emlen went into action. Dressed in a strapless slinky dress and eyes heavy with mascara, Caresse sat down at a dressing table that she and Emlen had dragged out onto the lawn, lifted her head, clutched her bosom, and writhed. A snapshot of this lustful pose was printed in the March 1954 article of *Holiday* magazine by Al Hine.

Poem 8 was included in a series of films presented in 1954 by Cinema 16, an organization founded in 1947 by Amos and Marcia Vogel, who had fled Austria in 1939 after the Nazi invasion. Films in the Cinema 16 series were first presented at the Provincetown Playhouse in Greenwich Village, and *Poem 8* was also shown earlier at the Paris Theater in New York City on October 9, 1949. Etting believed that this film created a poem "conceived directly in the language of visual symbols in action."[14]

By the mid-1930s, Caresse had reached a gaping impasse in her efforts to become a solvent independent publisher. As attached as she had grown to the full life that she was leading in France—a heady mix of work and play—she recognized that it was time to return to the United States. Although her personal finances seemed secure despite the Depression economy, she did not need anyone to warn her about fascist horrors brewing. In a 1931 trip to Berlin to purchase favorite paints for Black Sun Press books, Caresse had called upon George Grosz to see if she could interest him in a Black Sun edition of his satiric drawings about the emerging Nazi party. Five years later, she published 280 numbered copies of *Interregnum,* a collection of sixty-four black and white lithographs and one four-color lithograph, with an introduction by John Dos Passos. (Copy no. 1 was dedicated to Henrietta Crosby.)[15] The place of publication was New York City, not Paris.

Caresse's children made the move back to the States that much easier for her. Although her days at the Mill could still be exciting, with guests like Stuart Gilbert and Antoine de Saint-Exupéry mixing pleasure with the business of going about the translation of *Night Flight,* both Billy and Polleen wanted to establish American ties. Caresse's mother lived in New York. Billy was a student at Williams College, while Polleen pursued an acting career. She had already become a part of the elite New York social scene, having come out as a debutante. She appeared indifferent to taking the next step: settling down with a proper husband who would provide her with all the amenities her mother had taken for granted when she was the same age. Caresse arranged for Polleen to study with Edith Wynne Matthison at the Bennett School, officially known as the School of Liberal Arts and Applied Design. Matthison and her husband, Charles Rann Kennedy, both well-known British actors in their day, had established and taught in the drama department of the two-year finishing school in Millbrook, New York. The Tudor mansion had been built in the 1890s as a Hudson Valley luxury resort.

Besides publishing the surrealism anthology and George Grosz's *Interregnum* in New York, Caresse produced an exquisite edition of James Joyce's *Collected Poems,* designed, set by hand, and printed under her direction in New York. The entire book was printed in blue type, the binding cream-colored boards with a floral design repeated twenty-three times, the place marker a blue ribbon. The frontispiece was a crayon portrait of Joyce by Augustus John reproduced by Jacomet of Paris. Fifty of the eight hundred copies, printed on Japan paper with a gold-stamped cover rather than a blue one, were signed by Joyce and numbered. But six years would pass before the Black Sun Press would publish another volume.

It was easy for Caresse to get caught up the socialite life of New York City. She also enjoyed winter fishing in Miami, attested to by the fact that she was awarded a certificate dated February 17, 1936, from both the Miami Sailfish Club and the Miami Angler's Club for having caught an "Amber Jack" aboard the yacht *Friendship.* The fish weighed seventy-four pounds and was five feet two inches long.

However, by her early forties, Caresse manifested a strong nesting instinct. In order to satisfy her need for a place in the States to call home, she became a "country gentleman" who did not mind getting her hands dirty. She adopted a "back to the earth" lifestyle tempered by the dictates of her extravagant and selectively generous personality. And she found a new husband whom she thought would help her out.

9

Mind Over Matter

In the summer of 1936, Caresse told her longtime friend Constance Crowninshield Coolidge, Harry's "Lady of the Golden Horse," about two important changes in her life: she had set her future in the United States, and, to her delight, her heart had been claimed once again. With the sale of the Mill, she was without a permanent address in France for the first time in more than a decade. Her children's plans and the political crisis mounting in Europe certainly provided incentive for an overhaul. But in a larger sense, Caresse was continuing in mode, nurturing both the ambition that fueled the Black Sun Press and the healthy lust that had jump-started her relationship with Harry Crosby. This time, however, she would create a more rural setting where she could invite writers and artists to work and play. Her new lover was very different from Harry except perhaps for his capriciousness. As Constance put it, Bert was "untamed" and "entirely ruled by impulse."[1] Constance feared that Caresse would want to marry him precisely because she found such behavior invigorating.

Eighteen years younger than Caresse, Selbert Saffold Young—Bert—was a great-grandson of the first governor of Alabama. He had no gainful employment or particular accomplishments. He was broke. He dreamed of overseeing a large farm that someone else would buy for him. Caresse had formed romantic liaisons with younger men before she met Bert. Harry was six years Caresse's junior, and Armand de la Rochefoucauld and other lovers were younger, though not by nearly two decades. Also, Harry and Armand had

had sizable bank accounts. Perhaps Bert was closer in circumstance to Jacques Porel, also Caresse's junior, though not by so many years, and also dependent on Caresse for income. But what distinguished Bert most from Caresse's former loves was that he lacked any understanding about why Caresse would want to run a literary press. Constance felt compelled to advise Caresse of the risk that she was taking.

> I can't make up my mind what I think about your marrying Bert. He is very attractive & has the same elan vital which you have. But you are mentally far superior to him. What about your books & that side of your life. I am so afraid you will let all that slide if you marry him. But don't darling. You must have something besides a physical life—because all that cannot last while the other does.[2]

While Caresse was hardly oblivious to the dangers of marrying Bert, she was unprepared for the compromises of middle age.

Caresse met Bert in the summer of 1936. She was in Hollywood, California, having driven Polleen across country so that she could audition and take a screen test for a part in an MGM film. A stage mom Caresse was not. She does not bother to tell readers of *The Passionate Years* whether or not Polly got the job. Rather we learn that at this time that Caresse was cultivating her next author, a young, struggling writer, Tom Kromer, who had just gotten his first big break. His *Waiting for Nothing* was about to be published by Harcourt Brace. Before she returned to the States, Caresse had been corresponding with Kromer. Now that she was in California, she wanted to meet him.

It is difficult to imagine Caresse making an authentic connection with Kromer's Depression-era classic on purely political grounds. Indeed, her claim to have been left-leaning since the late 1920s was based on a skewed version of sharing the wealth, but with the wealthy still calling the shots.

> I believe I advocated a compulsory work week from nine to one Monday through Saturdays. Free enterprise, free education, free entertainment, from one to midnight. Picnics and parades on Sundays and lots of flags![3]

In Caresse's utopia, patronage remained a respectable venue for distributing money. The winter before she had sold the Mill, Caresse thought she could find a French publisher for *Waiting for Nothing* and an advance large enough for Kromer to get himself to France, where he could write his next book.

When Caresse realized that she would be in southern California the following summer with Polleen, she tried to arrange a rendezvous with Kromer, who was living in Malibu. Drawn to Kromer's prose and politics, his desperate circumstances, and his book jacket photograph, she contemplated a romance with him. The evening she thought she would be meeting Kromer, she stopped first with a young friend for a drink at a night club on Sunset Boulevard. She caught sight of "a blond giant, handsome as Hermes and militant as Mars." As soon as he saw her staring at him he approached her and asked her to dance. "As though pierced by the fatal arrow I rose and with a shiver was in his arms. . . . The need I had felt to plunge into an obliterating relationship had been satisfied."[4] A trip to promote her daughter's career and to rescue a starving writer turned into yet another opportunity for Caresse to demonstrate to friends and family that she was not ready to be reigned in. She did not care if she appeared capricious and irresponsible. She would have Bert.

Two months after Caresse announced to Constance her burgeoning love affair with Bert, she bought Hampton Manor, a huge, dilapidated mansion twenty-five miles south of Fredericksburg, Virginia, five miles from Bowling Green. Surrounded by five hundred acres of overgrown fields and towering magnolia trees, the place was virtually uninhabitable: filthy from decades of neglect, it featured crumbling ceilings, sinking floors, and no indoor plumbing. Caresse made a bid as soon as she saw it. She consulted only Bert for approval. Together, they planned the renovations—which included installing electricity and four baths—and booked rooms in a Fredericksburg hotel for the duration. That is, Caresse took rooms in the hotel, and Bert lit off for Florida, mission unknown.

At first, Caresse and Bert had thought they should marry. They drove to Montgomery, Alabama, in September 1936 so that Bert could introduce Caresse to his mother and get a marriage license.[5] But seven months would pass between the time Caresse bought Hampton Manor and their exchange of vows in Richmond, Virginia. During the interim, Caresse oversaw by herself the birth of the dream farm that threatened to ruin what remained of her financial security. She became frantic as Bert's absence stretched from days to weeks, but she could not acknowledge so soon that her Hermes-Mars lookalike was disastrous husband material. When she and Bert filled out their marriage license, Caresse shaved two years off her age (she was forty-four, not forty-two as she indicated on the license). Bert's frailties were more insidious.

Intended to be a showcase Virginia farm, complete with live cattle, Hampton Manor developed into a very expensive setting for Bert and Caresse (Mimsy, as Bert called her) to discover that they never should have married one another. Bert was a heavy drinker and periodically dropped out of sight, often after a nasty argument with Caresse. Caresse knew little about running a farm and relied on the "strong ebony hands"[6] of her farm workers to get the chores done. Yet during the frequent separations throughout their three years of marriage, Caresse and Bert wrote torrid letters filled with declarations of love and longing. They clung to the sentimental notion that they were made for one another.

In an impulsive attempt to shape up, and without telling Caresse first, Bert joined the army. "We'll have quite a time figuring out how you'd like to have the army run," he wrote in an undated letter announcing that he would be reporting to Camp Beauregard in Biloxi, Mississippi. Other letters followed beseeching Caresse for money, cigarettes, and new clothes to keep him operative. Caresse acknowledged the shattering reality of her situation: she was married all right, but she had no husband. She hauled herself off for eight weeks to the University of Nevada at Reno, where she audited a course in animal husbandry to find out if she could develop the expertise to run Hampton Manor on her own. More importantly, she initiated a legal separation and divorce.

At times she sank into emotional torpor. In a letter to Bert written on board the San Francisco Overland Limited, she mulled over the lyrics of a popular song of the day, "I'll never smile again till I smile at you," and the last evening they spent together.

> "I'll never love again I'm so in love with you" is in my ears as the train rockets over the endless miles of prairie that now separate us, and I don't want to go away from you a bit. I am just as miserable as can be. Why oh why did you force me into this? . . . I keep remembering you the night you left. How handsome you were, how terribly sweet, how your arms held me like steel in the dark alley way where we kissed goodbye.[7]

The nearly obsessive physical attraction that had initially bound them could not sustain them, as her friend Constance had warned. Caresse tried to be optimistic about Bert's army stint: "I do hope all goes well with you. That you are not discouraged by the heat and the discipline. I know you won't like taking orders all the time—but soon you'll be in officers training camp and that will be where you should be." Army officials did not share Caresse's estimation of Bert's potential.

Evidently, Caresse and Bert could not make a clean break. Caresse begged him to stop drinking: "Won't you *please*, I ask you like a prayer, *please* be a good boy. Don't drink anymore. It ruins and wrecks every effort we make to straighten out our life."[8] But she stayed hooked:

O how I love you darling
If you only knew
I love you
  love you
  love you
    a 1000000000000000000000000000 times.[9]

In turn, Bert would berate Caresse for playing Mother Superior: "I'm not overly fond of the way females of the species treat the one's [sic] they profess to love".[10] Then he would bemoan his sorry state: "I'm just going to write this without regard for spelling etc. Oh Mimsy—I can't explain how I've missed you. Its gotten now so it hurts inside I cant sleep, eat—I dream of you constantly."[11] Their relationship limped on.

On furlough to New York City, Bert agreed to meet with Caresse's lawyer, J. H. Philbin, at the bar of the Winslow Hotel in order to discuss how he and Caresse might proceed in formalizing their separation. Bert resisted efforts to resolve financial claims between them. He was ready neither to assume responsibility for his own debts and expenses nor to relinquish joint ownership of Hampton Manor. Perhaps for the first time, Caresse found herself financially strapped. In Reno, she could afford to rent only a rundown, tiny apartment with a leaky refrigerator and a gas stove that was "practically in the bed." For a brief period when she worked in an office six hours a day to cover living expenses, Bert asked her to send along $20. She did not bother to mask her anger: "I figure $20 means 2½ days of work for me plus rigorous economy whereas it will probably only mean KP for you, or at worst one or two days in the Guard House—and you can take the knocks better than I."[12] She resented Bert's insinuations that she deserved a little deprivation in her life, yet she continued to contrive a rendezvous in Tennessee or Kentucky where they might "find a little shack in some mountain lake for a wonderful vacation from all our problems, just live for the happiness of being together." Caresse knew she had given her heart and soul to the wrong man but held on to her fantasies a while longer.

Caresse's friends and family tried hard to support her through this new upheaval in her life even if they thought Caresse was foolish for wanting to be kind to this brash younger man who had used her badly. Among the most sympathetic to Caresse was Polleen, who could not stand Bert's presence in the same room. She refused to visit Hampton Manor even when Bert was absent because he often returned without warning. On the other hand, no matter how foolish her mother had been to take up with a gigolo in the first place, she responded sensitively to her mother's anguish.

In a March 25, 1939, letter, Polleen walked a thin line between telling her mother "I told you so" and offering constructive suggestions about how to lead her life. She recognized the intensity of her mother's suffering and feared that she did not have the stamina to endure much more.

> With all due respect to what might seem a perfect "set up" I can't ever believe that you and Bert are meant for each other even taking into consideration the violent "something" that brings you together.

Like Constance, Polleen urged her mother to remain true to her vocation as patron of writers and artists.

> What about your books . . . I hope you won't let that go for it might be an *answer to a lot of things*. Your marriage to the publishing world is one that you should never divorce for it is a far stronger liaison than that with Bert.

Perhaps even more to the point was Polleen's observation that Caresse's divided loyalties could never be reconciled. She would have to declare her primary allegiance.

In fact, Bert was interfering with Caresse's efforts to provide support for writers and artists, specifically Salvador Dalí, Henry Miller, and Anaïs Nin. Hampton Manor was big enough to comfortably accommodate visitors, but Bert had little interest in playing host. At the end of August 1940, Dalí and Gala were back in the United States looking to increase their fortunes. Caresse believed that the Black Sun Press could publish in conjunction with the Dial Press Dalí's autobiography still in progress, *The Secret Life of Salvador Dalí*. She invited the couple to Hampton Manor so that Dalí could work without interruption on the narrative as well as on some paintings promised to Julien Levy.

Oddly enough, Henry Miller had already settled in Hampton Manor, hardly a lodger compatible with the Dalís, who expected to be catered to and who by now were sympathetic, even enthusiastic, about Franco's Spain.[13] Adding complexity to this already exotic mix, Miller's friend and lover Anaïs Nin had joined him in Virginia. Miller was working on *The Colossus of Maroussi*, Nin on her *Diaries*. Miller's friends—poet John Dudley and his wife, Flo—also came down. The air was thick with creativity. Since Caresse was in Reno at this time, there was no host to ease the tension between the Dalís and everyone else, even if Nin could engage Dalí by speaking Catalan.

Actually, when Caresse, Henry, and Anaïs had met one another is not clear. One account by Caresse is somewhat corroborated by Henry Miller in a letter he wrote to artist and teacher Emil Schnelluck, his boyhood classmate at

P.S. 85 in Brooklyn and lifelong friend. Miller implies that he first met Caresse in Paris during the summer of 1932 when he was peddling *Tropic of Cancer.* He was traveling with Anaïs Nin. Their first stop was London, he told Emil, "to see the big literary lights. Rebecca West thinks very highly of [Nin's] book on Lawrence. And that failing, [Nin] will sell her fur coat and print it herself." He adds that he was "dickering with Caresse Crosby" over the publication of *Tropic of Cancer.*[14] In a letter to Anaïs, Caresse recalled meeting Henry in her Black Sun Press office, and telling him that his work "shocked and horrified" her. She confessed to Anaïs that at the time she did not realize that she "had the work of a genius" in her hands.

Both Nin and Miller remembered differently. Nin insisted in a September 14, 1967, letter to Caresse that she, not Henry, brought Caresse *Tropic of Cancer* so that she might publish it. On the other hand, she suggested to Miller in a July 31, 1932, letter that he bring the manuscript himself to Caresse along with a letter Caresse had written to Anaïs expressing interest in Miller's manuscript as an introduction: "She is bound to like you immensely, and if I know women well, she would rather be given a chance to judge for herself than be told by another women."[15] And in a July 27, 1968, letter to Caresse, Miller remembered that "Anaïs, you and I met in your home in N.Y. in 1940 when [John] Dudley and Lafe [Lafayette Young] appeared out of the blue. It was after that I went to your place in Va. (Still 1940)." Miller does not make clear whether or not this was the first time he and Caresse met.[16] The "home in N.Y." was a garden apartment in a brownstone on East Fifty-fourth Street that Caresse had rented, though she placed herself there earlier, in 1936, when she was in limbo between Paris and Hampton Manor, and between Bert and Hampton Manor.

In her *Diary,* Anaïs recalls another meeting with Caresse, at a party in the New York City home of American artist and patron of the arts Kay Sage and the surrealist painter Yves Tanguy in 1939. She captures Caresse's warm, magnetic personality, and her interest in collecting people.

> Stories surround Caresse like a perfume, a necklace, a feather. She always seems fresher and younger than all the women there, because of her mobility, ease, flowingness. D. H. Lawrence would have called it her "livingness." A pollen carrier, I thought, as she mixed, stirred, brewed, concocted her friendships by constant flux and reflux of activity, by curiosity, avidity, amorousness.[17]

In 1967, Anaïs was momentarily angry at Caresse for not mentioning her in *The Passionate Years,* especially since she had created a "full-length, charming, loving portrait" of Caresse in her *Diary.*[18] Caresse's explanation—that she ended *The Passionate Years* in 1940, before she had met Anaïs—only adds to the confusion since, by Anaïs's account, they had already met at least twice, in Paris and New York City. Whether or not Caresse left out Anaïs by accident or on purpose matters less than a goal they both shared: to write their own history before someone else created one for them. Despite intermittent bouts of jealousy over one another's personal success, Caresse and Anaïs remained good if distant friends and continued to support one another's professional ambitions.

A good illustration of their relationship begins with Caresse's gallant response to the fabrication Nin had designed to conceal the nature of her relationship with Henry Miller from her husband, banker Hugh Parker Guiler (who would become an engraver of copper plates and a filmmaker under the name of Ian Hugo). In 1934, while carrying on a love affair with Miller in Paris, Anaïs told her husband that she was visiting Caresse at the Mill. It did not matter to her that she and Caresse were as yet strangers to one another. Although Anaïs located Le Moulin at Fontenay-aux-Roses instead of Ermenonville, Hugo never suspect the ruse. Caresse's hospitality was well known among their group of friends.

Anaïs told Hugo there was no phone at the Mill so that it would be impossible for him to get in touch with her.[19] When Anaïs and Caresse met at that Tanguy party in New York, Anaïs feared that Caresse would undo her cover. Caresse vividly recalled Anaïs's mysterious behavior at that gathering in an account of what she regarded as their first meeting.

> it was a party, you came in late in a flurry and pulled me into the bedroom and agitatedly asked me not to mention the Mill when Hugo arrived—I couldn't imagine why, but I said "of course." I really don't know to this day what it was about.[20]

Caresse was cool in this sophisticated crowd; a less aloof reaction would have been gauche.

Many years later, in 1958, Caresse would not be as accommodating. She refused to allow Anaïs to loop her into the drama she had created by marrying Rupert Pole in 1955 in Los Angeles without divorcing Hugo in New York.[21] Sixteen years her junior, Pole was an aspiring actor turned forest ranger turned teacher. Caresse was hostile to the prospect of making Rupert's acquaintance.[22] Hardly the person to play judge, Caresse may have envied Anaïs's greater endurance for sexual escapade and intrigue. At the time, she was recovering from heart surgery at the Mayo clinic and had some sense of her waning energy. Moreover, Caresse favored Hugo, whose copper engravings she had exhibited in the art gallery she had opened after moving to Washington, D.C., in 1940.

Their desire to make public these episodes from their personal history, however, overrode any misunderstandings or rivalries between them. They remained colleagues in the literary life. Years later, when Anaïs's dairies were published, Caresse reassured the editors at Harcourt Brace that she would have no objections to whatever Anaïs had to say about her in the *Diaries.* If they could not agree on dates, they could appreciate one another's writing. Caresse was thrilled by Anaïs's description of her at Hampton Manor: "I feel like that bit of pollen floating in the sunny air after I read your description of me at harvest time." Caresse neglected to add that she doubted that Anaïs had in fact seen her "at harvest time.[23] She also ignored Anaïs's complaint that Caresse's support could be intermittent.

Caresse had wanted to publish Anaïs's collection of three novelettes, *Winter of Artifice,* in the United States, but after holding on to the manuscript for nearly a year, she could not raise the necessary funds. Yet somehow she found money to pump into the Gemor Press, the small hand-letter operation that Anaïs had started with her friend Gonzalo More in 1939 in order to publish her own work, beginning with *Winter of Artifice.* For Christmas 1942, Caresse arranged for Gemor to print under the Black Sun imprint one hundred copies of *Four Poems* by Sharon Vail, Kay Boyle's first of six children, called "Bobby." Caresse commissioned Gemor in 1943 to print an augmented edition along with fifteen hundred announcements of Paul Eluard's *Misfortunes of the Immortals,* translated from the French by Hugh Chisolm and illustrated by Max Ernst. Like the smaller Vail volume, this book bore the Black Sun Press imprint and Caresse controlled all aspects of its design, to Anaïs's dismay this time. Despite the income it brought, Anaïs lost "all interest" in the book once she attributed a less altruistic motive to Caresse's support: Caresse was using the book to "recapture her prestige as a publisher."[24] Caresse might not have agreed that her status needed bolstering.

Apparently, such barbed thoughts were not articulated. Caresse exhibited Anaïs's *Under a Glass Bell* at the show for Ian Hugo's copper plate engravings, and Nin helped her hang the plates. Years later, Nin published a poem by Caresse on the Russian cosmonaut Yuri Gagarin in *Epos* (winter 1967). Caresse would also bring Anaïs into her special circle of friends. Caresse introduced Nin to Colette at her Waldorf Astoria suite (after first providing Anaïs with a grey silk blouse to spruce up a mousy suit). In March 1941, she brought her to Canada Lee's nightclub, The Chicken Coop, in Harlem after

Lee's sensational opening night performance in Richard Wright's *Native Son,* directed by Orson Wells.

However, before any of these activities occurred, Caresse needed to extricate herself from Virginia and from Bert. The divorce had not put an end to their relationship. She felt responsible for his welfare even though his behavior had become menacing at times. While she was still in Reno, Bert phoned Hampton Manor with threats to come back. Henry Miller was the one to take his phone calls. Writing to Caresse on July 22, 1940, Miller indicated that he feared Bert's return.

> No, Bert hasn't appeared yet. We are on the look-out for him and not a little perplexed as to what his attitude will be. He spoke of seeing *his* place—and right away—you're goddamned right!—and we had visions of him coming in the middle of the night with a bunch of Virginia cronies armed with shot-guns to sweep us out.

He was expecting Anaïs the next day and assured Caresse that he would "telephone or telegraph if anything breaks." "Calm yourself," he added, "and come back as soon as possible." But Caresse did not get back to Hampton Manor in time to protect her guests from Bert.

In the middle of the night in early September 1940, Bert and a woman companion burst into the house drunk, scaring awake Miller, the Dudleys, and the Dalís. Bert wanted them to leave as soon as he got there and threatened to destroy all of Dalí's paintings if they didn't.[25] The Dalís packed up and left for the Shoreham Hotel in Washington, D.C., where they cabled Caresse for advice about where they should take up residence now that Bert had taken over Hampton Manor. In a hastily scrawled letter, Miller revealed how urgent their departure had been:

> We are all leaving now—in different directions. . . . I can't tell you more because it's no use. I hope you'll understand. I'll write you later from NY.

He added that he would stop the telephone service, as Caresse had recently asked him to. "I will take care of it—gladly," Miller wrote, aware that Bert was flat broke and expected Caresse to fund his welfare. Bert would plague Caresse and her friends with reckless behavior for at least another year.

The Dalís and Caresse were back at Hampton Manor later that fall. Dalí continued to work on five paintings that he completed by the end of his stay and to write his autobiography, *The Secret Life.* At first, Caresse thought she would translate the manuscript, but with Dalí's impossible handwriting and private spelling code, the task proved daunting. She cajoled translator and author Haakon Chevalier, who was teaching at the University of California, Berkeley, to take on the job.

She also welcomed to Hampton Manor an invasion by a crew from *Life* magazine for its April 7, 1941, issue. The reporters and photographers were perfect straight men for the surrealistic antics staged by Caresse and the Dalís, which included a tableau of the Dalís and Caresse and a prize heifer ensconced in the richly carpeted library, and an outdoor shot of a grand piano perilously hanging from a magnolia tree. That same spring, Dalí would exhibit his paintings at Julien Levy's gallery in New York. Bert would stir up more trouble over Dalí, this time against the background of southern California, where the Dalís had moved after the New York exhibition. Bert was at his worse.

After the divorce was decreed, Caresse passed a final winter in Hampton Manor. Although Caresse rarely lingered over descriptions of time spent with her mother, she fondly recalled a visit from Mrs. Jacob during this period, perhaps because it was such a peaceful one.

> now she was completely happy, knitting on the cooled, screened piazza, overlooking the busy life of kitchen doorstep and kitchen garden. She puttered in the flower garden and took frequent walks around the stables and barns. I was able to enjoy her visits without the tension of Bert's eruptive presence. Mother played chess, too.[26]

The allusion to "Bert's eruptive presence" was about as far as Caresse would go towards acknowledging that her marriage had been a disaster. Indeed, Caresse would insist that she had no regrets, but that she was only too ready to begin a new stage of her life, with or without a man. Such optimism belies the anguish she experienced while she eased Bert out of her life.

In the fall of 1941, Bert was in Los Angeles, wreaking havoc among Caresse's friends, and interfering with Caresse's efforts to sell a painting by Dalí. She needed the money and deserved it given the effort she had expended on easing his entry into the United States and providing him with gracious work space. Her broker was Miss Tone Price, one of four partners of Tone Price Rare Books, dealers and importers of fine books, first editions, manuscripts, drawings, and paintings. Their offices were on Sunset Boulevard in West Hollywood. Caresse had asked her "to look after" Bert, who had decided that he might have better luck in California than he'd had in Virginia. He did not wait until he got to Los Angeles before he cabled the book dealer for twenty-five dollars.

Bert arrived on a cattle train, sick with flu and looking like a drifter, "wearing the dirtiest pair of dungarees and boots—not even a hat."[27] He proceeded to dupe Miss Price out of money, clothing, luggage, and jewelry (he pawned her $2,500 bracelet for $125). He crashed her car, ran up her telephone bill, and used all her credit at the local liquor store. The final blow came when he tried to sabotage her attempt to sell the Dalí painting that belonged to Caresse. After he discovered that Caresse intended to share the profit with Miss Price only, he informed Julien Levy, Dalí's sole agent, about Caresse's intentions. In the meantime, Miss Price begged Caresse to let her keep the painting: she was close to selling it and desperately needed her commission for the deal.

Caresse never alluded to this episode. She preferred that readers of *The Passionate Years* believe that Bert was gone, out of her life. Nor does she refer to Bert in the unpublished sequel. However, in a diary that she kept for the first week of 1940, she makes clear the misery of disengagement. She was in New York City staying at the Dover, seeing family and friends. Her heart was not receptive to the festivities of the season, which she felt obligated to attend: New Year's Eve parties; an outing to Sneeden's Landing, an affluent community on the Hudson River south of Nyack, with Hugh and Bridget Auchincloss, Anaïs Nin and Hugo Guiler, and Yves Tanguy and Kay Sage; a meeting with Julien Levy; and a party that celebrated the Gotham Book Mart's twentieth birthday.[28] But she wrote in several places how lonely she was; "how she tried to find Bert on the telephone" when she got back to the hotel at 3:45 a.m. on January 1; how she was "torn between" her "need for his love" and her need "to keep clear of disaster." On January 3, she records that "Bert called about 12 from Washington in very bad shape—my heart is sick—I can never pull through if he doesn't help—2 pills." The next day, after Bert called again, she wrote, "I won't be nurse anymore—and my heart is like lead." On January 7, Caresse returned by train to Virginia. She had a forty-minute layover in Washington, where she refused an invitation to a gala at the Troika. She had her "best Balenciaga evening dress" with her, and if she had bought a curling iron at the local drugstore, she could have made a splendid appearance. But the idea of spending a carefree evening made her feel guilty about Bert. She fantasized that "all pretty and gay," she would run into him, "putting him somehow at a disadvantage." She ordered two whiskeys once she got back on the train and pondered over when she would "ever be free of this love."

Caresse had to sell and close up Hampton Manor by herself. But she described the experience as though it were one more adventure to enjoy. She sold her Herefords at a loss, chose enough furniture and household items to fill two moving vans, and auctioned off the rest. In a beat-up Ford station wagon with her dog Salar, she headed for Washington, D.C., the most interesting place she could afford. Like the hero she indeed was, she refused to allow the circumstances of her life to defeat her, even if that meant pretending that she had not made some very bad choices. She talked like someone who believed in the future, but also like someone who did not learn from her mistakes.

Correspondence during the war years (1942 to 1944) between Caresse and Bert suggests that they mused about restoring their romance. Nothing real materialized after the divorce. Bert did finally get into Air Corps Technical School. He continued to ask Caresse for cigarette money. They made a few aborted attempts to meet in New York City and in Florida. Declarations of love were exchanged periodically until Bert was shipped off to Korea. On the surface, Caresse remained aloof. She was silent about Bert's attempts to rehabilitate himself in her eyes and their consequent lukewarm efforts at a reconciliation. She had, after all, developed expertise in avoiding public humiliation when Harry died in 1929.

10

Old Friends, New Friends

Caresse had been leading a fairly secluded life for the past four years. Yes, she had played host to Salvador and Gala Dalí, Henry Miller and Anaïs Nin. She had spent a long summer in Reno, Nevada, and visited her mother in New York City, and her in-laws in Boston. But her contacts with larger worlds, with the many artists and writers she had met on the continent, had greatly diminished. She could hardly expect Polleen and Billy to keep her company.

In New York, Polleen had been struggling to break into theater or publishing but met with little success. She did make a splash when she was photographed as herself dressed in an elegant striped cabana costume for a Camel cigarettes advertisement. It was printed in a 1940 edition of *Modern Screen*, where she is described as a glamorous "gay young cosmopolite [who] has made thirty ocean crossings . . . attended school in France and Switzerland . . . had debut parties in Boston, New York, Paris." Polleen didn't have any money, however, and while, at the age of twenty-one, she was at least as sophisticated as any graduate from Radcliffe or Bryn Mawr, she did not have a college degree. She had hoped that her mother would provide her with more financial support than she did, but it was not to happen. In a May 16, 1939, letter, she allowed her resentment to surface.

> You see Mother, you have always had capital, an income, an inheritance to borrow against or something you could liquidate into money if you

> had to. . . . I am no longer a child that can depend on her family's wing at each instant, but a woman who has to make her way in the world in the place and state I was born in . . . and it is terribly hard to get started on next to nothing.

Caresse was not without sympathy for her daughter's plight, but she felt that she was in no position to give Polleen the $2,000 financial cushion that Polleen thought she deserved. Caresse was too concerned with preparing herself for a new stage in her own life to be really helpful or attentive to Polleen. Nor was she particularly receptive to complaints. Caresse was not especially cruel or selfish, merely consistent. She rarely had put motherhood first.

Polleen was living with her grandmother when she volunteered for the Women's Reserve of the U.S. Navy, not long after she posed "enjoying a cool smoke." Polleen was attached to a Danish Hospital Unit in Narvik, Norway, until an Anglo-French expeditionary force was forced to evacuate the port in June 1940. She made her way to France, where she volunteered for the Red Cross, and then by way of Lisbon, moved to London, where she landed a job with the B.B.C. Caresse was proud that her daughter's opinions were deemed worthy of broadcasting commentary: "She has been very wise in her observations so far, especially about Russia."[1] There was a fair amount of correspondence between Caresse and Polleen, but they were not to see one another the next six years. During that period, Polleen married Comte Albert de Mun (who had been among Caresse's guests at the Mill in 1932), lost her first child, and gave birth to her second, Lorraine.

Once she felt anchored by her own family, Polleen expressed little hostility towards her mother. She had wanted to write a memoir of growing up in Paris with Caresse and Harry, but when she asked Caresse for help on the project, Caresse informed her that she would be writing a memoir of her own covering much of the same material. Polleen was taken aback by her mother's attitude: "I thought you were going to help me to write it and not crib the idea."[2] Mother and daughter got past this dilemma because Polleen yielded to her mother's wishes.

Such rivalry did not exist between mother and son. Billy never thought of making the same kinds of demands on his mother that Polly did. His upbringing did not permit him to. He exuded the independence and charm of a handsome young man of his class who believed that some kind of success would eventually be his. Before he joined the U.S. Navy, he was working his way up the burgeoning airline business, starting out as a freight loader for American Airlines at La Guardia airfield. He could also be the occasional rake, borrowing without permission against his mother's credit to pay passage from Bermuda to Nassau to spend a week with his friends in a sublet house on the beach. Unlike Polleen, who had refused to visit Hampton Manor because Bert might show up, Billy stayed neutral, would send his "very best" to Bert at the end of a letter to Caresse.

There was never a tone of reproach in the correspondence between mother and son, never the suggestion from Billy that Caresse should reconsider whatever plans she was making—the marriage to and divorce from Bert, the move to Washington, publishing ventures, spontaneous junkets to New York, Miami, Nevada, Hollywood. "I haven't heard from you in weeks, are you still in Washington or have you the wander lust?" he inquired playfully in one letter.[3] During the war, he was based in Norfolk, Virginia, in Transport Squadron One, U.S. Naval Air Station. He was eventually sent to Puerto Rico, Trinidad, and Panama, where his skills as a French interpreter were commissioned for conferences with Free French leaders in charge of liaison for the Allied landing in Normandy on D-Day.[4] In one of the rare instances in her life when Caresse kept a journal, she admitted to herself how much she missed Billy, "though really his coming of age has overtaken me, with far too many gaps between the school years and the war years."[5] She was too honest with herself to express any regret that she had done little to avoid creating that gap.

Billy saw his mother in Washington, D.C., on several of his leaves. He escorted her to social gatherings and set Caresse up to meet his current girlfriend, Johnny Cotton, while he was back in Puerto Rico. In his correspondence, Billy was keen on keeping up with news about old friends and family, including his grandmother Mary Jacob and uncles Len and Buddy in New York City, his step-grandparents, Henrietta and Stephen Crosby, and Harry Crosby's sister Kitsa, for whom he retained a good deal of affection. Stuck in Trinidad for Christmas 1943, "not the 'Bard of Avon' / But just a salty lad," he composed a lighthearted poem to send as a greeting card. Just one stanza addresses the serious reason for his having to resort to such measures.

> Here's hoping by next Christmas,
> This war will have been won,
> That Hitler is a memory,
> Not to mention Rising Sun.

During Caresse's D.C. days, Billy was the much easier child, someone who gave Caresse solid emotional support, if not financial help. There is a letter written in September 1943 where he apologizes to Caresse because he cannot lend her $75. He would forfeit the role of model son several years after the war ended.

Caresse was not prepared for the cold reception of Washington, D.C. It took a few weeks for her to recognize how inconsequential her presence was regarded. Although she was a newcomer, she did have a small list of well-placed friends and acquaintances to call on, among them the new congressman from New York, Joseph Baldwin; her old Boston friend Connie Minot; and James Forrestal, at the time the Undersecretary of the Navy. Caresse had known Forrestal before she met Harry Crosby, and she tells a charming story in *The Passionate Years* about sitting beside him at an elegant dinner party in her honor given by Marie and Averell Harriman during the Christmas season in New York City after Harry's death.

Forrestal invariably turned down invitations to large dinner parties, but the Harrimans tricked him into attending the affair by saying that Caresse would be the only other guest present. Caresse had been determined to look elegant in a "demiduel" low-cut black crepe gown designed by her friend Elsa Schiaparelli. She chose a crème de menthe liqueur after supper to complement her diamond necklace (Harry's last present) and diamond-and-jade earrings: "I looked my best and I guessed that I was cresting the breakers of society's opinion. My path through the winter promised to be carpeted."[6] The other women present, including Mrs. Forrestal, who usually attended such occasions on her own, were kinder to Caresse than the Boston matrons had been when Harry was alive and making public his devotion to Caresse.

Caresse reported that she saw a good deal of Forrestal over the next several years when she visited New York. She credited him with introducing her to Canada Lee in 1934 by taking her backstage at the Fourteenth Street Playhouse after watching Lee play the title role in *Stevedore,* a powerful play by Paul Peters and George Sklar about mob violence. The play was notable for its integrated cast, and for "its mixed audience—black and white sitting both in the orchestra and in the balcony, perhaps for the first time."[7] Caresse's relationship with Lee grew into a serious romance during the wartime years.

Her friendship with Forrestal disintegrated when he became engrossed in preparing a peacetime navy to meet the demands of a world war. After he was appointed Secretary of the Navy in 1944, and Secretary of Defense in 1947, he was inaccessible to the general public, including Caresse. She later regretted that she had not pursued Forrestal more aggressively in Washington instead of relying on "orthodox" channels of communication available to any citizen. At Harry Truman's insistence, Forrestal resigned in 1949. In a state of severe clinical depression, he was admitted to Bethesda Naval Medical

Center. Two months later, he committed suicide by throwing himself out of the sixteenth-floor window of his hospital room.

Perhaps the most blatant snub in Washington came from Archibald MacLeish, who, after all, had been the person Caresse entrusted to identify Harry's body in Stanley Mortimer's studio at the Hotel des Artistes. And the Black Sun Press had published *Einstein* in 1929, and two editions of *New Found Land* in 1930, which contains "Ars Poetica," one of his most famous poems. By 1941, MacLeish had won the Pulitzer Prize for *Conquistador* (1932) and had published four collections of poetry and two radio verse plays. He was serving as Librarian of Congress when Caresse arrived in Washington, would become Assistant Secretary of State for a year, and filled other official positions before he was appointed to the faculty of Harvard University.

Caresse had sublet a pretty Georgetown house on Thirty-third Street. Ada and Archibald MacLeish lived across the street, and, once she settled in, Caresse expected to see them. But they apparently eluded her company.

> I was sure they would soon welcome me but they didn't. Indeed all that governmental hierarchy gave me a cold shoulder. I believe it was by mutual accord that they pronounced me "pas assez serieuse." I had, it is true, a reputation for hedonism, and, even more suspect, for surrealism and they were to deal with very serious opposites.[8]

Caresse would learn that she would be ignored on an official level also. It was October 1941, and Washington officials were not about to waste time on a woman whose most recent claim to fame was being photographed with Salvador Dalí and a piano stuck in a tree over a pond.

MacLeish did have fond memories of the days he and Ada MacLeish spent with Caresse and Harry. He had traveled some with Harry and Ernest Hemingway. He marveled over the Black Sun editions of *Einstein* and *New Found Land,* thrilled that two volumes of his poetry were physically beautiful works of art. Still MacLeish thought that Caresse had been "a pain in the neck but was touching" and that there were "a lot of silly affectations" about both Harry and Caresse."[9]

During their Paris years, he and Ada invited the Crosbys to their cold-water flat on the boulevard St. Michele for lunch after enjoying a meal with the Crosbys at their grand rue de Lille home. Caresse responded with regrets: "you know, my dears, we always eat lunch in bed."[10] Yet at the end of summer 1927, when the MacLeishes had returned to Paris after buying Uphill Farm, their lifelong home in Conway, Massachusetts, the Crosbys offered them their apartment rent-free.[11] MacLeish had not cut off Caresse indefinitely, but for the time being he could not pay her much attention. He did speak kindly about both Crosbys to his children even if one his lasting impressions of them was that they slept in a bed full of crumbs.[12]

Caresse was interested in more than filling up her social calendar. She wanted to contribute to the war effort. But attempts to work in some official capacity failed totally. Despite her fluency in French, and her experience in publishing, she lacked the required formal education and training. Her referees, like Jim Forrestal, were too busy, or embarrassed, to write for her. She was also nearly forty-nine years old, and missing three more teeth than she was allowed to in order pass a physical examination for the Women's Officer Corps of the Red Cross, a requirement she considered rather amusing. She had the gumption to think that another old friend, David Bruce, director of the Psychological Warfare Department of the Navy, would have a job for her "planning strategy," but he was only interested in reminiscing with her about Paris in the early 1930s. Her charm and earnest good will were leading nowhere.

An odd juxtaposition arises when Caresse's aborted attempts to work in wartime Washington are placed in the context of her family's conservative political orientation and Caresse's simmering pacifism, or as she put it, her instinct "to clog not grease the wheels of militarism."[13] Caresse voted for FDR both times that he ran for office. Her only reservation seemed to have been that he refused to accept Henry Wallace as his running mate on his ticket. Her mother and two brothers were horrified that she had supported any Democratic candidate, let alone a radical like Wallace. (Jim Forrestal was also anti-Wallace.) "The Wall-Streeters joined with the Social Registerites in the condemnation of my rebel act. I had always been considered a wayward member of the family, but never a renegade until then."[14] On the other hand, Caresse was also willing to socialize with Juan Cardenas, the ambassador from Spain, who was ostracized by many of Washington's elite because of his country's fascist government. She was often a guest at the Spanish embassy, unwilling to draw a line "between personal friendship and totalitarian appointment." Was Caresse a bundle of contradictions, an opportunist who took her favors as they came, or the person who defined for herself the guidelines by which she would live, even when they offended the people she least wanted to antagonize?

Caresse's relationship with Canada Lee could be viewed as another example of Caresse's rebellious spirit. Her lover was not only fifteen years younger than she, he was black. Born Leonard Lionel Cornelius Canegata in New York City on May 3, 1907 (he died May 9, 1952), Canada Lee studied the violin for seven years with the composer and singer J. Rosamond Johnson, the brother of writer and social activist James Weldon Johnson. He became a jockey, changed his name, and turned boxer, winning 265 out of 300 amateur bouts, including a national lightweight competition.[15] His career as a fighter came to an end in 1933 after he suffered a detached retina of the eye.

The following year, he appeared in *Stevedore* and later went on to become one of the most celebrated actors of his generation. On March 24, 1941, he starred on Broadway as Bigger Thomas in the Mercury Theater production of *Native Son* directed by Orson Welles. After ninety-seven performances, the play toured major U.S. cities, and then returned to New York City for another eighty-four performances.[16] Caresse would sometimes follow Canada on tour, thrilled to be in his presence and witness his rising popularity.

Miscegenation laws were still on the books in many states. Jim Crow was very much alive in Washington, D.C., less so in New York City, where subtler forms of racism were institutionalized. Caresse's mother tried to accommodate the couple. In 1934, the same year that Lee was appearing in *Stevedore,* Mrs. Jacob had invited Caresse and Canada for tea at her apartment on Seventy-second Street, but the doorman asked Lee to use the service elevator. "Mama was as indignant as only a Victorian grande dame could be. I, of course, was infuriated and humiliated for my friend."[17] She insisted that after their visit, she and Canada sit in the front lobby of her mother's building, but the hostile and derisive looks thrown by doorman and residents alike made the atmosphere unbearable.

Caresse's brother Walter ("Buddy") had a difficult time accepting the liaison, marking the dinner he shared with Caresse and Canada in Washington, D.C., in the early 1940s as the occasion after which he and Caresse lost touch for about ten years.[18] Caresse was not about to drop this affair of the heart to appease her brother or to yield to the pressure of a society in general that scorned relationships between blacks and whites. And, in a sense, Caresse was a victim of her free spirit, her motives likely to be misunderstood. As her relationship with Canada evolved, through the various stages of romance and friendship, Caresse's deserved reputation as a "hedonist," as she put it herself, interfered with what should have been other obvious aspects of her character, her political sophistication and integrity of commitment. A woman like Caresse would not always be taken seriously, especially when she freely partook in life's pleasures, and honored the sensual side of her character.

During the 1930s, Caresse and Canada would meet uptown in Harlem, mostly for lunch at the newly opened Frank's, an elegantly appointed restaurant with leather banquettes and quiet service, the clientele show people and other celebrities of the black community. Canada Lee was a favored patron, and he and Caresse enjoyed special treatment during their "jealously guarded" secret rendezvous. Caresse learned about the insidious nature of racist behavior and expectations, and how, unaware, she herself had a skewed perspective. When *Stevedore* was playing in Chicago, Caresse decided she would join the company for a weekend. She was writing a play, called "The Cage," a drama in one scene, about a doomed love affair between a black physician and an upper class matron.[19] She hoped to pick up an idea or two by living with the cast for a few days.

Without giving much thought to the matter, she assumed that she would have to find a suitable hotel that would accept her "colored friends." The only integrated hotels she could find were worse than shabby. She was stymied until one member of the troupe suggested that she stay where they always stayed—at the company's hotel near the theater, where she would be considered "one of them." Caresse got a quick lesson in what it means to be the person with power and privilege, no matter how delicately exerted. She was happily surprised by the graciousness of the "negro" hotel, of the "big bright corner room" she stayed in, the "perfect and polite" service, the delicious breakfasts in bed, and most of all, the easy comradery of cast and crew during after-theater hours. Caresse recognized that she had unintentionally fostered misconceptions about how black people lived and worked.

She now had to be careful about erring in the other direction. She records feeling "like a pallid flower that had been plucked from a gorgeous garden-plot to be transferred to a lonely vase on a varnished stand" when she returned to one of the Park Avenue apartments where she stayed during her various sojourns in New York.[20] But a look at "The Cage," the short melodrama she wrote in 1935, reveals that Caresse achieved some distance on the subject. The larger consequences of racism are illustrated in "The Cage," albeit in the precious context of a poor little rich girl plot.

In "The Cage," an unnamed white woman, the daughter of a physician, visits Jim, a successful black physician with whom she is having an affair. The woman tells Jim what a wonderful doctor he is, how even if she broke her neck, she knows that he would be able to fix it. The physician complains bitterly about their predicament, how they are trapped, always waiting for the occasions when she, his lover, can visit him in secret. The woman offers no solutions, only a list of reasons why their relationship must remain clandestine. Their discussion is interrupted by a call from one of the doctor's patients. The woman then calls home and discovers that her daughter is suffering with 103-degree fever from mastoid infection, the same illness mistakenly diagnosed for Polleen when she was a child. Jim offers to drive her home, but she refuses to risk exposing their relationship. She dashes out of the office to catch a taxi, she is hit by a car, and her neck is broken. Jim is not there to help her, and she will die, though not on stage. In a sense, she is killed by her cowardice and fear of family disapproval, by her own inbred racism.

About this time she also wrote a three-part short story in which the figure of the black physician Jim appears once again. Instead of an unnamed white woman for his lover, Caresse substitutes Cara Phelps, who is closely based on Caresse herself. Cara has returned from Europe with her daughter; her inspiring and "miraculous" "frail poet" of a husband, Larry (in the typewritten manuscript Caresse handwrites "L" over "H" every time Harry appears), has died recently. However, she lives on Fifth Avenue, in the home of her father, a distinguished physician and scholar. (The dwelling may be based on the Jacob brownstone that was near Fifth Avenue and Fifty-ninth Street.) In New York, she cultivates the same "gay brilliant successful international set" that she had left in France, but soon tires of their aimless frivolity and of her life as a "last minute girl," always ready for a good time. She meets Jim in her father's library, where he serves as a research assistant for her father. Jim and Cara are drawn to one another but fear the consequences of their attraction. Cara's father dies; Jim and Cara initiate and abruptly terminate an affair.

Not much of a story, it was never published. But it includes examples, allusions, and observations about the racial barriers a black professional encountered in the mid-1930s. When the doctor invites Jim to stay for lunch, Jim demurs at first and says that he can run over to a Second Avenue sandwich shop: "they'll serve me there." He fears that Cara will avoid him because he is black. The governess of Cara's child certainly hopes she will. The narrator of the story notes that, in the 1930s, "colored doctors" did not work at private hospitals in New York City, and that "only Bellevue, St. Luke's and New York Hospital subjected occasional charity patients to the touch of ebony fingers."

The narrator becomes entangled with racism herself. When Jim brings his own lunch to the Fifth Avenue house one day, she observes that it is mounds of fried chicken. Jim's sister also partially breaks the color barrier as an artist with an exhibition at "the Museum of Contemporary Art." Her sculpture is described as highly disciplined and inspired by "the wild beauty of her race."

Cara attends opening night, and who should be among the distinguished guests of editors, film directors, and socialites, but the celebrated actor Canada

Lee. Caresse wrote this story in 1937, three years after she had met Canada. The story had two working titles. The first was "As If Deprived," derived from the line in William Blake's "The Little Black Boy" that reads "But I am black, as if bereav'd of light." The alternative title was "Maybe in a Hundred Years." In her one-line preface, Caresse notes that the "characters in this story were drawn from life, the story is fiction." In 1960, Caresse tried to get this story and a few others published, but her agent, Gerald Pollinger, could not find an editor sufficiently impressed by them.[21] While Caresse was not particularly skillful at writing short stories, she was admirably disingenuous about their political edge.

In her unpublished memoir, Caresse confessed to one other occasion where she realized that she had been insensitive to the dynamics of social intercourse between whites and blacks. Canada had invited her to a charity ball that his mother and sister had organized for Children's Harlem Hospital. He asked that she bring along her two friends Max Ernst and Dorothea Tanning, with whom she had resumed contact since leaving Hampton Manor. Occasionally Caresse would stay at their Fifty-eighth Street apartment when they were living in Reno, Nevada. And during her years in Washington, D.C., when Caresse would resume her role as patron of the arts, she did so much to the delight of Dorothea. She had invited Canada to one her New York openings around this time, but he had been unable to go. Tanning had been disappointed, and Lee may have been trying to make amends by inviting her and Max Ernst to the ball.[22]

Crosby, Tanning, and Ernst did attend the charity ball, but their attire made them look as though they had not given much thought to the occasion.

> That night they were all magnificent—Canada master of ceremonies, his mother was very gracious and very handsome in black net, his sister quite exquisite in a white satin evening gown with orchids on her shoulder. Canada, his father and brother-in-law in dinner jackets while we sat in the box, the box of honor, in Monday tweeds, like sparrows in a peacock cage.[23]

In a moment of clarity, Caresse was mortified by her boorish appearance; after all, she had been schooled at a tender age in such matters of propriety, respect, and decorum. She promised herself that in the future she would appear "as soignee as possible" for any invitation she accepted, a small resolution perhaps, but to Caresse's credit, a sign of her deepening humanity.

Whatever the transgression, Caresse and Canada carried on a love affair through the mid-1940s. Canada wrote passionate letters to Caresse, telling her that he could no longer remember when she wasn't in his heart, and how much he yearned to be with her. He also reported that rehearsals for *Native Son* were grueling. If they guaranteed success, though, he did not mind the long hours. "It can mean so much to us—you and me," he wrote, adding "we won't have to hide so much, honey, and we can get a little of the happiness that I have wanted with you in this life."[24] Lee was in financial straits because he wanted to maintain his nightclub, The Chicken Coop, but could not get loans to pay for utilities. He grieved to Caresse about his predicament: "I tried to hock my soul, but nobody wanted my soul at any price." Unlike Jacques Porel and Bert Young, however, Canada Lee did not ask Caresse for money. He apologized for burdening her with his problems: "The only sunshine and softness about my life is you—and 'Native Son.'" Canada Lee's professional success, however, did little to ensure an easier path for their romance.

When Canada came to Washington, D.C., several years later, Caresse did all she could to protect him, short of pretending that they were not lovers. In 1941, blacks were barred entry from white restaurants. Caresse and Canada would be served together only in an African restaurant called the Bengazi, even though, by the early 1940s, Canada Lee was a Broadway star and *Native Son* a nationwide success. (A subsequent role as Caliban in Margaret Webster's Federal Theater production of *The Tempest* brought him greater critical acclaim.) It was not until June 8, 1953, that the Supreme Court ruled that restaurants in the District of Columbia could not refuse to serve blacks. Caresse set out in her own fashion to break down D.C.'s Jim Crow laws. Since she was not able to take on the restaurateurs by herself, she turned to art critics and theatergoers for support.

11

A Woman of Influence

After a dreary winter in Washington in 1942, Caresse realized that she would never land a position with a government agency to help the war effort. Wanting a change of scene to lift her spirits, she drove cross-county with Salar, her Afghan hound, to the S-Bar-S Ranch in the desert, north of Reno, and to Virginia City, back to her old haunts, where she had divorced Bert. Ironically, she found herself living as she never had before, among women only, "war widows," she called them, without connections to society or the arts. She cultivated friendships with four of them—Alice Berry, Phyllis Walsh, Helen Thomas, Cobina Wright.[1] They all decided that since sugar was rationed, it was the perfect opportunity to diet. Caresse commended herself for breakfasting on broiled tomato and tomato juice, giving up not just scrambled eggs and toast, but cream and sugar in her morning coffee.

Caresse enjoyed comparing the clutter of her small room with the others'. Caresse stocked about the same amount of perfumes and powders, but more books, paper, pencils, and ink, plus a typewriter, and a big bag of dog biscuits on her dresser. Unlike her friends, Caresse spent many days fishing, though she usually returned empty-handed. She was content to wade in the streams, the warm sun filtering through the willows.

> I tried to recall what Isaac Walton had said about rushing waters and whirlpools, but all I could remember was the book's binding, a beautiful

> willow green with gold lettering intertwined with a golden fish line—not the first edition by a longshot—but one that Harry had found in London, one of a deluxe edition whose cover must have charmed my eye away from the content.[2]

Caresse was never very far from thinking about books, those she read, produced, or tried to write.

Walking back to the ranch at the end of one particularly unsuccessful day of fishing, she surprised a group of mallards, who quickly moved upstream. Their squawk and their long, white necks banded with red reminded her of the funnels of the Cunard ships that she had taken between Southampton and New York, and how she incorporated that sound in the first poem of *Painted Shores,* an exquisitely illustrated volume of sonnets dedicated to Harry (Black Sun, 1927). The eighth poem in the sequence, "I Indicate the Storm but Long to Stay," recalls the rebellious persona that Caresse still cultivated.

> So often I have wondered would I dare
> Pull off my shoes and stockings in the square
> Or shout, "How stupid" through the tea-room doors
> Or say "How pretty" to the brave young whores.
> Or if by chance I met a charming man
> To whisper "Darling!" as away I ran.[3]

Nearly fifteen years after she wrote this poem, Caresse was still quick to take flight when she felt the strictures of convention closing in.

She drove home to Washington at the beginning of May. She had intended to stay until September, but life among the "war widows" had become too predictable. Moreover, the pastoral respite was broken by the arrival of navy officers with plans for constructing a new naval training base to be built at Pyramid Lake, about ten miles from the S-Bar-S Ranch. The noise would be deafening. She tried to muster up an adventure by telephoning Zoray and Eric Kramaer, the couple she had met during her first trip to Nevada. They had spent "escapist days" together in a deserted gold-rush brewery on which they had claimed squatter's rights.[4] The Kramaers were now living in Berkeley, and Caresse proposed that they take a quick trip down the Baja into Mexico. But gas was under ration, and the Kramaers were barely scraping by on Eric's shipfitter's salary while he attended classes at the University of California.[5]

Back in Washington, Caresse mapped out a more constructive life than she had been living out west. She lost patience with her social circle—the wives of diplomats, ambassadors, and officers who lunched at the Mayflower. Caresse needed a project. Without one, she was bored. She decided it was time to open an art gallery, not only to sell paintings, sculpture, and prints, but to provide a salon of sorts where writers and artists would mix with ambassadors of state, legislators, and other Washington officials. She was perfectly qualified for this position. She had a storehouse full of work (that included Dalí, Ernst, Chirico, and Tanguy) and vast experience as a social doyenne.

Not discouraged by the tight rental market in Washington, she wrangled a list of possible sites for an art gallery from the director of one of the largest realtors in the city. (She pretended that they had met at "the Gold Cup at Warrenton," the popular steeplechase race held in Virginia.) She found the place she wanted in downtown Washington, at 916 G Place, a renovated antebellum pink-and-brown gingerbread house, four stories high, facing the 1860 home of General Ulysses S. Grant. The only barrier that could prevent her from acquiring a lease was another individual who also, coincidentally, wanted the space for an art gallery, a young man named David Porter, whom she had met briefly at an art gallery on Dupont Circle.[6]

A native of Chicago, and an artist himself, Porter was an employee of the War Production Board. Porter wanted to show the works of midwestern painters as well as his own. He needed a place to live as well. When he and Caresse found themselves at 916 G place, haggling over who had the right to rent it first, they decided to lease the building together. The solution was spontaneous, and the partnership lasted little over a year. But it established Caresse as a serious patron of the arts now based in Washington, a position that she reinforced later with a gallery of her very own, the Crosby Gallery of Modern Art at 1606 Twentieth Street, near Dupont Circle.

That year with Porter was exciting. Once again, Caresse found herself involved with a younger man (by fourteen years) at the beginning of new venture. Porter was no Bert Young. Although he didn't have Caresse's financial resources and social connections, he was a hardworking and devoted colleague, at least for the year. As Caresse describes it, "all expense was scrupulously divided—David insisted on that—and the fun was to see who could make the mostest with the leastest."[7] Walls were painted and tinted, floors were sanded, living quarters mapped out. They planned that the first show would represent their chief interests: surrealism and the Chicago School.

Caresse interrupted preparations for the show when she left Washington that June (1943) for Long Island in order to run a small summer resort hotel in Southampton. Money was tight. If she were going to maintain her standard of living and start a business, she needed more capital. Also, she wanted to scout for a suitable spot in one of the nearby affluent summer communities where she and David might establish a branch of their art gallery. A summer at the ocean away from hot, muggy Washington did not look bad either. But Caresse allowed a few too many friends to stay, as a July 6, 1943, tease of a letter from Billy suggests: "I am delighted to hear that all is going well at the Post House, and I am sure you will continue to have attractive non-paying guests all summer." It seems that while she did want to make a success out of this temporary position, it wasn't her nature to put a price on hospitality.

Pete Powel, now Major Howard Hare Powel, commiserated with Caresse over the ugly necessity of money, how "disgusting" it was to be poor.[8] But he thought her stint as a hotel manager could be profitable now that gas was rationed. Even those with money could not drive long distances or hop on airplanes for holidays: "now they have to huddle in hotels." He reassured Caresse that she had a "wonderful talent for welcoming people and feeding and amusing them" and that she would come through "becomingly tanned [with] some money in your purse." Powel himself managed to visit Southampton and its "delights," but his predictions for Caresse's success were not entirely on the mark. Although he had warned that money should be "flowing in before it begins to trickle out," Caresse did not turn a profit. She tried hard to, rising with the sun in order to plan and prepare the day's menu, a radical adjustment for someone accustomed to eating breakfast in bed.

David Porter worked away at getting the gallery in shape for the first show. He also rented out the third floor for extra income, but that proved to be a headache since the tenant objected to the mattress on the bed, the slipcovers on the sofa and chairs, and the limited closet space.[9] Caresse trusted that David would manage without her, that she had chosen a sensible partner this time, who, as her friend Pete Powel agreed, would not "run off with the house, the profits, and the furniture."[10] Powel added that Porter was "the only wolf" Caresse would have to worry about for a while, and that he was "too young to have dangerously sharp teeth and claws," to do much damage anyway. Porter finally asked the annoying tenant to leave, even though he was hard up for cash and couldn't put together the fare to visit Caresse in Southampton. Sweet if not very passionate letters were exchanged. So that she would have company at night, David shipped to Southampton the new puppy he and Caresse had acquired before Caresse's departure. They had named the dog Vodka.

The first show at the G Place Gallery took place on Sunday afternoon, November 3, 1943. It was a double exhibition. On the first floor, Caresse arranged "Summer Work," surrealist paintings exhibited for the first time in United States by Max Ernst, back with Dorothea Tanning after a summer in Arizona; Yves Tanguy, who shipped his most recent work from his farm in Connecticut; Matta Echaurren, the Chilean-born French painter who was one of Caresse's lodgers in Southampton; and the Cuban artist Wilfredo Lam. The second floor was Porter's "Home Sweet Home," twenty works of everyday life by such painters as Flora Schofield, Mac Le Sueur, Gertrude Abercrombie, Copeland C. Burg, Eldzier Corter, Ann Wolf, Laura Douglas, Charles Sebree, and Dan Palumbo.[11] Ernst, Matta, and Tanguy were present for the opening. The exhibition was praised in the November 15, 1943, issue of *Art Digest* for providing Washington with a much-needed center for modern art.

The G Place Gallery served that function only too well, but without turning a profit. The gallery was open from two in the afternoon until eight every evening, "so that persons employed during the day have the opportunity to attend exhibitions."[12] The second exhibition was devoted to the early works of Giorgio de Chirico. It was a loan exhibit from a New York City show entitled "Art of the Century," paintings from private collectors such as Peggy Guggenheim and from a number of museums. None of the paintings, of course, were for sale, and a party atmosphere prevailed, establishing a bad precedent for business. Future openings and exhibits would be well-attended, when paintings actually were for sale. Champagne or martinis were served; talk and laughter filled the space. Prices were low and deluxe catalogs were provided free of charge. But there were very few buyers, even among the cultural attaches, and members of the Cabinet and Congress who stopped by.

Caresse and David Porter hung on through the spring of 1943, making next to nothing but creating a wonderful showplace for works by among others Buffie Johnson (Mrs. John Latham), Enrico Donati, Samuel Rosenberg, and Henry Miller. Anaïs Nin came down to help Caresse hang Ian Hugo's copper engravings. David Porter contributed his weekly salary of $75, Caresse the $500 interest she received every three months on her investments.[13] They were thrilled to broaden Washington's view of contemporary art, and to offer some respite from the grim affairs of the day, but sales remained stagnant. Caresse's concern over losses had as much to do with the welfare of the artists as her own and David's. Henry Miller was a case in point.

Caresse had written to him in December 1943 to find out if he had heard about her gallery and if he would be interested in contributing some work.[14] Through his agent, Clara Grossman, Miller offered fifty-two watercolors at fifty dollars each for the ten-day, one-man show. He had neither the time nor the money to come to Washington for the opening in May 1944. Living in the Beverly Glen section of Los Angeles, he was desperate for funds so that he could complete two manuscripts, "The Air Conditioned Nightmare" and "The Rosy Crucifixion."

At the opening, Katherine Ann Porter and Caresse both spoke about Miller, emphasizing the versatility of his genius.[15] Caresse also quoted from a letter that Miller had distributed to a select group of people that included former nuclear physicist and publisher Bern Porter; James Laughlin, the owner of New Directions Publishing Corporation; and Geraldine Fitzgerald. In the letter, he described his strapped circumstances and his determination to finish his books even if he had to beg for the money to do so. Miller was so optimistic about the show that he imagined giving away half the proceeds to artist Beauford Delaney, poet Kenneth Patchen, and Shep, the caretaker at Hampton Manor whom Miller had gotten to know when he was a guest there.[16] Sales, however, were not good, and Caresse had to return most of the watercolors to Miller. Miller and Janina Lepska did visit Caresse in the fall of 1944, shortly before they married that December.

During the summer, the partnership between Crosby and David Porter grew strained. By the time Caresse left for Southampton again, their affair was over as well. From New York City on September 14, 1944, Caresse wrote Porter a formal though cordial letter that gave him the lease on G Place for the following year. It would take another year before their finances were properly sorted out. Caresse struck out on her own with a gallery uptown, the Crosby Gallery of Modern Art at 1606 Twentieth Street, N.W. She created the same social atmosphere as before, even if the exhibits took on a sharper political edge.

Throughout this period, Caresse and Canada Lee cultivated their friendship and intermittent love affair. Canada, who was still married to Juanita Waller, came down from New York for gallery openings despite the strictures Washington imposed on his access to public facilities. Caresse usually dined with her friends after the gallery closed for the evening, often at such restaurants as the Salle du Bois, the Balalaika, O'Donnell's, the seafood restaurants along the Potomac, or the Trianon, a small, family-run bistro just above Pennsylvania Avenue on Seventeenth Street, and a favorite of Harry T. Moore.[17] Moore would later be known for his scholarly work on D. H. Lawrence and modern French and German literature, but during the war, he served as a lieutenant in the air force. Moore regularly attended exhibitions at the gallery and became good friends with Caresse. He would dine with Caresse and Canada at the Bengazi, the one restaurant that they knew would accommodate them. Another friend, Selden Rodman, would often join them. An enlisted master sergeant with the Office of Strategic Services, Rodman was a poet, playwright, art critic, and future influential collector of Haitian art. Soon after he was graduated from Yale University in 1931, he met Caresse in

Paris. She invited him to lunch with Paul Eluard and Louis Aragon.[18] When Caresse and her entourage grew tired of the Bengazi, she oversaw meals at her apartment or Rodman's small studio.

Caresse decided that it was time to protest against Jim Crow in Washington. In part, she was influenced by Canada's own activism concerning voter registration and equal treatment for black soldiers. Caresse made her gallery available for a reading of Selden Rodman's three-act play *The Revolutionists.* Set in San Domingue, Haiti, after the French revolution, the play depicts the struggle of three hundred thousand African slaves in Haiti who overthrow their white French masters. The chief character is Toussaint Louverture, an "educated slave" who belongs to a liberal plantation owner. He becomes the moderate leader of the revolution but is captured during Napoleon's unsuccessful attempt to reclaim the rich colony.[19] Canada Lee read the part of Toussaint and agreed to be available for other projects. Now bitten by the director-producer bug, Caresse staged *Othello* at the gallery. She cast herself as Desdemona, Canada Lee was Othello, and the part of Iago went to Harry Moore.[20]

By 1944, Canada was a member of the National Citizens Political Action Committee and Actors Equity. His parts in such plays as *Big White Fog, Lifeboat, Body and Soul, On Whitman Avenue,* and *Cry, the Beloved Country* had brought him great critical acclaim. He also caught the attention of the House Un-American Activities Committee, who regarded his plays as dangerously left-wing, and he was blacklisted.[21] Although Caresse would eventually broaden the scope of her civil rights activities, she apparently did not do anything to help end this harassment. His early death in 1952 goes unremarked upon in her memoirs. Caresse asked Anaïs Nin to avoid mention of her affair with Lee in the published diaries. Nin complied by describing Caresse and Canada as "good friends." In a June 11, 1968, letter, Nin wrote that she would honor Caresse's wish: "I understand the difficulties and respect them. Only a man can tell all and be respected for it. Witness Miller. Women have a long way to go."[22]

For now, in 1944, Caresse was not content using an art gallery for a theater. She wanted a larger space to stage future plays and readings with an integrated cast and an integrated audience. Harry Moore caught her enthusiasm: "Those of us who wore uniforms in the daytime were going to put on costumes at night to take part in the defiant project."[23] The first production was going to be *Oroonoko,* Thomas Southerne's 1696 adaptation of Aphra Behn's 1688 novel about the hypocrisy of Christian slave traders, based on Behn's experiences in the British colony of Surinam. It is not surprising that Caresse picked a work by Aphra Behn: she was often attacked for using lewd language and daring themes and for following an unconventional lifestyle before Virginia Woolf praised her in *A Room of One's Own* (1931) as the first woman professional writer. Unfortunately, Caresse abandoned plans to stage *Oroonoko* when a lease to a vacant movie house on Ninth Street fell through.

However, Caresse did not abandon the cause. She took it back to her art gallery, first with a collection of paintings and drawings by African American soldiers,[24] and then with a one-man show of works by Romare Bearden, who in 1944 was a combat infantryman and an unknown fledgling artist. While he was stationed in Pine Camp, New York, he told Caresse that most of his fellow soldiers believed that he was "nuts," and that if he showed his paintings to the army psychiatrist, he would probably get a discharge.[25] Caresse had more confidence in him than that: she was the first art dealer to show Bearden's work.

In a January 31, 1944, letter to Bearden concerning the opening date for "Ten Hierographic Paintings by SGT. Romare Bearden," Caresse reiterated her enthusiasm for his work: "Let me say again how fine I think your paintings are, and that I am delighted to be the first to show them." The path was set for a trusting and cordial agent/artist relationship, with Caresse receiving a 35 percent commission on sales. Bearden was quite pleased with the show's opening, thought it was "wonderful," and then, writing from a USO in Harlem, talked business in a very unbusinesslike fashion. Selden Rodman wanted to buy a picture but the price was too high. Bearden proposed that Caresse

> go about this like a doctor, and charge according to a person's ability to pay. Most of the people whom I like, and would like to have my paintings, have very little money. Maybe that is a curse of good (?) taste. In this, I'm sure you can exercise the best judgment.[26]

Caresse thought it best to set a "fairly reasonable ceiling" in order to encourage young collectors and followed through for the next Bearden exhibit, "Passion of Christ—Recent Gouaches" for June 10, 1945.

Caresse and Bearden were respectful of one another. Bearden sensed that he had a real listener in Caresse, someone who was not only sympathetic to his themes, but who also had an authoritative eye for art. He wanted her to know what he was trying to accomplish with his "Passion of Christ" series, which depicts scenes from the chapters of Mark, Matthew, Luke, and John in the New Testament.

> It may be thought strange that a soldier should . . . paint such a non bellicose series of pictures. But I hope every thing I have experienced in the Army is incorporated in the paintings in an emotional sense. For instance, this is certainly a sadistic age, evidenced not only on the battlefields but in the day to day relations of people. Some of the paintings express this.[27]

He explained that his approach was abstract, but not purely so. He wanted the paintings to be warm and spontaneous and "to display something of the personality of the painter." Now in Camp Edwards, Massachusetts, Bearden felt more isolated than ever. Caresse was a viable link to the life he wanted to live after his discharge.

Caresse was convinced that she was managing, for a time at least, the work of a great artist. After the "Passion of Christ" series of paintings arrived in Washington, Caresse told Bearden in an April 17, 1945, letter how thrilled she was to have the new work.

> Your development in technique and clarity is tremendous, and I am glad to see the same spiritual integrity is there. As you know, I was first struck by your painting because of a certain nobility of theme as well as a rich execution—and now added to this is experience in design and a clarification in color that is most exciting. I feel more than justified in my first enthusiasm.

Romare Bearden would go on to far greater vistas than the Crosby Gallery of Modern Art. But Caresse was confident enough to approach him a few years later for a new, and this time, interdisciplinary project that would again show that she was ahead of her time.

But first, the Crosby Gallery of Art shook up Washington in another fashion. In October 1946, Caresse exhibited a group of eleven modern paintings whose theme was the "Temptations of St. Anthony." The show received some unexpected publicity after the Copley Society of Boston announced that it had rescinded its commitment to show the paintings after Mayor James M. Curely described the exhibit as "an insult to the Catholic church and those having faith in the saint."[28] Paintings by a number of Caresse's good friends, including Dorothea Tanning, Max Ernst, and Salvador Dalí, were featured in the show. This was the exhibit that prompted Selden Rodman to become an avid collector of paintings by Horace Pippin. Chris Mathisen, who covered the story for the *Evening Star,* noted that while there was a good deal of nudity depicted, "none of the artists had indicated St. Anthony was being swayed by the blandishments of temptation." It is unlikely that Caresse would have declined to exhibit the paintings even if St. Anthony had looked as if he had succumbed to "undressed womanhood." Caresse had not listened to Boston's edicts when Harry Crosby was pursuing her in 1920. She had no reason to listen now, especially if she could improve her financial situation and challenge a distorted puritan ethic in the process.

More serious activities were also at hand. Her old friend Ezra Pound was in town, jailed in the criminal bloc at St. Elizabeths Federal Hospital for the Insane. He was accused of conducting treasonous broadcasts from Rome, pro-Fascist and anti-Semitic tirades to American troops between 1941 and 1943. After his arrest, he had spent the final seven months of World War II under guard in a specially reinforced outdoor stockade, the workplace for *The Pisan Cantos,* considered by some critics to be the most brilliant among all the *Cantos* and for which Pound would be awarded, amid much controversy, the first Bollingen Prize in 1949. At a Christmas party in 1945 in the apartment above her art gallery, Caresse was approached for help by Dr. "Tiny" Zimmon, assistant to Dr. Winfred Overholser, superintendent at St. Elizabeths and professor of psychiatry at George Washington University. They both thought that Caresse could improve Pound's case if she, as his publisher and friend, and as a "loyal American" would visit him and report afterwards on her impressions of his state of mind.

Caresse agreed to the visit but could not get past the uneasy feeling that she was spying on her old friend. Apparently she was expected to report on whether she thought Pound had changed much from the time she had known him in the early 1930s.[29] She was appalled by the grim conditions of Howard Hall, the tiny visiting rooms with barred windows and guards who never left Caresse and Pound by themselves, and perhaps most of all by Pound's filthy, ragged appearance. But Pound greeted her affectionately and they reminisced about old times in Paris. Caresse believed that he had not changed much, that he was not crazy, merely "as arrogant and as sure as he been ten years before—no cringe, no mumbling, no fault of memory, no change really."[30] All she could do for now was buy Pound some new clothes to wear for the hearing where the jury would determine whether or not he was sane enough to stand trial. She thought a suit would help tamp down his haughtiness. The jury declared him to be of unsound mind.

Along with many well-known figures and writers, including T. S. Eliot, James Laughlin (Pound's publisher), Charles Olson, and Allen Ginsberg, Caresse continued to visit Pound during his fourteen-year confinement at St. Elizabeths. Caresse told Charles Olson that Pound did not hesitate to correct her on dates of his publications, but that he also confided his troubles to her. She was taken aback when he speculated that his great mistake had been "to go on after Pearl Harbor."[31] Caresse never tried to excuse Pound's behavior, but she remained loyal in her efforts to help him return to Italy. When Pound's daughter Mary came to Washington in March 1953 in hope of getting her father released, she stayed at Caresse's home. Caresse brought her to St. Elizabeths and also engaged the services of her own lawyer in order to get Mary an appointment at the Department of Justice.[32] Caresse would later visit Pound when he resumed his life in Rapallo, Italy. She never stopped believing that he would ultimately understand the nature of what he had done, even if he would admit it only to himself.

12

Back in the Avant-Garde

Towards the end of the war, Caresse found herself in a peculiar position. During a period of great, worldwide disaster, she had done very well for herself. She had put an end to a destructive marriage, made a fresh start in a new city, cultivated friendships and romances, and established a reputation as a patron of contemporary art and as a civil rights activist. In the late 1930s, she had lectured to Howard University students about modern art in Paris, a tremendously gratifying experience for her. In the early 1950s, Caresse would be invited to discuss careers in the arts with the graduates of Paul Laurence Dunbar High School. She had flouted the color barrier and challenged prurient culture police, but she was not tough enough to defy Senator Joseph McCarthy. Before she could address the students at Dunbar High School, she agreed—albeit with great reluctance—to fill out a questionnaire about her political affiliations for the House Un-American Activities Committee. She had rarely been afraid to confront the establishment, but in this instance, the stakes were too high. In a sense, Caresse had conquered all that she could of Washington, and the charm of her victories, large and small, was wearing thin.

Caresse yearned to return to Europe, which she had left in 1938, and to visit Polleen, whom she had not seen in almost six years. Now married and settled in London, Polleen would be required to relinquish her passport if she returned to the United States. During the war and in the years immediately following, "leisure" travel for Americans was virtually banned. Caresse would have to figure out a way to make the trip herself. She tapped her connections to the upper echelon never considering that it was bad form to jump the line at the passport office. To no avail, she tried to persuade officials at the passport office that she would be helping to create an enduring peace if she were allowed to go to Europe. No one believed that her most recent experience as an owner of an art gallery would do anyone much good.[1] Nevertheless, Caresse remained determined to visit Polleen in London.

Harry Moore was sympathetic to Caresse's plight and suggested that she reclaim her literary reputation by starting an international cultural magazine: Caresse "blazed up at once and began organizing the project."[2] She enlisted Moore as assistant editor, and for editorial advisors, Henry Miller for prose, Selden Rodman for poetry, and Samuel Rosenberg for photographs. She had wanted Miller to assume the more prestigious title of West Coast editor, but he declined because he feared that he would be overwhelmed by submissions and correspondence.[3] Caresse was editor-in-chief and general publishing manager, with the right to veto any selection that she did not like. She forged ahead with a huge burst of energy.

Volume 1 was ready by the summer of 1945. The list of contributors was impressive: a who's who of currently (whether living and dead) or soon-to-be famous American and European writers and artists, including Henry Miller, Gwendolyn Brooks, David Daiches, René Crevel, Eleanor Clark, Alex Comfort, Demetrius Capetanakis, Karl Shapiro, Selden Rodman, Ruth Herschberger, Jean Helion, Romare Bearden, Pietro Lazzari, and Samuel Rosenberg, who provided a portrait photograph of Max Ernst. She called the publication *Portfolio* in order to indicate its eclectic content and its actual physical makeup. Paper was difficult to obtain in 1945, so Caresse went on a scavenger hunt. She took paper of different sizes and color, and used red plastic spiral for binders.

Caresse scheduled a party to celebrate the publication of *Portfolio* 1, which coincided with the recent surrender of the Japanese to Allied Forces. Her reluctance to describe the occasion in the sequel to her memoir was unusual and can be attributed to shocking circumstances. In two different but typed copies of a tentative table of contents for *Who in the World,* Caresse added a handwritten note to the list events for the summer of 1945. In one copy, she wrote "I was raped by a jubilant sailor" next to the line "Summer 1945, Hiroshima, August 6th, V.J. Day." In the other copy, she wrote next to the same line, "I am raped but escaped."[4] Caresse was determined to sustain the buoyant and confidant tone of her narrative at any price. Disclosing that she had been a victim of sexual violence (and that she never reported the crime) was impossible.

It should be remembered that the Black Sun Press had not been completely idle during the war years. In December 1942, Caresse had published through Gemor Press *Four Poems* by Sharon Vail, Kay Boyle's daughter; in 1943, *Misfortunes of the Immortals,* illustrations by Max Ernst, poems by Paul Eluard translated by Hugh Chisolm; in 1944, *Three Plays* by Ramon Sartoris. To coincide with a show of his work at the Crosby gallery in spring 1945, Caresse published *Horses,* four illustrations of etchings by Pietro Lazzari, the Italian-born American who had worked with the WPA and as a muralist at the 1939 World's Fair. He also appeared in *Portfolio,* volume 1.

Caresse relied on free labor to create *Horses.* The participants worked in a circle on the floor of her art gallery, "squatting on a handsome carpet . . . cutting and folding sheets of paper and cardboard, punching holes, assembling the components, and binding them with lengths of red ribbon. . . . Mrs. Crosby . . . presided unobtrusively, strolling the circle and chatting amiably with her band of volunteers."[5] The atmosphere was serious and festive at the same time, the reward a copy of the book.

Caresse returned to the passport office with *Portfolio* in hand and a number of letters from high-placed individuals such as David Finley, director of the National Gallery, and Huntington Cairns, head of the Censorship Bureau. She had also written to Archibald MacLeish, who was by then Assistant Secretary of State, expressing her wish to spend two months in Europe in order to gather material for the next volume. She wondered if he had any suggestions for future contributors, and would he be kind enough to put in a good word to the passport office about how the new journal could open avenues of cultural diplomacy. MacLeish would lend further support by asking Francis Lacoste, Charge d'Affairs ad interim, to assist Caresse in publishing *Portfolio* 2, which he was sure would help improve French-American relations.[6] Caresse got the passport.

There were no flights for civilians on American carriers, but for $500, Caresse secured passage on a BOAC "flying boat." It was Caresse's first transatlantic crossing by air. Everyone else on board was military and regarded Caresse as a pampered stowaway, probably encouraged by the Elsa Schiaparelli hat box she carried (which did not contain the designer's haberdashery but instead Pietro Lazzari's line drawings of horses, and Romare Bearden's "Passion of Christ" series in watercolor)[7] and by the red silk umbrella and zebra jacket she sported. She would count that trip as among her most comfortable crossings by air.

Caresse had pulled a few strings with government officials. But surely, they were impressed by the fervor with which Caresse described her plans. Caresse's approach was an eccentric mix of bald idealism and good-natured aggression. In the introduction to *Portfolio* 1, Caresse had listed her qualifications for embarking on a new journal, and she drew on this introduction for the speech she gave to the officials at the passport office. Referring to herself in the third person and alluding to Black Sun Press activities of the 1920s, Caresse declared that "the editor feels she is in some slight measure qualified to undertake such an enterprise because of her experience of many exciting years of specialized international publishing. . . . In those days, daring dreams captured in print and disobedient visions fixed upon canvas were our daily manna." She was not above romanticizing her mission, but her enthusiasm was refreshing. None of the authorities appeared to object to the dissident voices of *Portfolio*'s contributors. More than likely, they had neither the time nor the inclination to read the magazine.

Caresse reminded her listeners that the Black Sun Press had flourished in the decade following World War I by providing the first international outlet for writers such as James Joyce, D. H. Lawrence, Hart Crane, Archibald MacLeish, Kay Boyle, Marcel Proust, Constantin Brancusi, and George Grosz. Translations of Antoine de Saint-Exupéry and René Crevel were made available to readers in the United States. *Portfolio* would have similar goals at the end of World War II. The fluid, cross-disciplinary format of *Portfolio* would, with each "moveable unit," "bring into focus an expression, whether grave or gay, scientific or emotional, of the world of ideas today."[8] Alluding to the imagery of one of her favorite authors, Caresse said that now the world was rising once more from the ashes of war, "Phoenix-like," and ready to follow the "courageous vision of the artist." The writers, the artists, and cultural historians to be included in subsequent volumes of *Portfolio,* clad in "the full amor [*sic*] of light," would reveal what was needed to maintain a lasting peace between nations. In retrospect, Caresse regarded herself as a predecessor of UNESCO. Her endeavor was not nearly as grand, but her global perspective on community was in sharp focus.

Caresse's summer in Europe was a success. First, she got to see Polleen, who even though she probably knew better than anyone else that her mother had never let the word "no" stop her before, was amazed when she saw her mother standing at the front door of her small house off Sloane Square in London. No time was lost popping the champagne, which Caresse noted was in more plentiful supply than it was in Washington.[9] She was happy to see Albert de Mun again, now in his role as son-in-law. But there was also personal tragedy to acknowledge over the miscarriage of Polleen's first child. Nevertheless, the day was filled with the joy of reunion, hope for the future.

And although Billy was not there, a toast was made to his recent engagement to Josette Janacopoulos. Born and brought up in Paris, Josette was living in Brazil, where her grandfather had been the Greek consul. Josette's brother had gone to school with Billy at L'Ecole de Lille de France, and together they had attended the six-day bicycle races with Harry Crosby.[10] After Billy and Josette married, they planned to resettle in the apartment of Josette's aunt in Paris. So it appeared that the Crosby/Peabody family as a whole was yearning once more to expand the dominion of home.

Caresse wasted no time putting together *Portfolio* 2, which she edited from Paris in the fall of 1945. *Portfolio* 1 had been well received in Chicago and Los Angeles, and Frances Steloff of the Gotham Book Mart on West Forty-seventh Street in New York City sold out the entire first order.[11] Since 1942, Steloff had stocked Black Sun Press editions with the volumes and little magazines of avant-garde literature she proudly sold. Although the bookstore was a profitable enterprise, Steloff often waived the bookstore's commission, as she did for Caresse's issues of *Portfolio*.[12] Over the years, Caresse and Steloff would become devoted friends.

Caresse found lodgings in Hotel California on rue de Beri and resumed business with her "perfect printer," Roger Lescaret, who had fought with the French Resistance. He set the type for one thousand copies from his reopened offices on rue Cardinale, quite a feat considering how difficult it was to obtain paper and to arrange finances. Whatever the difficulties, Caresse was exhilarated to be back in France and told Henry Miller in a September 14, 1945, letter that Paris was as "beautiful as ever. . . . I wish you and Lepska could join me this evening at the Café Flore for a glass of good wine and some bread that even at this time is better than any in the U.S.A."

The contributors to volume 2 of *Portfolio* were no less impressive than those to volume 1. No doubt, there had been a dearth of outlets for writers and artists during the war, and Caresse did not have to spend much energy persuading them that they should appear in her new journal, whose subtitle was *The Intercontinental Review of Art and Literature*. As she would later write to Henry Miller, "*Portfolio* was received in Paris like rain in drought."[13] It should be emphasized that she was spending her own precious money with the dream of maintaining a forum that would ultimately disabuse readers of the idea that there could ever be a war fought to create peace. The journal was officially a nonprofit quarterly publication. Remuneration for use of original material was limited to $25 and a year's subscription, although that would be gradually increased. Each issue sold for $3, or $10 for the year.

Among the contributors were Jean Paul Sartre ("The End of the War"), Albert Camus ("Letter to a German Friend," his earliest appearance in an English-language publication), Henri Matisse, Paul Eluard, Pablo Picasso, René Char, and Henri Cartier Bresson, whose major exhibition at the Museum of Modern Art was still another year off. Picasso contributed not only portraits of Stéphane Mallarmé and Paul Verlaine but also a prose statement arguing the inextricable connection between art and politics. Actually, Caresse was humble about the second volume. She told Henry Miller that she thought *Portfolio* 1 was "fresher, more hopeful, and vigorous. I had to use known factors in II as I had to work quickly without looking about."[14] A more accurate editor's compass than Caresse's would be hard to locate. And she was receptive to the suggestions of her editorial board, and of her friends in Paris. As she told Man Ray in a February 12, 1946, letter, Paul Eluard had been especially helpful. She had written to Man Ray with the hope that he would be interested in contributing to a future issue of *Portfolio:* "I know many of your friends in Europe will be anxious to see some of our recent work."

Soon to be appointed poetry consultant to the Library of Congress, Robert Lowell was one of the Americans included in volume 2. Lowell would later attend a Washington dinner party given by Caresse in honor of St.-John Perse, where he would meet Carley Dawson, a wealthy Georgetown neighbor with whom he would have an affair that lasted six months.[15] Another poet Caresse featured was Weldon Kees, whose poems, short stories, and criticism had been published in the *New Yorker, Partisan Review, Harper's, Time,* and the *Nation.* His poem "The Ambassadors" appeared in both English and French.

As professionally rewarding as her trip to Europe was, Caresse had sacrificed her good health for the cause. When she came back to the States, she landed in the hospital with a case of pneumonia that lasted a month.[16] While she recuperated, Caresse worked on volume 3, another strong mix, which included previous contributors such as David Daiches, this time with a piece on wine, and Selden Rodman, who, very much against the current, panned Evelyn Waugh's *Brideshead Revisited.* Romare Bearden designed the cover for a special deluxe edition of three hundred copies. Kay Boyle, whose translation of a section of René Crevel's *Babylon* had appeared in *Portfolio* 1, submitted a story of her own entitled "Military Zone."

Caresse also printed a brief selection from Harry Crosby's diaries, *Shadows of the Sun* (1929), Harry's own rendition of Walt Whitman's "Whoever

You Are Holding Me Now in Hand" (1860). It was an exercise he thought would help him comprehend the kind of devotion he expected from his lovers. In the third section of the poem, of particular interest to Harry, Whitman warns a disciple that he must forsake all allegiance to his former life if he is to follow him: "I alone would expect / to be your sole and elusive standard, / Your novitiate would even then be long and exhausting." Taking such action could be destructive, Whitman warns, and suggests that perhaps it might be best for them to cease and desist. Caresse's motivation for including Harry's version—"I alone / expect to be your Sun-God, sole and exclusively"—is not clear. She may have wanted to reveal the conditions that "perfectly mirrored her relationship with Harry."[17] To what end, however, is another issue. Apparently, Caresse wanted to reiterate eternal allegiance to Harry, to renew her vows to the life and values they had shared. She may have been reflecting on how much she owed Harry, but that she had paid too high price because ultimately he did leave her. Was there any room in Caresse's emotional makeup to allow resentment into her adulation? Was she suggesting that she had transcended Harry's influence, that she felt that she was a leader in her own right?

Other contributions in volume 3 included three poems by Stephen Spender; "Chant's Secrets," poetry by Jean Genet, who was still nearly two years away from being released from a sentence of life imprisonment; Natalia Ginzburg, whose first novel, *E Stato cosi (The Dry Heart),* about the kinds of unhappiness endured by women, would appear in 1947; and Federico Garcia-Lorca. Caresse selected "Lament for the Death of a Bullfighter," Lorca's powerful statement about the tragic sense of violent death, written the year before he was murdered by Falangist soldiers in the opening days of the Spanish Civil War. It became one of Lorca's most anthologized works, considered by some critics to be among the greatest elegies in modern Spanish poetry. England, France, Italy, and Spain were represented by these four writers, providing an international scope but hardly with voices of the establishment. Caresse would stay true to this unorthodox course of action for the duration of *Portfolio,* publishing writers whose social concerns corresponded to her own.

With a scattered editorial board, limited resources, and little secretarial assistance, Caresse could irritate her contributors. Letters were lost and writers' fees not always speedily dispatched. In May 1946, she received a harshly worded letter from Kenneth Rexroth after he discovered in a San Francisco bookstore that his dance play, *Iphigenia at Aulis,* had been published in *Portfolio* 3. In his capacity as poetry editor, Selden Rodman had served as intermediary between Rexroth and Caresse. In an undated letter to Caresse, Rodman mentioned that he would be sending her some material by Rexroth, "the most exciting discovery in years." Rexroth had never received a formal acknowledgment that his play had been accepted for publication. However, he was under the impression that if it were to appear in *Portfolio,* he would receive $50 and author's copies. He had already published two volumes of poetry, *In What Hour* (Macmillan, 1940) and *The Phoenix and the Tortoise* (New Directions, 1944), and expected to be treated with respect and consideration.

Rexroth saw no reason to conceal his anger and irritation. He told Rodman that he did not enjoy "being kicked around by millionairesses" and that Caresse should not run a magazine by "reducing its contributors to literal buggery—but then—that is what she does it for, and they in turn simply love it. But not this boy."[18] He continued in this vein to Caresse, stating that he despised her "world of cocktail literature and art" and that her reputation as a "simply fascinating woman, and one of the world's leading art patrons" was created at his expense and that of others like him "who could not possibly afford $3.50 for your simply fascinating magazine."[19]

Portfolio 3 had been out only two weeks when Rexroth saw it, and Caresse sent the $50 to him as soon she learned what had transpired. Mollified, Rexroth apologized to Rodman, but his attitude towards Caresse—that she was a callous, wealthy dilettante—remained unchanged until he allowed Rodman to introduce him to Caresse in the fall of 1948. Rexroth was on the poetry circuit and had stopped in Washington, D.C., to visit Ezra Pound at St. Elizabeths. At their meeting, Caresse kept her initial impressions of Rexroth in check—she had speculated in an undated letter to Harry Moore that Rexroth suffered from a "great big inferiority complex." She made clear that despite the flack over its publication, she had been excited about publishing *Iphigenia at Aulis* and expressed an interest in directing a student production of the play at Howard University. Given the circumstances of their meeting, and their shared interests, Caresse and Rexroth decided to be friends.

Later that fall, Rexroth encouraged Caresse to visit him in California and suggested that Howard students listen to recordings of Japanese Noh plays to get a sense of the appropriate music for *Iphigenia.*[20] He and Caresse would meet again, but not at Rexroth's home San Francisco, rather in Rome.

An earlier trip to Italy, however, would occur two years before that reunion, in the course of her collection of material for volume 4 of *Portfolio.* Volume 2 had been noticed by the cultural attache from Italy, and he approached Caresse with the request that she do the same for his country that she had for France, that is, demonstrate that Italy was brimming with new writers and artists waiting to be discovered or more widely acknowledged. As was her nature, Caresse was immediately attracted by the prospect of publishing an Italian *Portfolio,* even though initially she realized she had not given much thought to the possibility of what the attache assured her was an Italian renaissance.

Booking passage to Europe was not a trial this time, but traveling within Europe presented a problem or two. Caresse flew to Paris. Her only chance of getting to Rome was by military transport, which meant that she had be to be packed and ready to depart on two hour's notice. She was notified of her flight in the middle of the night, after dinner with friends from long ago, Mai and Frans de Geetere. They were still living on their barge, the *Marie Jeanne,* now docked near the place de la Concorde. With the exception of three elderly Greek women who were inching their way home to Athens, Caresse's traveling companions were all military personnel. The plane, a converted bomber, "a bucket-seat job," arrived in Rome in the early morning hours.

Again, Caresse's appearance was as startling as it had been when she landed in Paris the previous year. With her Elsa Schiaparelli hat box, fur coat, and umbrella in tow, she aroused a fair amount of animosity while she tried to find porters to carry four suitcases, not to mention "several bundles of books."[21] She managed, nevertheless, to make her way to the formerly glamorous Excelsior Hotel, which was to be her home base for the two months that she stayed in Italy. She had great plans for meeting the new Italian avant-garde, but she also thought she might get a special audience with Pope Pius XII and make a film about the Vatican. She saw the pope, but the movie never materialized. She did, however, take several photographs of the ceremony for the sainthood of Mother Cabrini.

The role that Caresse was developing for herself was a peculiar one, yet consistent with the pattern of her life. Although Washington had not taken her seriously as a commentator on political issues, by the end of the war, she had turned herself into a cultural ambassador of sorts, promoting pacifism and a global community with the publication of *Portfolio.* Although she had no official status, she enjoyed some of the privileges of a delegate of the United States government—passage from Paris to Rome on the military plane and a room at the Excelsior, where military personnel were billeted. She had entry into the army commissary and officers' mess, where she lunched alone on her first day in Rome: the meal was "decidedly PX," she recorded, "but the two martinis at 50 lire ($.20) each were definitely P[re]-war."[22] She was courted by Rome's elite, most of whom, according to Caresse, "lived at the top of noble balustraded stairways, and received *al fresco* on flower-laden balconies overlooking those hazy roofs of the Eternal City." A reader would hardly know that Caresse was surrounded by a population devastated by world war. And yet, she was completely serious about the mission of *Portfolio* and truly believed that her efforts could promote a permanent world peace.

Portfolio 4 was another beautiful production, enhanced by a photograph taken by Romolo Marcellini of Caresse standing beside a Roman fountain, a copy of *Portfolio* in hand. As before, she gathered contributors whose work would soon gain wide recognition, like Carlo Levi, whose yet-to-be-published *Christ Stopped at Eboli* would piercingly capture the devastating poverty of Italian peasants in the south of Italy; and Alberto Moravia, whose prolific career was still in its early stages. Robert Fasola and Giorgio de Chirico were among the artists represented. Caresse reported that a good deal of cultural activity was occurring outside Rome also, that small theater groups and chamber music orchestras were creating a new Italian renaissance. Caresse returned to Washington in the fall. The U.S. embassy assisted her by shipping the material she had gathered.

Caresse was still pressed for funds, and like most ambitious editor-publishers, she urged potential subscribers to keep up with recent developments in the arts by putting up $12 for four issues. Without ever having taken a course in marketing management, she knew how to sell her product: she personalized the letter, aiming for a spontaneous yet gracious tone. She was chatty, reporting that she would soon be off to Greece for an upcoming issue. Nor was she beyond trying to instill a little anxiety into potential subscribers: "I forgot to say at once, that if you are not interested in modern trends and experimental art, then PORTFOLIO is not your meat, but if you are in the 'avant garde' you are doing yourself a disfavor to neglect it."[23] Although there are no figures that indicate how many subscribers she had, Caresse behaved as though she could always find a way to pay the printer for unlimited numbers of copies.

In the spring of 1947, before she flew off to Athens, Caresse published another issue of *Portfolio* from Washington. Harry Moore's lead article, "Why Not Read Lawrence Too," was neatly complemented by a photograph of Lawrence taken by Harry Crosby in 1929 at Le Moulin du Soleil. Eight love poems by Crosby were also printed. Other material included an excerpt of Emmanuel Carnevali's autobiography (perhaps at the urging of Kay Boyle) and an excerpt from Anaïs Nin's *Children of the Albatross,* published by Dutton that same year. Also included was a print of a recent Max Ernst painting and a rayograph by Man Ray, whom Caresse had met in Paris.

Some fresh names appeared on the contributor's list as well, like George Leite, editor of the West Coast little magazine *Circle,* and poet Charles Olson, whom Caresse had come to know through Ezra Pound and on visits to St. Elizabeths. Olson had worked in the Office of War Information and was then director of the Foreign Nationalities Division of Franklin Delano Roosevelt's 1944 reelection campaign. When he rejected a political career for the life of writer and teacher, Olson turned to Ezra Pound. During the late 1940s, he assisted Pound as secretary in exchange for Pound's mentorship. Eventually, Olson would be regarded as a leader of postwar experimental poetry. He served as the rector of Black Mountain College from 1951 until its closing in 1956.

When his poem "Moebius Strip," inspired by a sketch by his friend Corrado Cagli, appeared in *Portfolio* 5, Olson had not yet published a volume of poetry. In 1948 and 1950, the Black Sun Press published two editions of *Y & X,* his first chapbook of five poems, illustrated by Cagli. Furthermore, Caresse advanced Olson a much needed one hundred dollars on *Y & X* and helped pay some medical expenses for his wife, Connie.[24] Few copies were sold, and Caresse lost $1,200 on the book, despite heavy promotion on Olson's part and hers—she sent copies to T. S. Eliot, William Carlos Williams, and, of course, Ezra Pound. But financial matters did not affect the friendship that developed between Caresse and Olson, and he was often a guest at the dinner parties that Caresse held when she was in town.[25] Although Olson may have initially questioned Caresse's intellectual qualifications to be a publisher of contemporary poetry, his letters to Caresse in the 1950s indicate a concerted effort to stay in her good graces.[26]

Caresse intended to publish three more volumes of *Portfolio.* Volume 6 would be dedicated to Greece, volume 7 to "Negro" culture, and volume 8 to Ireland. Selden Rodman stepped down as editorial adviser, and Romare Bearden came on board. But Greece was to be the final number, and the trip Caresse made to the country in May 1947 had an unanticipated and radicalizing effect. While, in her usual manner, Caresse made contact with the higher end of the social community, she was confronted by the poverty of the general population and the rampant corruption that sabotaged postwar international efforts of aid.

Caresse had been to Greece before, in the spring of 1932 with Polleen. They were guests of Andy Embericos, the wealthy, adventurous nephew of a shipping tycoon whose fleets sailed between Greece and Italy.[27] He had assembled an assorted, international group that included Lady Mendl, the Paris playwright Marcel Achard, pianist and composer Jacques Fevrier, a German professor and his wife, and a few stars of the society page. Caresse believed that she and fourteen-year-old Polleen, American widow and daughter, added "the Daisy Miller touch." With the exception of an overnight passage from Brindisi to Venice on a ship freighted with hazelnuts, they had traveled deluxe from Paris and were indulged with appropriate travel items from the houses of Hermes and Schiaparelli. Caresse was able to revisit places where she and Harry had gone six years earlier—Palermo, Pompeii, and Amalfi—and to watch her daughter take in the sights around her with fresh and innocent eyes.

When the Embericos party had arrived in Athens, Caresse separated from the group. The Black Sun Press was never far from her thoughts, and she went in search of undiscovered authors to publish. She located Aetos, the bookstore with the greatest international stock, introduced herself to the owner, and asked him if he would lead her "to the literary rebels of Athens."[28] He was happy to oblige by introducing her to Nicholas Calamaris. The young poet was their "constant cavalier" while they were in Athens (Caresse was delighted to discover that he was "solvent as well as poetic"). He eventually visited Caresse in Paris and at Le Moulin, where she introduced him to surrealist André Breton. Much to Caresse's amusement at the time, Breton enjoyed fishing in the pond at the Mill even though it had no fish.

Now, more than fifteen years later, Caresse was back in Athens collecting material for an issue of *Portfolio.* She returned to Aetos, the bookstore she had visited in 1932, hoping her good fortune in discovering new talent would be even better than before. She also consulted a list of potential contacts given to her by Nicholas Calamaris, the Nico Calas who was teaching at Columbia University. Unlike the trips to France and Italy, her journey to Greece was not sanctioned. One American diplomat told her that she would be wasting her time, that there was no poetry or painting to be found in modern Greece.[29] Caresse would of course prove him wrong.

Caresse's recollections about her month in Athens in 1947 have a different drift than those about other research and development trips she made on behalf of *Portfolio.* She allowed her impressions as a well-heeled, sensitive outsider of postwar Greece to color many of her observations to the extent that the significant literary and artistic material that she gathered got second billing. There were several themes that she touched on: the social hierarchy that kept a small portion of the Athenian population well fed, housed, and entertained; the dire poverty that oppressed the rest of the population; the corruption of official agencies that prevented the proper distribution of international aid; and finally, the driving artistic spirit of the Greek people.

She also demonstrated the qualities of a good travel writer, with her vivid, picturesque language. She described a delicious supper of pigeon wrapped in vine leaves, spiced baby artichokes, Attica wine, and baklava that she relished in a humble taverna under the Acropolis. Walking back slowly to her hotel, she remarked on how at the sight of the "moondrenched Parthenon . . . she could hardly believe that the poverty-stricken morning sights had been true or that the starving partisans were dying in the hills in defiance of that corrupt minority of quislings who then held Greece in their grip."[30] Soon after she visited the bare studio of Diamantopoulos, an artist who had suffered starvation and incarceration during the German occupation. He had persevered, devoting years to his paintings, but had never had the opportunity to sell any of them. All he could serve Caresse was a glass of water, but she felt the graciousness with which he offered it was palpable.

Caresse had numerous opportunities to observe children and displaced adults living under the most deplorable conditions in orphanages and hospices. Nobody really bothered to hide the fact that much of the money and food supplied by UNNRA never got past government officials. She also traveled outside Athens by bus, in one of the "crippled little derelicts," broken down by years of using wood for fuel instead of gas. She visited Kessrinni, the stronghold of the Resistance during both world wars, and bemoaned the fact that citizens were still dying for freedom and democracy. She admitted that a day did not pass without someone telling her about a friend or relative who had been arrested on trumped-up charges by "jittery leaders of an empowered minority."[31] She added that these policies were supported by American money and munitions out of a misplaced fear that the Communists would gain control of Greece.[32]

But Caresse insisted that she would not go on in this vein: "I am not writing about war and its blighting wake, but rather about those men and women who in Athens were contributing spiritually and actually to the promise of a new world."[33] And indeed, she told wonderful anecdotes of meeting the people whose work she would publish in *Portfolio:* Ghika, a painter from the modern Greek School and a professor at the University of Athens; Engonopoulos, the surrealist painter and poet; and the poet Angelo Sikelianos. She helped the struggling artists as much as she could. She gave supplies, and small amounts of financial assistance to the most impoverished, like Takis Vassilakis, a young, homeless artist who managed somehow to leave Greece in the 1950s for London and Paris. Caresse would ask her son, Billy, now an executive at American Overseas Airlines living in Paris with his wife Josette, to help her protégé, "an absolute darling and an artist of great talent. . . . I asked him to call on you and I sent him in my last letter a check for $20, which I told him you would cash. It could help him get the necessary materials that he needs, but I think he also needs a friend or two."[34] In the early 1960s, he was artist-in-residence at the Center for Advanced Visual Studies at M.I.T.[35]

Caresse visited Sikelianos at his retreat on the island of Salamis. Anna Sikelianos, the artist's wife, accompanied her. It was a hot, two-hour bus ride from Athens along rocky roads bordered by roses "bursting into bloom," and then a row-boat crossing from Eluesinia. Caresse swam in the Aegean with her eyes wide open to watch "the sun shine through." But she would return again to commenting on the poverty, to the botched distribution of UNNRA supplies, and closed the chapter by describing her lunch with Queen Frederika, who herself was working furiously to correct this awful situation.

A reporter for an Athens periodical noted that Caresse was "indefatigable" in her efforts to publicize current Greek art and was completely amazed that in the short period of time Caresse had been in Greece, she had familiarized herself with the work of numerous writers and artists, that she had developed an uncanny ability to "spy value in the unknown, in poor and despised painters and authors."[36] Among her discoveries was the Arts Theater founded by Charles Koun in 1942. The company, a vibrant, subversive cultural force during the German occupation, producing in translation such plays as Tennessee Williams's *The Glass Menagerie* and Eugene O'Neill's *Mourning Becomes Electra* despite the ban on American plays.

Caresse had announced that a supplement to *Portfolio* 6 would follow, an anthology of poems by two poets who were relatively unknown by American readers—George Seferis, who would become the first Greek to be awarded the Nobel Prize, in 1963, and Odysseus Elytis, the second Greek to be so honored, in 1979. Caresse also planned to include the prose of Nikos Kazantzakis before his reputation had been established in the English-speaking world. Although *Zorba the Greek* was published in 1946, it would not be translated into English until 1952. However, the supplement never appeared. *Portfolio* 6 turned out to be the final number. It had been difficult to produce, largely because Caresse had had trouble getting fluent translations, with the exception of Derek Patmore's rendition of "The Woman of Crete" by Andrea Cambus.[37] Caresse had run out of money and could find no financial backers. In 1948, the Black Sun Press published the Greek *Portfolio* and Charles Olson's *Y & X*. The final Black Sun publication would occur three years later, in 1951, a folio of four portraits by Modigliani, accompanied by a critical introduction, a brief biographical note, and a bibliography.

One of Caresse's liveliest adventures in Athens involved a late-night visit to the studio of surrealist poet and painter Engonopoulos. She had seen his work in a shop across from the Grand Bretagne Hotel. By chance, he walked into the store while she was studying his painting, but he dashed out immediately, giving her no chance to talk to him. He had a reputation for being eccentric and unpredictable. The shopkeeper agreed to tell Engonopoulos that he should telephone Caresse so that she could see more of his work. Engonopoulos eventually invited Caresse to his studio on the same evening that she had accepted a dinner engagement. They agreed that she would come afterward.

The party did not break up until midnight, but it wasn't too late for Caresse even if the studio was on the opposite side of town. The taxi dropped her at the end of the long narrow street where she was supposed to find Engonopoulos. She walked towards the narrow column of light, found the door to what looked like a tool shed and pushed it open:

> by the light of a center bulb, hung from the rafters, a whole surrealist world of brilliant colors and dreamlike shapes appeared. Thirty or more huge canvases ranged along the walls, standing, leaning, hanging and bending forward from the four corners above my head, canvases of such vivid unreality that I actually gasped. And in the center at a low table . . . the artist, pen in hand with pages of writing strewn about him, and from behind the largest, wildest painting issued the low voice of Bing Crosby crooning "Good Night, Sweetheart."[38]

Conversing in a mix of French and English, they spent the next two hours discussing his paintings and poetry, some of which Caresse took with her to translate from the French. It was past two a.m. when Caresse walked back to her hotel through "ghost-packed streets." She was fifty-five years old and undaunted by the possibility that her safety was at risk. She had never been afraid to pursue what she wanted. So then, Caresse may have come to the end of the Black Sun Press era, but she was not destined to retreat into a quiet, private life. It was never too late in the day for Caresse. She revived Crosby Continental Editions in order to publish something of a very different nature.

13

Mondialization

By the end of May 1947, Caresse had gathered all the material that she needed for *Portfolio* 6. She flew to Paris to visit Billy and Josette, now married. The threesome spent the better part of June together and motored down the Loire Valley to view the chateaux and to sample the local wines.[1] For July, Caresse joined Polleen and young granddaughter Lorraine at the Villa Capponi in Florence. She was back in Washington, D.C., by September, after a stop in Dublin. Caresse still entertained the hope of producing an Irish *Portfolio.*

Once *Portfolio* 6 was printed, Caresse started preliminary work on the "Negro" *Portfolio.* Over the next few months, she finally acknowledged to herself that she could not afford the risk of funding another issue of the magazine. She decided to shut down. The trips to Europe for promoting an international exchange of culture had been gratifying but unprofitable. However, her firsthand observations of the devastating consequences of war moved her to become a political activist. She was not exactly geared for a grass roots campaign.

> The more I traveled and met and talked with the intellectuals of Europe the more I realized the great hope they cherished that the United States might offer to the world some spiritual ideology to which they could all adhere, working toward peace through a united intelligentsia.[2]

She regarded herself as a leader, an ambassador of good will, and a peaceful troublemaker. But if she wanted to influence an antiwar movement, she needed to reach a wider audience than the readers of *Portfolio*.

Serendipity was on her side. In January 1948, a young couple, Rufus and Janice King, came to her editorial office in Washington looking for an independent publisher who would print and distribute a political manifesto that they had written. King, recently graduated from the Yale University law school, had served in the Coast Guard during World War II.[3] Mainstream publishers had summarily rejected their manuscript, entitled "Manifesto for Individual Secession into World Community." Although Caresse knew she would never make a penny on it, she felt that she had just been presented with "the corner-stone of a new world order."[4] Caresse promised to print it when she returned to France that spring. She was off to a new start.

Caresse was in Paris by April, and the 104-page version of "Manifesto" was published on May 15, 1948, under the Crosby Continental Editions imprint. Rufus King soapboxed world citizenship at Speaker's Corner in London's Hyde Park, and in Paris, he helped Caresse with distribution. One reader was Garry Davis, a young man of twenty-one whose experiences as a bomber pilot during World War II had transformed him into a pacifist. Inspired in part by the tract written by the Kings, he publically renounced his citizenship at the passport division of the American embassy and staged a protest all on his own. He parked himself on the steps of the Trocadero, then the site of the United Nations, thus designated international territory. From there he proselytized about the need to prevent the build-up of armaments and to replace national identity with global community. Caresse printed pamphlets on his behalf, and Rufus King offered him legal counsel. For a year, Davis managed to remain visible with the help of such high-profile French citizens as Jean-Paul Sartre, Albert Camus, Roger Sarrazac, and André Gide. Caresse printed world citizen "passports."

When Caresse returned to Washington in June, she had acquired a new kind of notoriety, this time for signing on as a world citizen. In the daily paper, she published an open invitation to anyone who wanted to discuss world citizenship. The forum would be held at her editorial offices in her house at 2008 Q Street, N.W.

> About fifty people showed up, a cross section of human society, the religious man, the artist, the soldier, the diplomat, the housewife, the business man, the student; it pointed the way to a new and better understanding among men and women.[5]

As down-to-earth as Caresse was about the venture's capacity for producing financial headaches, she was flying high over what she considered to be the spiritual benefits for all who participated.

Caresse got a small clue of the difficulties she might encounter when the June 27, 1948, issue of the Sunday *News* featured a photograph of her with Garry Davis next to a shot of two Americans who had given up their passports to become citizens of the Soviet Union. In a letter to the editor that she wrote on July 18, 1948, Caresse expressed anger at such an overt effort to portray her as a communist sympathizer. She then went on with her mission. Within a year, she had shed Davis and created her own agenda for achieving a "World Commonwealth of World Citizens under world law with freedom for all."[6] Rufus King became a distinguished Washington attorney devoted to protecting individual rights within the criminal justice system. He provided legal counsel to Caresse while she built her movement, and she designated him as her literary executor. She worked within the United States, but she also established headquarters abroad in a rundown, magnificent castle in the Italian foothills of the Abruzzi, forty miles north of Rome and ten miles south of Rieti, the very geographical center of Italy.

Caresse first visited the castle at Roccasinibalda in the summer of 1949 at the urging of her friend Pietro Lazzari, whose work she had showcased in *Portfolio* and at the Crosby Gallery of Modern Art.[7] She had spent that summer in Europe, mostly touring Italy, ostensibly to write a feature story on national elections for her friend Blair Clark, who at this time was editor of the *New Hampshire Herald.*[8] Caresse usually employed chauffeurs to escort her on her travels, especially to Italy, where in 1946 she had run over an elderly man (she took him to a nearby clinic where he recovered) and on another occasion had sideswiped a truck loaded with oranges on its way to the export docks at Genoa.[9] Sometimes her drivers were younger men who were artistically inclined and could use the cash. For this trip, Caresse found that Kenneth Rexroth was available for the job, the past contretemps now completely forgotten since their meeting with Ezra Pound at St. Elizabeths. Thanks to a Guggenheim fellowship, Rexroth was spending the summer in Europe touring Provence and the Riviera with English friends. He arranged to meet Caresse in Rome. Together, they drove northeast seventy kilometers along the Via Salaria (which ends at the Adriatic), then another six kilometers east on the Carsole road to Roccasinibalda.

Caresse was as thrilled with il Castello di Roccasinibalda as Lazzari had expected her to be. Built between 1530 and 1560 according to a design by Baldassare Peruzzi, the castle stands on solid rock eighteen hundred feet above the winding Turano River. The walls are stone and brick with massive beams supporting the tile roofs. "Breathtakingly beautiful and peacefully remote," the castle had been closed for years and was obviously in great disrepair, "but the weaponless grandeur of its battlements and the brooding promise of its rooms and corridors seemed a haven and a promise for future citizens of the world."[10] Caresse put down one million lire, about $1,800, on the place and took many photographs.

Rexroth and Caresse headed for Florence, explored the great museums of the city together, and moved on to Ravenna and Venice.[11] They drove through Vicenza, Verona, Bergamo, and Milan. They passed beautiful Lake Maggiore and stopped in a hotel in Domodossola, the last town below the Simplon Pass. Their ultimate destination was Paris, from where they would both return to the United States, Rexroth to San Francisco and Caresse to Washington, D.C. During the trip, Caresse became Rexroth's confidante and encouraged him to spend the second year of his Guggenheim with his new love, Marthe Larsen. She suggested that the couple might want to spend some time at Roccasinibalda.

Although Rexroth reassured Marthe that she should not be threatened by his traveling companion—he wrote to her that Caresse, who was fifty-seven, was a very old lady—he and Caresse had a brief affair. He would address her as "Dearest Girl," "Dear Honeybear," "Dear Cutie," and "My little honey lamb" in the few letters he wrote to her over the next six years.[12] But he also made it clear to Caresse that he was an alien in her world of "countesses and couturiers" and that he—a longtime anarchist/socialist/pacifist—thought the World Citizens movement "harmless folly."[13] He was most appreciative when Caresse sent him a copy of Olson's *X & Y* so that he could review it for radio station KPFA. And he would also try to help her tape programs for KPFA about the Black Sun Press, Harry Crosby's poetry, and even her new organization.

Back in Washington, Caresse encountered the same kind of barriers that she had faced when she moved there in 1941. Officials were not inclined to take her seriously. And as before, their resistance did not deter her from starting a new campaign. Except that this time, Caresse decided that women would be her best allies. She announced the formation of a new worldwide organization, "Women of the World Against War." She would refine its agenda over the next year as reflected in this excerpted list of goals that appears on one of the flyers that Caresse distributed in Washington.

1. To form rallying centers around the world, in all countries, for enrollment, so that all women in all countries will be members of the Women of the World Movement.

2. To vote for women representatives in all important assemblies.
3. To denounce war as mass murder.
4. To deflate the egoism that kills as uncivilized and bestial.
5. To protest by voice and vote against armaments. If the women of the world unite against war, there could be no war; therefore, armament for defense would be unnecessary.
6. To decree that atomic energy be used only for progress and peace.
7. To abolish nationalism in favor of World Citizenship.
8. To educate our children in the knowledge and belief that they are Citizens of the World.
9. To admire and support goodness wherever we find it, and to judge power in relation to it.
10. To guard and increase our individualism and feminine qualities and to use them as instruments of power for good.
11. To organize volunteers in all countries to enlist members and to overcome barriers.[14]

How remarkable is it that Caresse had reached such a perspective in 1949? The political climate in Washington offered little support. The Cold War between the United States and the Soviet Union was in full swing, the North Atlantic Treaty Organization had just been formed, and Senator Joseph McCarthy was only a few months away from charging that more that two hundred Communists had infiltrated the State Department.

Caresse's conservative family had never encouraged her to adopt such pacifist/feminist views (though later on, her granddaughter Lorraine did come to her assistance). They viewed her latest activities as a continuum, a misguided mix of idealism and defiance. But they had taught her about the power of self-confidence. Caresse was consistently fearless about carrying out her plans. She boldly presented what ostensibly amounted to a global peace proposal to celebrities and people in high places—from Harold Stassen, Dwight D. Eisenhower, and Adlai Stevenson to filmmaker Maya Deren, journalist Edward R. Murrow, and Dorothy Norman, former editor of the avant-garde journal *Twice a Year,* who had been part of the bohemian crowd long ago at Romany Marie's.

Among those she petitioned in late 1949 was Joseph Clark Grew, one-time U.S. Ambassador to Turkey, distinguished career officer in the Foreign Service, and Harry Crosby's first cousin. His response to her was familiar—that the United States had no choice but to be prepared militarily, that if the country let down its guard, it would invite attack from the Soviet Union. However, Grew also expressed admiration for Caresse's efforts, which he placed under the category of "moral and spiritual preparedness."[15] Caresse might have enjoyed such a response from Grew, since it was a good indication that she had rattled his outlook on international relations. Caresse rarely sought affirmation of her actions, but she secretly seemed to want it, sometimes from the most unlikely people.

While in Washington, she honed her skills as a political activist. In February 1950, she registered with the U.S. Congress as a lobbyist for peace in the name of Women Against War.[16] She circulated letters to both houses of Congress in order to ascertain whether she could gather interest for a "Peace Act of 1950" and "Peace Bonds" to support the bill. Just as there was a Department of Defense—which in 1949 had incorporated the Department of War—there should be, she believed, a new executive department to be called the Department of Peace.[17] Such a department would initiate cultural, educational, and health programs within the United States and exchange programs around the world that would promote peaceful relations and better understanding between all peoples. The budget for the Peace Department would be "not less than 3% of the total sum and made available for the National Military Establishment" each year. In addition to a Secretary of Peace, there would be an Undersecretary and an Assistant Secretary, one of whom would be a woman. There was no mention of any economic policy. Money for the budget would be generated in part by Peace Bonds, just as War Bonds had been issued for sale during World War II and Victory Bonds during World War I.

The proposal was hardly embraced. In an October 28, 1949, letter, E. H. Foley Jr., Undersecretary of the Treasury, suggested that she might use Savings Bonds as a model for the Peace Bond. Caresse suspected that she was being stonewalled. She wanted to know if it was possible to prevent the income accrued from the sale of government bonds from being allocated to armament and military expansion. She felt certain that Savings Bonds would be under the same restrictions as any other bond, with the military making a big claim on the revenue. "It is not a soubriquet I am looking for, but a reality," she admonished Mr. Foley.[18] Surely Caresse sensed the belligerent climate that was firmly settling across the country, but she refused to concede to its strength.

In order to put her proposal into the formal language required for presentation before Congress, Caresse enlisted the aid of Katharine Price Collier St. George, the representative from New York's 27th district. She wanted to create a solvent account in the Treasury for peaceful uses exclusively. On March 7, 1950, St. George presented the Peace Bond Bill under the serial number HR 7596 at the 2nd Session of the 81st Congress. It was shelved by the Ways and Means Committee, although it did receive support from two prominent women, Frances P. Bolton from Ohio, and Edith Nourse Rogers from Massachusetts.[19] St. George promised that she would present the Peace Bond Bill again to the 82nd Congress but upon reconsideration never did.

Caresse would devote the better part of the last two decades of her life to Women Against War and Citizens of the World. She expended the major part of her capital and risked her safety and well-being. Although she was often surrounded by friends and admirers, she would never again have a longtime companion. On the surface, she had no regrets. She returned to Roccasinibalda in the summer of 1950, making the commitment to her new cause that much firmer. The castle would be the first site where she would raise the Citizens of the World Flag, the town the first to be declared a Citta del Mondo.

Caresse's second arrival was much more dramatic than the first. She had acquired two "chauffeurs," Bill Barker, an aspiring writer and actor, and his friend Deighton Higgins. Caresse had met Barker at Constance Crowinshield's villa near Villefranche, on the French Riviera. It turned out that Barker was also friend of her son Billy—they had been classmates at Rosay, the exclusive boy's prep school in Switzerland. Originally assigned to intelligence duty during World War II, he witnessed the liberation of the Dachau concentration camp. Undone by the experience, Barker had been living a peripatetic life since his recuperation.[20] He became one of Caresse's most loyal friends.

On April 20, Caresse's fifty-eighth birthday, they started off from Paris, where Caresse had shipped her "doe skin pink" Kaiser sedan from the States. Caresse was brimming with excitement at the thought that her new mission might actually work. Her arrival, apparently, had been anticipated by the entire village.

> I was greeted like a matriarchal liberator; the mayor, the lawyer, the school teacher, the pharmacist and the village bard were first in line and behind them the grocer, the shoemaker, the miller's daughter and the baker's wife. . . . Everyone was attentive, everyone was ruddy and scrupulously clean, threadbare shirts were snowy white. . . . The walk from the car to the castle was a triumphal procession. I was the Americana who had, with magic dollars, bought the mummied pile that hung above their lives like a somber tapestry of glorious past and gone, but now—wonder of wonders—their stage was set again.[21]

With the help of the local innkeeper and his family, Caresse moved into the castle on the day of her arrival. The rooms that she slept and dined in had been abandoned thirty years before, and the abandoned furniture crumbled into pieces when moved. By the next day, Caresse had found "a gay little maid" to help her unpack, "two scurrying urchins" to take care of errands, and "an old crone for a cook." If the people of Roccasinibalda were offended by Caresse's airs of superiority, they kept it to themselves, perhaps because she seemed to be filled with a surplus of good will and American dollars.

Caresse started shaking up the village over the next months by gathering recruits for her One World movement. She was appalled by the pervasive poverty around her, that more than half of the five hundred people who lived there were dependent on a monthly check of approximately $4.00 from the government. But she also recognized that she could not find a more suitable audience than the women of Roccasinibalda to rally to her cause. By her account, all she needed to do was tack a petition to the post office wall, persuade the priest to support the plan publically, and invite two hundred women to the castle for a glass of wine. The town council unanimously voted to designate Roccasinibalda as the first Italian Citta del Mondo. Pledged to "one Citizenry of the World for the good and the peace of all," the town recognized Woman Against War as the agent of its mondialization, of its joining a global community with no borders.[22]

Caresse would devote enormous time and energy to converting the castle into a small, autonomous work place, transforming about seventy-five of the 352 rooms into habitable space. Right off she realized that she would have to give up her habitual eight hours of sleep a night. Five hours between sundown and sunup would be her allotment if she were going to oversee the elaborate physical scheme for renovations.

To begin, she wanted to gather a team of young people who would transform the "rubbled homes" of the poorest citizens in the vicinity of Roccasinibalda into "liveable dwellings."[23] She was quite specific about what she wanted in a form letter that circulated from her Women Against War headquarters in Washington: an engineer, an architect, handymen, whitewashers, and "one or two women to sew curtains"; paint, spray guns, calcimine and whitewash, a buzz-saw, a cement mixer, and a sewing machine. She required twenty people in all, for whom she would provide shelter, pasta, and wine. They would have to bring their own sleeping bags. Her goal was to rehabilitate twenty-eight homes in four weeks, starting July 4, 1950.

As for the castle itself, she wanted to carve out large studios for writers and artists. Guests there for the experience of living in such a community would be charged modest fees. Even daughter Polly in London caught Caresse's enthusiasm and offered to contribute $200 to the project.[24] There would be a library, gardens, a swimming hole, horses for riding, an avant-garde theater, and a screening room for an international festival of contemporary films. She would also establish such cottage industries as carpet weaving and lace making. She would install a kiln for ceramics and a printing press. The sections of the castle that had been a prison would be converted to a clinic and a nursery for the children whose mothers worked on the looms. The tavern keeper from Rieti would take over the wine cellars so that local people and visitors alike would have plenty of good wine to wash down the trout they caught in the stream that ran through the property. Caresse could barely wait to get started.

However, in October 1951, when she made a formal offer to buy Roccasinibalda outright, the Catholic Church outbid her.[25] All plans for the castle were put on hold. Thwarted but not defeated, Caresse diverted her attention to recruiting members to her cause. Over the following eight years, she traveled within Italy, and to India, Greece, Egypt, Yugoslavia, Germany, Wales, France, and England campaigning for Women Against War and Citizens of the World. She tapped all sources whether or not they were prepared to listen to her. She tried to enlist the support of poet and translator William Jay Smith when she visited him and his wife in Florence one summer in the early 1950s. Though taken by Caresse's "bubbly, effervescent" personality, Smith was not receptive to her campaign.[26]

Smith had first met Caresse in Paris, and they had since corresponded about her publishing his translations of Jules LaForgue's *Pierrot.* It never happened. Together in Florence, the Smiths and Caresse drove to Siena for the Corso del Palio, a brilliant parade and horse race around the main square with the riders dressed in medieval costumes of their respective city districts. During their three days together, Caresse talked nonstop either about her efforts to promote a global community or Harry Crosby. Smith could not engage in Caresse's politics, and in the February 6, 1963, issue of the *New Republic,* he published a gently derisive poem about Harry's suicide.

Caresse's encounters with other audiences were more successful. She was interviewed on radio in Rome and Delhi, visited schools and ministries of culture in Bangalore City and Jaipur, and met with government officials on both sides of the Berlin Wall. At a 1955 meeting of the "Commonwealth of World Citizens"—the umbrella organization of the movement—Caresse was appointed Counselor to the Unites States. In that capacity, she opened a World Citizens Information Center in Washington, D.C., the same year. The following summer in Cardiff, Wales, she was elected first President of the Council.[27] She would get into serious trouble once. When she tried to establish a capital for Citizens of the World in Delphi, the Greek government regarded her actions as a violation of its sovereignty. Subsequently, she shifted her intended site to Cyprus.

The number of "citizens of the world" who actually joined the movement remains a mystery. Prospective citizens could register with the International Registry at 20 rue Corneille Montrouge, Paris, or by directly contacting Caresse or presumably other administrators of the organization.[28] In any number of forums, Caresse wanted to persuade people that she was not promoting any existing ideology. She did, however, favor some established systems of thought more than others: communism was a "fanatic belief," capitalism "a just system," and socialism a "democratic ideal."[29] In a letter from Paris on December 3, 1951, she stated her case to Secretary of State Dean Acheson. She wanted her "one woman" campaign to be regarded as an apolitical crusade. On the other hand, she emphasized that what the world needed was not just "a dollar economy" but a "belief that could transcend the appeal of communism," a "world ideal that transcends all isms." The ingenuous rhetoric did not go far. When she returned to Washington that December, her request for an appointment with one of Acheson's assistants was denied.

Caresse needed a capitol for this world ideal, a symbolic physical presence. If it was not going to be Roccasinibalda—she would continue to make bids on it—why not Delphi? It was the ancient site of the Amphyctionic League, an association of neighboring states that was primarily religious but exercised a political influence through its membership oath that forbade the destruction of member cities, or the cutting off of water supplies, even during warfare. Under no circumstances were women and children to be harmed. In honor of "the spirit of unity and humanism that inspired the ancient Greeks to build their thesauros—a spiritual bank for engraved documents of governance and philosophy—2500 years ago in Delphi,"[30] Caresse would build a symbolic thesauros on the slopes of Mount Parnassus overlooking the port of Itea on the Gulf of Corinth. It would house periodical exhibitions of works by contemporary artists from all over the world. Demetrios Pikionis, professor at the Polytechnic School of Athens and a specialist in ancient buildings of Greece, drew up a tentative architectural program for the center.[31] Pikionis also envisioned simple, modest administrative buildings, study halls, libraries, and guest houses, "autonomous units to serve for isolation and contemplation." Above all, the structures were to harmonize with the surrounding austere beauty of Delphi's landscape and reflect the three basic tenets of Delphic ideology: "the demands of the prophetic, the retrospective, and love."

Caresse purchased two acres of this land from the family of goat herders who had owned it since 900. She announced the opening of a World Gallery of Art for Saturday, May 23, at five p.m., where one hundred contemporary drawings by such artists as Miró, Calder, Picasso, and Tanguy would be exhibited. The following day, she scheduled a World Citizen Ceremony dedicating her land to friendship, enlightenment, and the service of humanity.[32] She had assumed that she had the right to schedule such an event according to Law 6323, November 3, 1934, of the Legal Bulletin Archives of Greece. All that was required, she thought, was formal official status, and so she merged with the legally established Commonwealth of World Citizens founded by Dr. Hugh Schonfield, a British historian and scholar of what the West called the Near East.[33] The Minister to the Prime Minister of Greece, the Mayor of Delphi, and the Archbishop of Amfissa agreed to attend. Caresse would present the dedication and unfold the World Flag, and Hugh Schonfield would make the acceptance speech.[34] However, the Greek militia arrived before the ceremony began and arrested Caresse.

Caresse had not counted on the possibility that the Greek government would suddenly feel threatened by the formal establishment of a center for World Citizenship, that the World Citizen Center would compromise their dominion. The Superintendent of the Gendarmerie ordered the men of the home guard to take out their guns and drop the flowers they were bringing to the ceremony. Guests were barred from climbing the hill from the town of Delphi to the site, reporters were physically restrained from continuing their coverage. Caresse was first placed under house arrest and then asked to leave the country.

From Athens, Caresse consulted the embassy of the United States to ascertain her rights as an American citizen under Greek law and to determine whether she had any legal recourse over her expulsion. On May 28, she filed an application with the Ministry of the Interior that would prevent the Gendarmerie of Delphi from interfering with "the operation of her artistic exhibition" or of the gathering of friends to discuss "spiritual and artistic subjects . . . and the pure ideologies of the Citizens of the World."[35] Back in Washington, D.C.—after a motor trip through Yugoslavia with Bill Barker and photographer Michael Law, both witnesses to the Delphi fiasco—she pursued her suit against the Greek Minister of the Interior. Represented by Angelo G. Procopiou, an attorney in Athens, she filed a petition on July 12, 1953, that she be permitted to continue her mission in Delphi. She returned to Greece to attend the public hearing on December 3, 1953, at which time the court ruled against her on the grounds that the Citizens of the World was a "movement conceived and initiated by aliens yet tending toward the creation of a super-national organization which may exercise international political influence." Caresse went home. She had suffered a setback, but she kept her mission alive from her offices in Washington, D.C. She was not yet finished with mondialization.

14

Fame

The 1950s for Caresse then were hardly a silent decade. Indeed, her rallying efforts on behalf of Women Against War and Citizens of the World did not consume all of her energy. Caresse had started writing a six-part memoir that began with her "crystal chandelier" childhood; following were sections devoted to her marriage to Richard Rogers Peabody and life as a Back Bay matron and mother of two; her seven years with Harry Crosby in Paris and the founding of the Black Sun Press; her merry widow years in Paris and New York as an independent publisher; her marriage to Bert Young and "farming by ear" in Virginia; and finally her years in Washington, D.C., and travels abroad as publisher of *Portfolio* and an art gallery owner. She intended to include reminiscences about her encounters with one hundred well-known writers, artists, musicians, and scions of society.

Malcolm Cowley, then editor at Viking Press, worked with Caresse during the first stages of her manuscript. She and Cowley had maintained a distant but cordial relationship since their first meeting at Hart Crane's Brooklyn apartment in December 1929, three days before Harry Crosby's death. However, when Cowley first published *Exile's Return* in 1934, Caresse heard, before she had had a chance to see the book herself, that Cowley had relied heavily on Harry's diaries in order to write his chapter on how neatly Harry exemplified the American expatriate writers of the 1920, an observation already noted to which Caresse objected. She had been more than willing to lend Cowley three volumes of the diaries but never expected him to quote extensively from them and possibly divulge aspects of her marriage that she preferred to keep private. Cowley assured her that he had tried not to pick out the personal passages, "just the ones that helped to interpret Harry's character. . . . Harry was an extraordinary person and I don't think the world ought to forget him."[1] Caresse had been mollified, especially after she learned that the French postal service had lost her advanced copy of *Exile's Return,* that in fact Cowley had wanted her to have the book before anyone else could tell her what was in it.

Actually Caresse had already begun work on *The Passionate Years*—an alternative title had been "I'll Never Forget"—as early as December 1946 at Craig Air Force Base, Alabama, where she was staying as the guest of Harry and Beatrice Moore. Still in the air force, Moore took Caresse to military parties, where she was "as successful as ever in conveying her magnetic personality."[2] During the day, however, Moore "virtually closed her in her room, telling her that she must write her autobiography." Caresse wrote some early segments there in Alabama, and Moore suggested "The Passionate Years" as a title.

Malcolm Cowley encouraged Caresse to step back from the story, if she could, and speculate about why she and Harry had behaved as they did. In a letter of November 19, 1949, Caresse admitted that she did not know how to interpret her relationship with Harry or with anyone else for that matter. She would try introspection, but she had never been inclined "to judge motives, only actions. I am 100% extrovert (or was); if I had been otherwise, I doubt I could have weathered the 20's."[3] And yet she took Cowley's advice to heart.

A little over two weeks later, she wrote to Cowley: "I seem to be turning myself inside out, a thing I had no intention of doing in public."[4] She had hoped Cowley—"you are the doctor"—would advise her through to the end, but he was about to go take a leave from Viking to teach a course at the University of Washington in Seattle. He did offer strong words of encouragement: "Do you know what old Dr. Cowley prescribes? Just more of the same medicine you've been taking this last month. I am very pleased with your revisions."[5] He gave her some good pointers on writing biography (for example, to take as much care presenting the people in her life as she would developing the characters in a piece of fiction) and pushed her to explain her dreams and ideals, and to elaborate on the details of the times, especially the 1920s. Caresse turned over the completed manuscript to Pascal Covici and George W. Joel, both editors at Dial/Viking.

First published in 1953, *The Passionate Years* contains thirty-nine short anecdotal chapters. It follows the general pattern that Caresse originally proposed in her six-section outline.[6] Critics generally admired its vivacious style and intimate rendering of 1920s Paris. One of the strongest reviews appeared in the *New York Times,* which praised Caresse as writer and publisher: for "straight reporting" on Charles Lindbergh's first flight across the Atlantic and for her "fostering of unknown or otherwise unpublishable writers (Crane, Joyce, D. H. Lawrence)." The *New York Herald Tribune* called the book "entertaining" and "an essential document of its era."[7]

Furthermore, in a prescient observation, the *New York Herald Tribune* noted that this wife's account of a literary era could be considered on equal footing with her husband's: "[Harry Crosby's] posthumously published journals are a source book, often quoted, for his times and customs. His widow's memoirs are likely to be just as necessary to the literary historian." On July 15, 1953, Delia Bye, another editor at Dial Press, told Caresse that the reviews in these two leading New York newspapers were a good publicity break for the book, and that sales were slow but steady. Caresse was pleased. Her major objection to Dial's handling of her manuscript had been resolved. Photographs of Bert Young and Hampton Manor had been sandwiched into the middle of chapter 27, the short chapter that covers Harry's death. Finally, though, the pictures were pushed ahead sixty-five pages, placed right before chapter 37, which is devoted to Caresse's three years with Bert.

Caresse wrote the preface while she was arranging her gallery opening in Delphi, testament to her ability to focus on more than one task at a time. It is a peculiar introduction insofar as Caresse allows that while she depended solely on memory—she points out that she kept neither diary nor journal and never subscribed to a clipping service—she could "vouch that these remembered years are played straight." She wraps the people who appear in the autobiography and the prospective readers into an allusion from *As You Like It:* "I hope, as every wishful mummer must, that they [the remembered years] will be played to a full house. May I thank the cast, one and all, for making this wish possible." The fashionable and affected young Jaques is not speaking here; rather a strong, spirited, and talented woman in love with romance, literature, art. She was also ready to fight for a good cause. Rebellious, sometimes reckless, she was rarely if ever cynical.

The Passionate Years contains inaccuracies and inconsistencies, some of which have already been mentioned in passing. Caresse was too old to be the debutante she claims to have been in 1914. Rousseau did not live in the Mill, as she claims, but in another building on the estate. Her relationship with Frieda Lawrence ended in rancor not mutual admiration. Harry's wedding ring was found crushed on the floor in the studio at the Hotel des

Artistes, not on his finger where he promised Caresse it would always be. Some of these errors seem more innocent than others.

Caresse was sensitive to the demands of verification. At the back of *The Passionate Years,* there is a facsimile of the original application she filed on February 12, 1914, for a strapless brassiere patent. There is a reprint of a letter by Ernest Hemingway that confirms a chaotic episode over lost passports that Caresse relates in the book, and another letter from D. H. Lawrence that alludes to a pleasant visit with the Crosbys also referred to in the book. Also included—a standard marketing practice—is a series of blurbs by such luminaries as André Maurois, T. S. Eliot, Jean Cocteau, and Aldous Huxley, collected under the heading "What Famous Authors Say About Crosby Editions." Behind the outward and charming bravado lurked a human-sized portion of insecurity and an extra portion of knowing how to play with form and convention.

The Passionate Years had its share of detractors, whose reactions could be summed up with a statement made by Maurice Richardson in the December 1955 issue of the *New Statesman:* "Mrs. Crosby rattles on about [celebrated writers] in an utterly harmless, only moderately informative but pleasant book." Yet the book would serve as a resource for biographies of James Joyce, Anaïs Nin, Henry Miller, Harry Crosby, Salvador Dalí, Kay Boyle, Ernest Hemingway, and others. Caresse succeeded in making the first fifty years of her life story difficult to forget.

The 1950s for Caresse were also charged with terrible tragedy. Her son, Billy, died on January 25, 1955, in his third-floor walk-up apartment on rue du Bac. Billy and Josette had settled into a pleasant routine in Paris. Billy was in charge of the Paris office of American Overseas Airlines and had recently hired two ticket agents and an accountant to take routine tasks off his shoulders and his secretary's. For a social life, he and Josette entertained at home or accepted dinner invitations from friends, which they far preferred to going out on the town. Josette was a master card player and often organized an evening's entertainment around a bridge game. They did go to the theater often but were usually disappointed by what they saw, and the theaters themselves were uncomfortably cold.

Billy and Josette had trouble heating their own apartment. In a November 21, 1954, letter, Billy wrote to Caresse that he and Josette were "still very pleased with our apartment in spite of the fact we have no heating except an open fireplace and a small stove, but the ceilings are very low and so far we have made out all right." On the cold night of January 25, 1955, Billy retired early while Josette and some friends continued to play cards. She fell into bed much later. No one had noticed the smell of a gas leak from the oven that they had turned on to keep warm. The police found Josette comatose, but she was revived at the hospital. Billy died of asphyxiation, two weeks away from his thirty-ninth birthday.[8]

Devastated, Caresse left for Paris to attend the funeral and to help Josette survive the first weeks. Josette attended Billy's funeral on the arm of Polleen's ex-husband, Albert de Mun, who had been part of the crowd at Le Moulin du Soleil in the late 1920s and had remained a friend of the family. Billy left no will, no instructions for a funeral service. Caresse thought that Polleen might know where Billy would have wanted to be buried. On February 3, 1955, Polleen wrote her mother: "I don't know *what* Bill's wishes were?? but I can't help feeling that he would *much* rather rest near 'Grandma' [in a Brooklyn cemetery] than at Arlington Cemetery."

Because Billy died intestate, French law stipulated that his estate be equally divided between his mother and his wife. Caresse insisted that she wanted no war stocks or bonds in her portion of Billy's investments; no "ammunition plants, builders of fighter planes or bombs or guns such as Colt Manufacturers or U.S. Steel," she told her brother Len in a March 25, 1955, letter. "There are plenty of food stocks and bonds that support a progressive, peaceful economy," she added. Polleen took great exception to the possibility that Peabody money would be deflected from the family and threatened to sue Josette for murdering Billy if she did not turn over her portion to Polleen.[9] A settlement was reached. Josette supplemented her income by playing in bridge tournaments and eventually remarried. She and Caresse never lost contact. Indeed, Caresse would come to Josette's assistance when the need arose, as Henrietta and Stephen Crosby had come to her aid after Harry's death.[10]

Caresse herself did not write immediately about her son's death. There are few letters of condolence among the files of correspondence she saved. Bill Barker responded immediately with a telegram: "I know this cannot help much but please remember you have another son love always."[11] Her dear friend Kay Boyle did not learn of Bill's death until the spring. "Poor darling," she wrote Caresse on June 7, 1955, "you, for so much courage has been asked of you, and you have somehow summoned." She had not heard from Caresse since December, when Caresse mentioned that she would be visiting New York for New Year's festivities. It was the last Kay Boyle had heard from Caresse for months. Lifelong friend and correspondent Constance had written to Caresse over the previous summer about the surgery Caresse underwent in July to remove her thyroid. Caresse recuperated her strength and her voice—the loss of which Constance had speculated was the consequence of "physical shock and fatigue"—at her brother Walter's home in Cape Elizabeth, Maine.[12] Four years would pass before correspondence resumed between them.

There are similar gaps in her correspondence with Anaïs Nin and Dorothea Tanning, to whom Caresse wrote on December 7, 1954, about her "bad" operation and how she was raising money by selling books, drawings, water colors, "and the Picasso that Max and I bought together some time ago." No doubt Caresse's friends were filled with compassion and respected her need for privacy. Caresse kept herself busy, perhaps too busy to maintain a steady correspondence that would keep her grief raw and exposed.

A combination of good fortune and well-deserved recognition did help her along. Nearly two years before Billy's death, Millicent Bell, a young Hawthorne and Melville scholar at Brown University, had contacted Caresse after reading *The Passionate Years*. She was engaged in writing a book about Edith Wharton and so far had been dissatisfied with the casual manner that other scholars had treated the relationship between Walter Berry (Harry Crosby's uncle) and Wharton. Bell was struck by Caresse's vivid account of Berry: "Your sketch, with its wonderful comic-grotesque vignette of Berry's funeral," or the episode of "the big grab" for Berry's library, was "a rare gust of fresh air into a room closed too long and too unnecessarily."[13] Bell wanted to know if Caresse would be willing to correspond with her about Berry and Wharton, and if she had any letters or documents that she could show her.

Caresse read Bell's letter in London, where she was visiting Polleen, divorced from her first husband and now married to the Honorable John North. Delighted with Bell's inquiry, Caresse assured Bell that as soon as she returned to the United States, they could meet in New York or Washington, where all her papers were stored. A meeting in April 1954 turned out to be fruitful for both Caresse and Bell. Bell found the interview edifying. In an April 14, 1954, letter, she wrote: "I return to the Wharton book with a far clearer view of my subject and her friend Walter Berry as a result of our conversations," adding that she took great pleasure in meeting Caresse. She also set in motion the first exhibit in the United States of Black Sun Press books.

Caresse was exhilarated by the prospect of a Black Sun Press exhibit at Brown and cooperated fully with Bell and David A. Jonah, the head of John Hay Library, in arranging the agenda. The library had acquired many Black Sun Press books, and Caresse promised to complete the list. She also provided copies and some originals of letters by Ezra Pound, T. S. Eliot, James Joyce, Hart Crane, and D. H. Lawrence. The exhibit ran four weeks, from

November 18, 1954. Bell picked up Caresse at the train station on the 17th and drove her to the Brown campus, where she would spend the night at the guest house. She was looking forward to the cocktail party in Millicent Bell's apartment that would follow her lecture that evening, even though she warned Bell that there was "only one hitch in that I have lost my voice since my illness and may have difficulty in being heard."[14] She had also arrived early enough to help the library staff with any questions that might arise while they arranged the exhibit.

If Caresse had expected a larger crowd, she never let on that she was disappointed. The evening was frigid and blustering, and the publicity for the event had been mismanaged.[15] About forty people sat in metal folding chairs opposite the glass exhibition cases of the Special Collections Room, the majority of them faculty, graduate students, and members of the Brown English Club. As usual, Caresse made a striking and gracious entry. One audience member, Jane Baltzell, then a graduate student, described her manner as "valiant and weather-wise." She likened Caresse's appearance to "the exquisite Greek head on a newly minted dime, if you can imagine that Grecian goddess with a pert nose, a giddy smile and Mediterranean blue eyes."

Despite a wheezy voice, Caresse delivered a lively, animated lecture, a mix of straight literary history and personal reminiscence. Of course, writing *The Passionate Years* was excellent preparation for such an event. And as Bell had reminded Caresse in an October 21, 1954, letter, "You can't imagine how it thrills scholars to listen to one who has seen Joyce plain."

Indeed, Caresse captivated the audience with her anecdotes about James Joyce, D. H. Lawrence, Hart Crane, and the heady life of Paris in the 1920s. Afterwards, she carried on with the same wit and charm. As Jane Baltzell described Caresse, she continued her lively chatter "curled up on the Bell's living room sofa," answering every question "with the hoped for rare and intimate glimpse of a great man behaving like an ordinary person and this seemed to mellow and reassure everybody." One of the last guests to leave around midnight wondered aloud about how dull his professors would seem the next day in class.

Millicent Bell also performed the great service of writing "The Black Sun Press: 1927 to the Present," a six-thousand-word essay to be printed as the introduction to the January 1955 edition of *Books at Brown.* Enormously pleased with the piece, Caresse was able to catch a few minor errors before it went to press. Bell recounted some anecdotes that appear in *The Passionate Years*—how at the request of Black Sun Press printer Roger Lescaret, Joyce added lines to *Tales Told of Shem and Shawn* to fill out the last page of the text; and how the Crosbys discovered D. H. Lawrence by picking up a copy of *The Plumed Serpent* in a Cairo bookstore. More importantly, Bell discussed what she called the Crosbys' "responsibility to the text," the care and delight Harry and Caresse took in conceiving the book as a whole, and of creating "successful fusion of the writer's, the illustrator's, and the designer's point of view." She also pointed out how the Crosbys invited the authors to participate in the production of the book and mentions that the frontispiece for Lawrence's *Sun* is his own watercolor of an Aztec sun worshiper, and that Archibald MacLeish chose his own portrait by Paul Emile Becat for *Einstein*. One unfortunate omission exists: when the Crosbys ran the press together, Caresse, as managing editor, labored longer hours than Harry. In addition to creating the Black Sun list of titles with Harry, she was the one who did the leg work, oversaw the design, and negotiated terms of contract with authors and artists.

The November 19, 1954, issue of the Providence *Evening Bulletin* ran a full-page story about the exhibit, entitled "A Black Sun Shines at Brown." It is dominated by a large photograph of an "alert, zestful" Caresse, holding forth, open book in hand, "still seek[ing] for new things under the sun." Maurice Dolbier, who wrote the piece as literary editor for the newspaper, was in awe of the treasures before him, including the edition of *Alice in Wonderland* with illustrations by Marie Laurencin, a book that had originally sold for five dollars. He took pleasure comparing the "small and precise handwriting" of D. H. Lawrence, to the "lines that marched in smart formation down a right incline" of Ernest Hemingway, to the "lines that went this and that way, upside down and downside up . . . in the wide tortured scrawl of Hart Crane." The exhibit contained more than one hundred samples of poetry, fiction, art, letters, and often rare documents

Caresse had known—even if she kept it to herself—the disappointment of rejection, of what it meant to propose a project, literary or political, only to have it ignored or, worse, ridiculed. Here she was in Providence, Rhode Island, receiving accolades for achievements, acknowledgment for her own hard work. Even now though, she seemed content to share the attention with Harry, to bring him out of the scandal of his death. In early January 1955, at the invitation of Professor Hannah D. French, she brought the exhibit to Wellesley College. She participated in other Black Sun exhibits, at the University of Buffalo on March 22, and at Black Mountain College on April 3, 1955, where Charles Olson was serving as rector. Billy died between the Wellesley and University of Buffalo exhibits. The ghastly contrast between events could have paralyzed an ordinary individual.

Caresse did turn down an invitation from the University of Texas, although her sorrow over Billy's death was not the reason. She learned that Dean Harry Ransom had rescinded his offer of a position on the faculty of classical languages to Joseph Franckenstein, Kay Boyle's husband.[16] Boyle and Franckenstein had recently won a long battle with the State Department affirming their allegiance to the United States, but apparently their image was too tarnished for the University of Texas. Caresse told Boyle that in addition to her letter of refusal to Ransom, she would send William Morris, editor of the *Daily Texan,* the World Citizen Credo for comment.[17]

That year, Caresse helped her dear friend out of financial debt by sending her a portion of the check she had received for reprint rights to Boyle's translation of *The Devil and the Flesh.* And the following spring, she sent Boyle six Matisse lithographs. Boyle was able to sell two for $150 each to friends, one to the University of Rochester for $125. She gave one to a McGraw-Hill editor to whom she felt indebted, and another to her dentist in exchange for care of her children's teeth. The sixth remained on sale at a Madison Avenue gallery.[18]

By no means had Caresse given up efforts to promote world peace. She still owned land in Delphi but, for the time being, saw little hope of establishing a world center there. Her lobbying activities out of Washington, which included mailing strident letters with the World Citizen Constitution and Credo attached, were ignored by such personages as Eleanor Roosevelt and Nelson Rockefeller. Caresse looked again towards the Mediterranean for headquarters and came up with what she thought was a brilliant idea. She would approach Archbishop Makarios of Cyprus with what she called "The Cyprus Peace Plan." If the British gave up their control of the country, Caresse would establish a Center for Peace. Cyprus, with its diverse population and strategic location as gateway between East and West, could be the physical embodiment of One World ideology. Caresse intended to purchase a suitable piece of land to build a basilica from which to fly the One World Flag.

Before Caresse could pursue her latest scheme, however, she attended to health matters. She had already spent time in a London nursing home and at Salvator Mundi International Hospital in Rome for respiratory illness and irregular heartbeat. In the spring of 1957, she underwent heart surgery at the Mayo Clinic in Rochester, Minnesota. Taking a small holiday first, she flew to the West Coast, where she stayed with Bill Barker at Whitley Terrace in Hollywood. Together they drove to Sidona, Arizona, and visited Dorothea

Tanning and Max Ernst, who since the late 1940s had tried to spend part of each year working in the beauty of the dry, colorful desert.[19] Heading back to Hollywood, Barker dropped Caresse off in Flagstaff, where she caught the train to Rochester. She told Barker that she would be listing him on the hospital papers as next of kin.

To celebrate the successful operation, Kay Boyle dedicated to Caresse "A Poem of Gratitude," which was first published in the March 1959 issue of *Poetry*.[20] Set on the beach at dusk during ebb tide, the poem celebrates the renewed strength of Caresse's heartbeats: "Where you now lie, the tide of ether ebbs, / And the small door of your heart opens and closes, opens, / But now it is the south wind of your blood that fans it wide." Boyle also expresses tender happiness over memories of Caresse, sure now that new ones would be in the making.

Caresse also endured two operations on her eyes, one in 1956, the other in 1959. Never one to succumb to setbacks, she was rewarded for her perseverance by an unexpected source. After nine years outbidding Caresse, the Vatican decided it would relinquish its claim on Roccasinibalda. Caresse bought it for $15,000, a very low price. Untouched since Caresse had been forced to abandon it in 1950, the castle was in even greater disrepair than before. It was time to dig up Washington roots and start anew once more. The Crosby Gallery of Modern Art had been sold in 1957. Crosby would wait another four years before completely severing her ties to Washington. But she knew that she would never be considered more than a human interest story in the nation's capitol.

A glaring illustration of her predicament exists in a the twenty-minute interview of March 6, 1958, for radio station WWDC. Steve Alliston introduces Caresse as a "very charming lovely lady who has a few ideas bout how we can make peace."[21] Caresse conducts herself with impeccably good manners, speaking at a quick enough pace to keep her listeners' attention, enunciating each syllable as no doubt she was taught at Miss Chapin's. She does not rise to Alliston's goading when he asks her if it is true that "Paris has loose morals." "Heavens," she replies, "I don't know." She does not ridicule Alliston even though after she identifies herself as a humanist and a Deist, he does not know what she means. She does not permit him to align her with any political party. Rather she takes advantage of the air time by presenting her manifesto for world peace. When Alliston presses her for details, she demurs. He is skeptical of her outline for global community: as far as he can tell, if two men were to be confined to an island, "one will be the servant, the other the boss." Caresse responds that it would be women, not men, who would work as ministers of peace. Caresse may have impressed the audience with her style, but at 11:30 p.m., the time the program was broadcast, it is unlikely that she got any more mileage out of the interview than she had gotten with her other lobbying efforts. She was eager to return to Europe.

15

A Thirty-Year Plan

Upon her return in 1959 to Roccasinibalda as owner outright, Caresse initiated her "Thirty Year Plan," based on the program she had mapped out nearly a decade earlier. Trepidation was never part of her temperament; so be it that she would have to live to 107 if she were to see the plan through to the end. She still dreamed of converting the castle into a self-supporting community with cottage industries, even though to some people, her idea of community sounded more like a gentle fiefdom than a cooperative. With the title to the property, she had acquired the rank of "Principessa," an irony for a woman who regarded herself as a world citizen.

Repairs to the roof, battlements, floors, and walls; clearing the rooms; and creating a kitchen and bathrooms that worked took enormous energy and resources. Caresse planned to spend September to April in the United States, so an elaborate heating system was unnecessary at Rocca, as the castle came to be called. But some provision besides open fireplaces needed to be made for heating. She employed several young men to oversee the construction and the hiring of local craftspeople, mason, carpenters, and plumbers.

Over the next few years, Caresse raised enough money to run the castle by dissolving securities and selling artwork, including a Degas print that Sotheby's determined was fake.[1] She asked her brother Len to arrange that payments from an aunt's trust be made monthly rather than quarterly. As she wrote in a May 31, 1960, letter to him, the "two lean months in between are really not adequate to cover monthly expenses here." She was relieved to learn that another $25,000 would be added to the trust. The house in Washington had not been rented and she was losing $250 every month.

She nurtured her dream of creating a haven for writers and artists where by day they could work in solitude, and in the evenings linger on the terrace for cocktails and draw around the refectory table in the dining room for a simple dinner and lively conversation. She designated Rocca a "Humanist Center for the Creative Arts," and anticipated that one day it would house a library dedicated to the memory of Harry Crosby. The huge basement prison would be transformed into a clinic serving the region. Because she had suffered another heart attack in the winter of 1960, she was too weak and short-winded to walk up the hill to the castle. Instead, she required two men to carry her sitting in a palanka constructed by Bill Barker. Nothing, apparently, would deflect her ambitions.

Caresse defrayed expenses by charging guests room and board, although she always had a cadre of artists who lived there on scholarship so to speak. The first summer season ran through October 1. One of the first inquiries she received was from Harvey Fite, the sculptor connected to the Associated American Artists Gallery on Fifth Avenue in New York. He had restored ancient Mayan sculpture for the Carnegie Institute in Washington, designed sculptural landscape at Overlook Mountain in Saugerties, New York, and was a professor and chair of the Arts Division at Bard College. He seemed like an ideal, paying candidate to invite to the Humanist Center.

The terms for paying guests were as follows.[2] Board, lodging, and a studio to work in cost $125 a month. Breakfast consisted of coffee, fruit, and pannini on the veranda overlooking the valley. Lunch was brought on a tray in the studio, or a meal could be arranged at the village taverna. Dinner was served no earlier than 8:30 after an optional aperitif in the garden. Plumbing work was still going on in the private apartments of the southern wing. At this point, Rocca could accommodate no more than eight "working" visitors at a time. Guests could also stay by the day. A family of four—two adults two children—would pay $20. Gilbert Chase, a cousin of Anaïs Nin, spent the night with his wife, Kathleen, $4 each with meals. A separate room cost $5. All plans included meals. Caresse was serving the arts and humanity. She was also ensuring that for spring and summer, she would have stimulating company.

During the summer of 1960, Caresse's longtime friend Elsa Schiaparelli stayed at Rocca. Although better known as a fashion designer, she was preparing a show of her paintings for an exhibition in New York City the following winter. Other guests included Takis, the young Greek sculptor whom Caresse had befriended while putting together the Greek *Portfolio* twelve years earlier in 1948; Bill Barker, now working on a first novel; and Lillian Segal, an American painter. Robert W. Mann, an American composer living in Rome since 1948, came to the castle in order to write music for Takis's fall exhibition in Paris. He had recently stepped down as the general secretary of the International Society for Contemporary Music.

Through the 1960s, Caresse managed to keep the Humanist Center open for the season, despite sparse amenities and rooms with leaking roofs. Caresse created an atmosphere that was irresistible to young, idealistic, aspiring artists. Rocca was elegant and earthy, an inexpensive (sometimes free) retreat for hard work and discipline in a setting that reverberated with history and culture. Indeed, fifteenth-century frescoes were found under the calcimine that had been spread over the walls to avert the spread of plague. Fiona Dudley, a student at the Uffizi gallery, visited Rocca to see if she could restore the frescoes and determine their origin. Caresse hoped they were by Raphael, or at least by the school of Rafael, but Dudley was never able to confirm that.

Other residents included Sandra and Jack Gabriel, two artists who had met in Paris—Sandra was originally from Mississippi, Jack from Haiti. They worked on paintings and collages while at Rocca. Painter and poet Irene Rice Pereira was preparing for a surrealist exhibition. Professor Sy Kahn from Raymond College in Stockton, California, wrote in March 1962 to inquire if he could visit Rocca and became a regular guest over the years. Caresse thought highly enough of his work to publish it in Castle Continental Editions, her next publishing project yet to be born. Kahn would eventually write an article on the correspondence between Harry Crosby and Hart Crane, and edit a selection of poems by Harry Crosby.[3] Another candidate for Castle Continental Editions was Bill Barker, who in addition to writing his first novel, had already composed a sufficient number of poems for a book. He also helped Caresse to manage the daily running of Rocca during those first years.

A day in the life of residents at Roccasinibalda was captured in the documentary film *Always "Yes!" Caresse* made by Robert Snyder in 1963. Snyder had heard about Caresse and Roccasinibalda while he was in Rome filming his documentary on the Sistine Chapel, *The Titan: The Story of Michelangelo,* which received an Academy Award for Best Documentary Feature in 1951.[4] More than ten years later, he returned to Italy to produce *Always "Yes!" Caresse* in 1963. Codirected by Nancy Thompson, the twenty-six-minute documentary celebrates Caresse's history and ambitious plans for the castle. With voice-overs by Caresse, the camera takes viewers on a tour of the grand if dreary common rooms, including a shot of the vivid face of a beautiful dark-haired woman in a fresco undergoing restoration. Visitors such as the Gabriels, Fiona Dufy, and Bill Barker are shown working on their projects, the background music a mix of stately baroque and modern jazz.

At seventy, Caresse was statuesque, posture-perfect. Her gray hair was gently waved, held back on each side with combs. Whether she was dressed in a prim shirtwaist or gauzy gown, she appeared elegant, proud, and down-to-earth all at the same time. At lunch on the terrace, she sat at the head of the table wearing large sunglasses, looking very much the movie star. In the cavernous dining room at evening, she was back at the head of the table, directing conversation and never touching the food on her plate. She entertained her guests with tales of her glamorous past: clad only in a bathing suit, rowing Harry down the Seine to his office at the Morgan, Harjes bank, baring her bosom and eating dahlias as the figure "Passion Plus" in Emlen Etting's short film *Poem 8,* dancing with Ezra Pound at the Jockey Club in Paris, walking the grounds at Le Moulin du Soleil with D. H. Lawrence, sitting for a portrait by Max Ernst, running out for a 200-watt lightbulb so that James Joyce could proofread copy for *Works in Progress,* laughing with Bob Hope at the Coq Rouge party (also known as the Surrealist Ball), where as he was about to help himself to what he thought was a portion of frogs legs, whole frogs started jumping off the serving plate.

But Caresse was far more interested in what was going to happen next. As she had repeated on many other occasions, she wanted visiting poets and painters to exchange ideas for creating lasting peace and sanity, to find a way to break down national boundaries through art. Roccasinibalda would be one of several world centers. She was ready for more action, especially resurrecting *Portfolio.* From the top of the castle, she flew the One World Flag—a blue globe against a white background. "I am queen mistress of my own small realm," Caresse declared, missing the inconsistency between the democratic nature of her political dreams and her need to create settings where she would shine, be adulated. A sense of humor did come through the film: to make sure no one would think that she was taking herself too seriously, she stated that after she was through with Roccasinibalda, she might consider traveling to the moon.

Caresse's delight in living at Rocca can also be seen in her response to a request for two favorite recipes to be included in the *Artists and Writers Cookbook.* She composed a charming rendition for baby artichokes and freshwater shrimp. The first ingredient was "a castle with an artichoke patch and one preferably around whose feet winds the Turano River where *gamberi* (fresh water shrimp) abound."[5] The recipes were simple and appropriate for the month of May only, when the artichokes were the size of walnuts and the shrimp tiny. Late summer had its rewards though. By then the *gamberi* were large enough to be steamed, split, brushed with butter, sprinkled lightly with fresh sage, and browned for a minute under the broiler. They were to be eaten in a hanging garden above the artichoke patch. Caresse promised not only a joyful dining experience but also a transcendental one. While eating the shrimp, Caresse urged fellow diners to contemplate the shrimp's "birthplace far below in the valley, knowing that next year and the next artichokes will bloom and *gamberi* will multiply . . . until perhaps some future day, ad infinitum, they will dine on us." After such a meal, visitors at Rocca might feel inclined to transcend the perspectives of the projects they had brought with them.

Caresse had never abandoned the plan to create a World Citizen Center on the property she had owned in Delphi since 1952. She also considered the wisdom of enlarging the modest house that came with the property so that she could comfortably escape the cold of winter. In October 1962, she traveled to Greece hoping that she might also plant trees and build a verandah on the small house that overlooked the Grove of Apollo. Catching the ferry at Brindisi, she was met by armed guards at Corfu, where she was forced to disembark. Placed under house arrest at the Corfu Palace Hotel at her expense, with police beneath her window, she was incommunicado for three days. Her chauffeur and car were taken into custody. Once again, she was told that she was not welcome in Greece. She was ordered to leave the country on October 25.

All she could find out from the American consul in Athens was that after ten years, she was still "considered dangerous to the economy and politics of Greece."[6] Never one to lie down after a fight, Caresse wrote on November 16, 1962, to her old friend and attorney in Washington, Rufus King, to inform him of her latest predicament, and to give him copies of the letters she sent to the consulate and the ambassador. She would tell Alexander Xydis, Greece's ambassador in Washington, that she could not understand why his country should feel threatened by her antiviolence politics and her belief that cultural exchange would be the best way to ensure freedom for everyone around the world. Among other people with whom she discussed her predicament was Alfred Barr Jr., director of the Museum of Modern Art. In New York City in February 1963, she had invited Barr to 109 East Ninety-first Street, the home of Helen Simpson, her host whenever she was in town, and where she was introduced to Alexander Kerensky, who was in residence there for many years. Barr was sympathetic and offered the name of another lawyer in Athens who could help her. Encouraging Caresse to put the incident in perspective, he observed that "some minor Greek official" might find her manifesto subversive and added, "I suspect that our consuls throughout the world have blocked foreign visitors to this country for less, especially in the McCarthy period."[7]

Caresse left Roccasinibalda for Madrid, where her daughter and grandchildren were spending the holidays. Her new chauffeur, William Chapman, was English, "just right for my needs," she told King, "as he is quiet, a cautious driver and has a lot of know-how, speaks three languages and is a perfect Jeeves."[8] His salary was $150 a month. Caresse needed to make as much cash available as she could since, as she reported to King, she was "in no way backing down on my beliefs and ideals, nor my legal right to express them." To that end, she had written to Chase Bank to sell seven hundred shares of the thousand Chase Fund securities and to deposit the proceeds (approximately $4,000) into her checking account. That was in addition to another 333 shares she had sold recently. Caresse was convinced that her real enemy was "Mr. Hilton or some business tycoon" who wanted to convert her hilltop property into a luxury hotel to accommodate Greece's booming tourist industry.

While Caresse was in Madrid that Christmas, she was appalled to learn that tales of her latest experience in Greece had preceded her arrival. She was called on by Prince Atulfo Orleans-Bourbons, an old friend, who with his parents had stayed with Caresse's "family in Boston" in 1928.[9] She told him about her troubles with the Greek government, but he already knew about her arrest. Representing Spain at a royal wedding in Athens, he had been asked by the queen of Greece if he knew that his friend Caresse Crosby was "a fellow traveler."[10] Fearing trouble ahead—she was surprised she had not been stopped at the Spanish border—she was adamant that her name be cleared. To her dismay, while she was in Washington, D.C., she had been listed as a spy on the police list in Athens because of the incident in Delphi that had occurred in 1960.[11] In 1965, the Greek government allowed Caresse to return to her property, which she had intended all along to leave to the citizens of Delphi.

By then, however, Caresse had become involved in intricate negotiations to build a Citizens of the World Center in a location close by—Cyprus. Astonishing as this may seem, in 1957, she had captured the attention and support of Archbishop Makarios, who was living in exile in Athens, two years before he was to become the first president of the Republic of Cyprus. She was actively endorsed by Buckminster Fuller, who in his lifetime was called "the planet's friendly genius," and who was the inventor of the Dymaxion house, a factory-assembled, air-deliverable structure that contained its own utilities; the three-wheeled Dymaxion car; and the geodesic dome, based on the idea that the triangle, not the square, is the basic unit of natural structures. He designed the U.S. Pavilion for the 1967 World's Fair in Montreal. A continual theme in the many books that he published (which also included poetry) was the warning that advancing technology needed to be guided by social good; otherwise, the planet would be destroyed by a power-driven elite.

Fuller and Caresse had maintained a respect and fondness for each other over the years, since their brief affair in the 1930s, when they first met at Romany Marie's, a café in Greenwich Village.[12] Rumor has it that in those days, the reward of a free meal a day was enough compensation for Fuller to decorate the walls with drawings of all kinds of Dymaxions.[13] It is likely that Caresse and Fuller saw one another when Caresse gave her Black Sun Press talk at Black Mountain College in 1955. At the time, Fuller was on the faculty. Fuller was now teaching at Southern Illinois University with another friend of Caresse's, Harry Moore.

It was to Buckminster and Ann Fuller's Dymaxion house in Carbondale that Caresse wanted to go on November 22, 1963, the day John F. Kennedy was assassinated. Over the years, Harry and Beatrice Moore and Caresse had visited back and forth in Washington, D.C., London, Paris, Rome, and the Moores' home in Carterville, Illinois, near the Southern Illinois University campus. Moore would ask Caresse to speak to his students of modern literature about her publishing days in Paris and her friendships with James Joyce, Hart Crane, D. H. Lawrence, Kay Boyle, and others. The morning of November 22, she and Harry were about to leave for campus when they learned that Kennedy was dead. Heading for Fuller's house "was a marvelous idea," Moore recalled. "We were going to see old friends (for, like Caresse, I had known Bucky before either of us came to SIU-C) and it was the best possible thing anyone could have done that day."[14]

The following day, the Moores did not cancel the party scheduled in honor of Caresse's visit, because "it was a dreadful time and people needed to be together. Caresse was grand as always and became an unforgettable part of the SIU-C community." Actually the party was an annual, by-invitation-only event. About seventy-five people were in attendance, mostly faculty and graduate students. Caresse held forth from a comfortable armchair in the corner of the living room, while those guests who could not get close enough wandered through the house, which was lined with 100,000 books, the largest library in the state of Illinois.[15]

Fuller had visited Roccasinibalda in the summer of 1964. Even more coincidentally, Robert Snyder was Fuller's son-in-law and had shown "Bucky" (as he was called by those who knew him) his documentary about Caresse. Fuller was fascinated by it but wanted additional important episodes of her life added, including the opening of her art gallery in wartime Washington. He told Caresse that "the ramifications of your life are great. Your conservation and nourishment of the creative faculties of man have been historically powerful."[16] By the mid-1960s, Fuller was at the height of his fame, and Caresse knew that Fuller's support could go very far.

Caresse suspected that if she held on, she might get a World Center, the culmination of what she was now calling her "30 Year Plan" for peace. She had never before won the support of a famous architect and theoretician, or a head of state. She could also count on Xenon Rossides, the ambassador from Cyprus to the United States. It is amazing that the negotiations for a "World Man Center," Fuller's revised name for the center, went as far as they did, given the divisive political strains between Greek and Turkish Cypriots. March 1964 marked the beginning of the decade-long presence of the United Nations Peace-Keeping Force in Cyprus. Numerous incidents of violence were initiated by an offshoot of the National Organization of Cypriot Struggle, which had fought for union with Greece, and by Turkish Cypriots with a near invasion by Turkey in 1967.

Makarios's chief interest was to keep Cyprus independent, but he was obliged to accept a Turkish Cypriot Provisional Administration, which managed Turkish minority affairs outside the jurisdiction of the central government. Although Makarios was reelected twice, talks between the Turkish and Greek communities remained deadlocked over the question of local autonomy. During the mid-1960s, when Caresse was lobbying her 30 Year Plan, she seemed oblivious to the reality that she could not propose to Makarios that she herself seek cooperation from the current leader of the Turkish Cypriot community, Dr. Fazil Kutchuk.[17] In a May 19, 1964, letter, Makarios had to remind Caresse, however gently, that while he deeply appreciated her interest in Cyprus, and hoped it would remain constant, uppermost in his current agenda was "defend[ing] the "territorial integrity and freedom [of Cyprus] which are constantly threatened by Turkey."[18]

Caresse also needed to exercise a diplomat's restraint when discussing the progress of establishing the World Man Center. Even though the plan was far from official approval by Makarios, she spoke about Fuller's commitment to donate a design for the World Man Center to a journalist from the *Chicago News* all too eager to share the information with a world news wire service. Fuller became "terribly worried" when a reporter from the *Washington Post* led him to believe that Caresse had leaked a story that an international peace center was soon to be established in Cyprus.[19] Although Caresse maintained the affection and good will of Makarios and Fuller, their support could only be conditional. Caresse had drive and humane aspirations, but even while she had gained some political credibility, she lacked any leverage. Her money might have made up in part for missing credentials, but her funds were lower than ever.

That being said, Caresse not only captured the attention of Fuller, Makarios, and Rossides but, through Fuller, also inspired an articulated interest from United Nations Secretary General U Thant, and also from Indira Gandhi, Willem DeKooning, and Isamu Noguchi.[20] She garnered moral support from Alfred Barr, Anaïs Nin, Hugo Guiler (one of Nin's husbands), Cyril Connolly, Elsa Schiaparelli, and Dorothy Norman, editor of the avant-garde publication *Twice a Year.* Her efforts to establish this center extended over the entire decade, with the first tangible step occurring in 1965, when she visited the northeastern coast of Cyprus with Ambassador Rossides and purchased eight acres of land for $4,000, that is she paid $2,000 and Archbishop Makarios paid $2,000.[21] Soon after, she met with Fuller in London for preliminary discussion about the geodesic dome, which he would design to sit above Kyrenia. In New York City, she and Rossides and Fuller met. Caresse learned that in addition to the eight acres, the archbishop proposed that he give the center sixty-eight acres of church property closer to the harbor of Kyrenia and an additional $200,000, on the condition that Caresse would procure an additional $200,000 of matching funds. Makarios made his offer public at a July 7, 1966, press conference at the presidential palace.

At the suggestion of Buckminster Fuller, the World Academy of Arts and Science, to which he had been recently elected, were asked to serve as trustees of the property. Caresse met with Robert Dowling of Park-Bernet in order to arrange a benefit auction. A not-for-profit corporation, World Man Center, Inc., was set up by Rufus King with Caresse as president, Fuller and the Greek American artist Michael Lekakis as vice presidents, and Rufus King as secretary and treasurer. Among the distinguished people that Caresse recruited for the fund-raising committee were Marcel Duchamp and Norman Cousins, editor of *Saturday Review* since 1942, and responsible for expanding the scope of the magazine so that it included articles about other arts in addition to literature and about world affairs.

Peggy Guggenheim also signed on. Caresse had seen a good deal of Guggenheim in Venice. Guggenheim's renovated eighteenth-century palazzo on the Grand Canal housed her extraordinary collection of works by artists such as Calder, Giacometti, Picasso, Braque, Duchamp, Gris, and Brancusi. It was open to the public as a museum on Monday, Wednesday, and Friday afternoons. Caresse was one of many private summer visitors who enjoyed Guggenheim's exotic dinner parties and soirees, along with writers Nancy Mitford, Cyril Connolly, and Mary McCarthy; actors Ruth Ford and Zachary Scott; poet (and brother of Ruth) Charles Henri Ford; art critic Clement Greenberg; abstract painter Buffie Johnson; and Helena Rubenstein, who with millions made from cosmetics became a serious art collector.[22] Caresse liked to ride with Peggy in her private black gondola, along with the many Lhasa Apsos that were Guggenheim's constant companions.

A photograph of Caresse and Peggy in the gondola, taken by the young Canadian photographer Roloff Beny in the mid-1950s, shows two middle-aged women, well-kept, dressed casually, with hair dyed dark and swept up and away.[23] Peggy holds a cigarette in her left hand, and her eyes cut away from the photographer, not quite peering at the water, a slight smirk across her lips. In a sleeveless, tailored sundress, Caresse stares out directly, and so does one of Peggy's Lhasa Apsos sitting on her lap. Slouchy handbag beside her sandaled feet, with toenails painted white, bare slim legs gracefully crossed, Caresse appears to be the younger of the two, around forty-five and a little vulnerable, though she is past sixty and Peggy's senior by six years. The two friends appear at ease with one another, and beyond any rancor between them, given that Peggy's heart was broken by Laurence Vail and Max Ernst, both of whom married good friends of Caresse's—Kay Boyle and Dorothea Tanning. Caresse apparently did not envy Peggy's greater prominence, though she probably wished she had her money.

Kay Boyle, Dorothy Norman, Roloff Beny, and Constantin Doxiades also offered Caresse support. Artists from whom she received contributions included Jean Helion, Calder, DeKooning, Cartier-Bresson, Romare Bearden, and her old friend Henry Miller. However, before fund-raising activities, which included the art auction, could begin, the corporation sought not-for-profit status so that all contributions could be tax-exempt. The Treasury Department rejected the application, essentially signing a death warrant for the center. Caresse still owned four of the eight acres that she had bought with Archbishop Makarios. She could have built a private residence on the land, but she continued to hold out for a World Man Center. After all, in reserve, she still owned the magnificent castle Roccasinibalda.

16

How to Run a Castle

Caresse had been able to call many places home—New York City, Boston, Paris, Ermenonville, Fredericksburg, Washington, D.C., Delphi, and now Roccasinibalda. With the exception of Delphi, she had demonstrated a remarkable ability to nest well. The several flats that she shared with Harry she furnished sumptuously, but with far less money, she was also able to convert a New York City sublet into a pied-à-terre featured in *Better Homes and Gardens.* The Mill was uninhabitable when she and Harry took it off the hands of their friend Armand de la Rochefoucauld, but Caresse transformed it into a charming if sometimes raucous retreat. A more difficult space to civilize, Hampton Manor became a comfortable, hospitable domicile, complete with indoor plumbing, under Caresse's careful direction. The several apartments in Washington, D.C., were barely a challenge, except for designating rooms for the furniture and artwork and placing what could not be used in storage.

Roccasinibalda was more problematical. While the place and Caresse's plans for it were enormous, Caresse's financial resources were modest. The castle was not a cozy space. Caresse was absent for at least a quarter of each year, and it required a caretaker. She also needed the practical and emotional support of a partner. Although Caresse and Polleen and her family spent winter and summer holidays together, Polleen had no desire to participate in her mother's latest scheme. On visits to Rocca, the oldest grandchild, Lorraine de Mun, did help her "dearest gran" with maintaining files and writing publicity for the World Man Center and Women Against War. Caresse's brothers had been guarded in their support of the World Center from its inception. Bud appreciated her idealism but advised her to ascertain that from a legal perspective her plans were not "in conflict with, or contrary to our own constitution and the laws of our great United States."[1] Len felt "no antagonism whatsoever" to the concept of world citizenship and wished her "all success" in turning Rocca into headquarters for the center. But he knew that her personal resources alone could not support the effort.[2]

In fact, Caresse needed full-time assistance. For a while, William Chapman, the English chauffeur, was caretaker, with Caresse giving instructions by post during the cold fall and winter months. She wanted him to keep the castle's books and oversee the renovations. As was typical for Caresse, she kept dogs wherever she lived and worried about their behaving themselves when she was absent. "To complicate the castle life with illegitimate puppies would be a disaster," she wrote Chapman from the Virgin Islands on February 21, 1963. She was also concerned about the garden, particularly the rose bushes, which she assumed Chapman had cut back to about six inches, "as I think they should be—my brother is a great rose grower and that is what he says."[3] Caresse's reference to her brother's expertise sounds odd since she was not one to consult family. She also signs off as "M[ary]. J[acob]. Crosby." When she deemed it appropriate, she pulled rank. Her relationship with Chapman was strictly business.

Bill Barker was a candidate for a different kind of "job." Caresse had long regarded Barker as a surrogate son. She appreciated his elegance and charm, his writer's aspirations, his love of travel, and his eagerness to take chances with the future and with stock market profits that funded his adventures. He was also an aspiring actor with suave good looks to go with the role. In Athens in 1959 with his wife, Diane, and poet Gregory Corso, he won a "meaty part" in a Michael Cacoyannis film *Eroica,* for which he would earn $200 for two weeks' work.[4] Corso and Diane had bit parts, and together, Corso, who had met Caresse the summer before at Peggy Guggenheim's palazzo in Venice, scribbled to Caresse, the three of them were "the most handsome irresolute starvelings in Athens."[5] By then, Caresse had figured out that young friends helped her remember the times of her own flamboyant youth. Indeed, at Corso's urging, she wrote to Lawrence Ferlinghetti at City Lights Books to see if he wanted to publish Harry's diaries.[6] They would be a testament to her most precious years as well as his.

In a rough draft of the foreword to Barker's first collection of poetry, scheduled for Castle Continental Editions (it was never published), she praised Barker for his worldliness and passion and a "determined will to achieve."[7] She reserved judgment of the poems until later, only suggesting that the poems "may seem dated as they run because this poet must express the passing scene that moves ever faster and faster, and he always with it." No doubt she preferred to rely on Barker than Chapman for duties such as driving and keeping the household ledger, services he had provided in earlier times at Rocca. (Barker also used her car to get to Athens in 1959). Barker was too free a spirit, not one to be tied down to an aging patron, as much as he loved her. He returned to Rocca every summer and never regretted the professional opportunities missed because of his devotion to Caresse. He was an official world citizen, number 7 on the registry. But he also knew what it meant to restore a fresco and spoke fluent Italian (among several other languages, including Turkish).

The most suitable substitute for Barker was Robert Mann, the young composer and translator based in Rome, who had been one of the earliest visitors at Rocca. His home base was Trastevere, and while he enjoyed travel, he did not have the funds to wander very far from Rome. He had no plans for returning to the United States, and an arrangement with the castle that allowed him to pursue his music and translations at the same time would be convenient. Caresse was delighted at the prospect of securing a steady overseer, especially one as talented and sensitive and young as Robert, who was fluent in Italian. By 1965, the multitalented Mann had slipped into a comfortable helper's role at Rocca, but not without first facing a few problems.

Caresse was running Roccasinibalda on the fly. While she was fine at figuring out what the physical plant needed, she was lost when it came to raising and allocating funds. With a musician's head for figures, and the knowledge that Caresse was vulnerable to requests by needy artists, Robert designed a hard-line proposal for the castle's future. Caresse had never been interested in laying a firm foundation before she tackled a new project, and Robert was determined that she confront some hard realities. After writing nearly five pages of suggestions, he may have also been forcing himself to figure out how deep he wanted to get into Caresse's dreams. He had already achieved a kind of intimacy with her that he had not anticipated.

By the end of August 1963, and the fourth season at the Castle, Robert had developed additional ideas about how this humanist center could survive and achieve a formal, recognized standing as an international retreat for artists.[8] The underlying premise of his plan was simple: Caresse had to find the funds to run the center without depending on the center itself to make a profit. He suggested that she sell the Black Sun Press collection to the highest bidder, since so far Caresse's tentative inquiries to university libraries, including the University of California at Riverside and the State University of New York at Albany, had been fruitless. Her hopes had been high for the University of Texas, as she told Frances Steloff, but the final outcome "was very much like *Waiting for Godot*."[9] She was under the impression that Texas wanted to print a catalog of the collection whether or not they purchased all the books. When they insisted that Caresse sell them the entire collection at a price she could not accept, they refused to print the catalog.

She was dismayed over their hard bargaining and, had she known their style, might not have suggested to them that they approach Man Ray, whose work would be a valuable addition to their archives. Included in Man Ray's collection were two pastels of Caresse drawn in 1959, depicting her as a shadowy, dancing, butterfly-like creature. The last Caresse heard, Man Ray was offered $50,000, but he would be required to turn over the not only prints but negatives as well, his source of steady income.[10] Robert was aware of these negotiations as they faltered to a halt. He was serving as Caresse's secretary, taking dictation and typing the letters. He warned Caresse that she was running out of time and urged her to consider dividing the collection and selling the more valuable part.[11]

As it turned out, with the help of Harry Moore, Caresse sold the collection in July 1965 to Morris Library, at Southern Illinois University, for $21,000. Before she signed the contract, however, Moore had to reassure Caresse that all students, professors, and independent scholars would have access to the collection. She feared the university might observe Jim Crow laws, as many southern universities did, because "Southern" was part of its name. On the occasions that Caresse had visited the Carbondale campus with the Moores, she had never seen black students or faculty eating in the local restaurants. Moore promised her that "there was no segregation on the SIU-C campus, that black students were allowed access everywhere."[12] Caresse may have sounded naive with such a question, but she also remembered the early forties when she and Canada Lee could not dine together in Washington, D.C., restaurants.

Before the sale of the collection, Robert proposed a plan for running the humanist center that sounded more sensitive to reality, but not altogether feasible. He had seen how arbitrary Caresse had been about fees for guests, and about determining who should be invited in the first place. According to Robert's new plan, all applicants needed to be closely screened; no more than twelve artists should be accommodated from July through September; the artists would be given free room and board. In addition, a senior artist would be in residence for the season to serve as general mentor. Spouses, pets, and children would not be welcome. A business administrator would have to be employed, a job Robert had no intention of taking. Robert would be glad to oversee the screening committee that judged applicants but stressed that his presence should not be essential to the general success of the place. Indeed, he needed to devote his energies primarily to his music and to the translations that paid his bills.

Despite his efforts to persuade her that she needed a more efficient mode of operations, Caresse proceeded as usual, preferring a more extemporaneous agenda. Robert continued to assist her as time allowed but never initiated the selective application process that he thought would enhance Roccasinibalda's reputation. Gradually he disengaged from his role as Caresse's assistant, even though there would be talk of his visiting Caresse in New York during the winter, or accompanying Caresse on a trip to Athens. Caresse did manage to maintain some semblance of a schedule of fees. She informed Kay Boyle's daughter, Bobby (whose *Four Poems* the Black Sun Press had published in 1942), that she was welcome as long she agreed to "be of assistance to the castle." Her "Swedish artist friend" would have to pay full fare.[13]

Caresse could not reject established if struggling artists whose work she respected. Through artist Irene Rice Pereira, she had met Julian Beck and Judith Malina, founders and directors of the Living Theater. Anaïs Nin had also recommended the group, full of talent and originality, perfect to stage a performance at the castle. The experimental theater company, first housed on Fourteenth Street in New York, was usually in trouble, its plays banned and performances shut down on obscenity charges and other bogus reasons. On October 24, 1964, Julian Beck wrote to Caresse to ask if the Living Theater could use Rocca for rehearsal from November 18 to January 1. In London at the time Beck wrote the letter, Caresse did not learn about Beck's request until the middle of November, when she returned to her small Rome apartment in 37 Angelo Brunetti.

Caresse was so excited by the possibility that the Living Theater would use the castle for rehearsals that she sent both a telegram and follow-up letter to Beck: she was delighted to cooperate but cautioned that winter conditions made "comfort uncertain."[14] She could not have sounded more obliging in her letter.

> I wish the castle were heated or even liveable in winter, there is plenty of room and tons of space to practice and rehearse. . . . I know I couldn't house or feed thirty people at present . . . you would be welcome to use the place to work in. I would have to see you myself and show you the

> castle before I take off for Madrid on December 1. I'd have to charge you for electricity and open fires and telephone not too much about $50 for a month, but where could you sleep or eat?[15]

Caresse already had the answer. The company could rent the rooms in the village over the bar and trattoria, and the little house near the gate accommodated about eight "in a pinch." They could eat a full dinner at the trattoria for about $1.25 or buy groceries to cook in the kitchen of the little house. She also offered them the use of her pied-à-terre in Rome until January 10, when she would return from Madrid. "If you could manage it, it would be lovely," she added.

For the better part of winter 1965, the Living Theater worked and lived in Roccasinibalda. They prepared for a spring tour that was supposed to include Rome, Triest, Turin, Milan, Genoa, and Venice. By April, Beck and Malina were in different living quarters, Lungotevere delli Armi 23, but a few women in the company remained in the little house with their children. Against Caresse's advice, some of the troupe had slept in the castle itself. Expenses soared. The actors kept fires, gas, and electricity going all night; ran up a terrific bill at Spataros Trattoria; and left piles of dirty bed linen in their wake. According to Caresse's estimate, she had advanced the Living Theater more than 240,000 lire ($700).[16] She would be flying from New York to Rome on April 7 and could wait to settle accounts then. More vexed than outraged, Caresse remained concerned about the Living Theater's welfare.

Beck and Malina greatly appreciated Caresse's support and patience. As Beck told Caresse in an April 6, 1965, letter, the Living Theater would not have been able to get through the winter together without Caresse's help. They were more than grateful for the "pleasures" that she provided: "living in a great castle, living in the perfect cottage in Rocca, falling into a hotel with rooms reserved the night we tiredly entered Rome, and the dinners, and the coat, and the bottle of Scotch."[17] Caresse did not press hard for expenses to be honored, or as she subtly put it in a July 12, 1965, letter wishing them a successful run in Berlin, "I see that your financial status is still flexible and I do still hope for eventual payment from you." She also invited them to stay the night at Rocca when they returned to Rome. If that was not convenient, perhaps they would meet in New York over the winter. Caresse walked into this situation with eyes wide open. She could not depend upon herself to run a tight ship and probably never really wanted to.

By this time, Robert Mann, who had always understood her great if selective generosity, had given up any hope of reforming her. He belonged to the group that genuinely understood what she was hoping to accomplish at

Roccasinibalda, even if he demonstrated far more interest in her artistic projects than in her political activities. He was not after personal gain. He was not a user, like, long ago, Jacques Porel or Bert Young had been. Over the next years, he maintained his affection for Caresse without either of them compromising their ambitions. Letters to Caresse are full of warmth and tenderness right through the end of 1969. In essence, Caresse and Robert were completely independent of one another, but they enjoyed the idea that regardless of the difference in age, they could enjoy a special friendship.

Anticipating Caresse's return to Roccasinibalda in April 1966, Robert urged her to make haste. He reassured her that they there were good times ahead for them.[18] Not one to reject overtures of love (or, for that matter, blueprints for artists' colonies and One World centers), Caresse would not yield to the fact that her state of health was compromised. She had been to the Mayo Clinic in December 1965, where Dr. R. O. Brandenburg recommended that she undergo heart surgery to replace faulty valves with plastic ones. She had already undergone a mitral commissurotomy, which she blamed for the thickening of her waist.

The following summer (1966), Caresse was back in Roccasinibalda. She was a youthful seventy-four. She had never been averse to coloring her hair and through the years had maintained tasteful shades of brown. As the holder since 1914 of the patent for a brassiere, she knew how to take advantage of the slimming effects of a girdle. More to the point, Caresse's spirit for life and action counted far more than how well she preserved her physical beauty.

Dr. Brandenberg's medical report revealed that Caresse suffered from progressive bouts of fatigue, dyspnea, asthma, bronchitis, hypertension, and recurrent mitral stenosis (heart failure).[19] Yet he noted that "Mrs. Crosby was a remarkably animated, youthful, and zestful person with ruddy cheeks," an observation that could only be reinforced after he read a letter Caress wrote to him from Jerusalem on February 10, 1967. She was returning to Italy by way Beirut, Cyprus, and Athens, a trip that was proving to be more difficult than she had anticipated: getting from one side of a room to another was a challenge.

> In fact I'm tired mentally and physically and I want to fight against it or else snuff it out. I am seventy five, or will be on April 20, and need another fifteen years of active involvement in living.

She wanted the "miracle" plastic valve as soon as she could be scheduled for it. "I want the very latest model valve," she added in a postscript. In a letter that reached her in Athens, Dr. Brandenburg suggested a repeat operation on the mitral valve instead. Three times the operation was scheduled—in April and July 1967, and in January 1968. Caresse missed all. Her decision against the operation was supported by her New York doctor, Louis Bishop, as well by a Dr. Evans in London. The risk may have been too great, the recovery time too long.

Caresse was traveling through the Middle East in constant search of support for the doomed World Man Center. She visited her friends Isobel and John Fistere, who operated a public relations firm from the St. George Hotel in Beirut. They had been guests at Rocca and supported the World Man Center agenda. Buckminster Fuller was a mutual friend, and the Fisteres kept Caresse informed of Fuller's crowded itinerary. Future publishers of a cultural magazine to be called *Jordan Quarterly,* they would consult Caresse for her editorial expertise. After Caresse told them that the cover of the first issue "had very little allure. It looks like a dispirited tree in any desert," they sought better staff for color and layout. That proved too optimistic, and the journal folded.

Caresse's skills as a drama critic were also called upon. For Beirut's *Daily Star,* she wrote a review of a reading at the British Library of Edward Albee's play *Who's Afraid of Virginia Woolf?* (Caresse and Albee had met in spring 1964, when they both sailed to Europe on the S.S. *United States.*) Reprinting the review, the *Beirut Times* turned the event into a human interest story about Caresse, who used the opportunity to promote the World Man Center as a place where artists, intellectuals, and scientists from all countries could gather together. The goal, as she had stated over and over elsewhere, was to break down divisions between these groups in order to avoid war. Her sense of humor intact, she added: "We may even invite a few politicians to stay with us."[20] Caresse was ailing inside, but to the world, she appeared a miniature dynamo, highly polished.

As Caresse had told her doctor at the Mayo Clinic, there was still so much that she wanted to do. She had been writing a sequel to *The Passionate Years* and was looking for a publisher. The manuscript, thirty short chapters that cover the years 1941 to 1960, is an unwieldy collage of personal anecdotes, travel writing, and informal political discourse. Her family barely appears in "Who in the World! A Personal History of World Citizenship." Billy's death is noted in the outline of the manuscript, but there is no allusion to the tragedy in the text itself. She may have been respecting her family's wishes for privacy. They had not been particularly responsive to *The Passionate Years.* Her brother Bud refused to read it.[21] She discusses none of her several romances. There are far fewer participants in the sequel.

She wanted a contract and an advance before she embarked on the heavy revisions that she knew would be required, although it is not at all evident that she would have personalized her "personal history" any more than she already had. *The Passionate Years* had established her credentials as an interesting, lively memoirist, but a good deal of the strength in that book lies in Caresse's talent for giving faces and personalities to people who in other contexts seem abstract or other-worldly or too famous for detailed description. (For example, her portrait of Ezra Pound in the published and unpublished works is sharp.) Both Kenneth McCormick at Doubleday and Kenneth Ewing of Fraser and Dunlop read and rejected the manuscript. It is a wonder that Caresse had been able to put together anything even resembling an addition to her autobiography given the frenetic, sometimes nomadic quality of her life during this time period.

17

Keeping the Faith

The castle, however, continued to serve as home base. Caresse would visit friends like Roloff Beny in Rome and Peggy Guggenheim in Venice. She took small motor trips to Spoleto, where she enjoyed the annual summer festival that attracted so many artists, writers, and musicians from around the world. She looked forward to seeing Ezra Pound there, even though she knew he had become withdrawn and silent since his release from St. Elizabeths and would probably not talk to her. Pound refused to engage in any conversation at one luncheon for him attended by nearly thirty people, including Charles Olson, Caresse, and poet Desmond O'Grady, also a friend of Caresse's and a regular at Rocca. Pound would not eat a morsel of food despite exhortations from Caresse and Olga Rudge, Pound's companion. Finally left alone at the table with O'Grady, Pound announced that he did not like being pushed around by women and ate his meal.[1] Not one to take Pound's behavior personally, Caresse made sure to attend the festival that would honor Pound in 1966.

In fact, Pound had been to Roccasinibalda in the summer of 1963. Frances Steloff was visiting the castle at the same time and became greatly saddened by Pound's depressed state of mind. (After Steloff's visit in 1961, Caresse and Robert Mann voted her the most charming guest of the summer). Pound's affection for Caresse had been reinforced by her support during his confinement at St. Elizabeths, and by her refusal to concede to authorities that Pound was insane (even though the plea of insanity is what saved Pound's life).[2]

During the visit, Caresse tried to revive an interest in Pound for yet another project of hers, first entitled "Letters to the Editress," then "Letters to the Editor." It would be a collection of the correspondence between Caresse Crosby and D. H. Lawrence, James Joyce, Hart Crane, Ezra Pound, Ernest Hemingway, René Crevel, and Kay Boyle. A reprint of Millicent Bell's history of the Black Sun Press would introduce the volume. For the section on Pound, Caresse would include excerpts from *The Passionate Years,* ten letters, two photos, and a narrative of her meetings with him in St. Elizabeths and in Italy. Earlier she had suggested to Pound that he might want to edit the essay,[3] but nothing indicates that Caresse's idea went beyond a prospectus.

Another project collapsed. Faithful to the memory of Harry, Caresse intended to create a library at the castle in his honor. She wanted to initiate an annual $500 Harry Crosby poetry prize, with entries in French, Italian, Spanish, Greek, Russian, and Portuguese, forty of which would be translated into English. Caresse aimed high when she drew up a list of poets she wanted to serve as judges: Charles Olson, Allen Tate, Lawrence Ferlinghetti, René Char, St.-John Perse, Eugene Montale, George Seferis, Pablo Neruda, and Allen Ginsberg, who Caresse decided should be chief judge for the Russian entries. Inspired by the efforts of Gian Carlo Menotti, founder and organizer of the Spoleto Festival, Caresse planned to announce the first winner the week before the June 1967 festival, which many of the judges would be attending. No matter how the prospective judges were charmed by Caresse at social gatherings, few were inclined to sacrifice the time and energy that the task required. The Harry Crosby prize turned into another good-hearted idea that never got off the ground.

Still searching for money to manage the castle, Caresse turned to Frances Steloff, who counted Caresse among her best friends. Steloff was eager to purchase Black Sun books and ephemera as well as anything else Caresse owned that would be appropriate for the avant-garde and rare books and manuscripts section of the Gotham Book Mart. Steloff had opened the landmark bookstore on January 1, 1920, when she was thirty-three. In 1967, Steloff resolved that the time had come to sell it to Andreas Brown, a young book appraiser.[4] Although she stayed very much involved with the place—she was listed as "president" on the shop's letterhead—she was now free of the daily grind of running a business. Brown acted as negotiator between Caresse and the Gotham Book Mart.

In May 1968, Steloff took a three-week holiday, stopping first in London and Paris for a few days, then continuing to Israel, saving the last three days to be with her "precious one" in Roccasinibalda.[5] The visit proved to be gratifying for them both. Steloff especially enjoyed a tour of Robert Mann's private apartment in the former prison of the castle. The following summer, Steloff was interviewed by the *New Yorker.* She talked primarily about the Gotham Book Mart but also mentioned how exciting her recent travels had been. In passing, she put the spotlight on Caresse and Harry Crosby.

> I spent a few days with my old friend Caresse Crosby in her castle at Roccasinibalda. . . . She and her husband, Harry Crosby, who was a nephew of J. P. Morgan's, ran the Black Sun Press back in the twenties and thirties. They published all the Moderns—Joyce, Pound, Lawrence. They also published the first edition of Hart Crane's "The Bridge." They brought out exquisite books. People buy them now just for their beauty. Isn't that wonderful that he spent his money that way, instead of becoming a playboy? Caresse has had the first floor of the castle done up as studios, which she gives free to anyone creative. Isn't that wonderful.[6]

Of course, Steloff knew more about the Crosbys than she was revealing. But she captured a sense of the Crosbys' genuine dedication to the press, and Caresse's idealism in general. She may have also hoped to sell some books.

Dependent upon the interest of family trusts, the $21,000 she had received from Morris Library, and uncertain royalties from the sale of Black Sun Press books and manuscripts, Caresse could not keep Roccasinibalda much longer. She spent about $1,000 a month for basic maintenance, taxes, insurance, and telephone. In addition, she had to set aside enough money for her own personal expenses, food, and the salaries of the people who worked in the castle.[7] She put together a one-page announcement that the castle was for sale, briefly describing its glorious setting and reassuring prospective buyers that the edifice had been inspected "by a leading architect for the Vatican and declared in excellent structural condition" and that all titles and related matters of legal ownership were in order. Delyte Morris, president of Southern Illinois University, considered the possibility of establishing a summer institute at Rocca.[8] At his request, Harry Moore had made an informal report on the feasibility of the idea after his last visit. In his "subjective appreciation of the place," he noted that the castle "was full of young people staying there, painting and writing: Caresse had even put in a swimming pool." His interest piqued, Morris visited Caresse at the castle with the intention of negotiating a sale, but he and Caresse failed to agree on a price.

When no other serious buyers surfaced, Caresse thought about creating a "Castle Club." If she could secure sixty memberships, annual dues would be $1,200 a year. But she never mustered the energy to start a new campaign, so to speak, and limped along with things as they were. She maintained a steady correspondence with Andreas Brown, who now controlled acquisitions at Gotham Book Mart, and she unloaded a cartload of material in May 1969. In addition to Black Sun Press ephemera, it included items such as volumes of *Black Mountain Review,* a broadside of Robert Duncan's "Song of the Borderguard," and Ezra Pound's *Analects.* Thirty copies of Caresse's own *Crosses of Gold,* published in 1925, swelled the lot, which brought her $200.

But Caresse was hardly ready to retire. Far from yielding to financial troubles and medical setbacks—her bronchial asthma had landed her in Salvator Mundi hospital more than once—Caresse maintained a remarkable level of activity. In October 1968, she organized a happening, to be called "Threshold for Peace." It would be her next to last public contribution towards establishing a global community. On the invitation, which she mailed to world dignitaries, directors of peace organizations, writers, artists, and journalists, she announced that during the ceremony a marble plaque inscribed "LOVE, TRUTH, BEAUTY, JUSTICE, CHOICE" would be placed in the earth of the courtyard of the castle.[9] The circle of land surrounding the plaque would be designated as "extraterritorial" and would be held in trust by her beloved Citizens of the World, or by the International League for the Rights of Man, an organization that she had not worked with closely but that she admired greatly. She avoided any reference to the World Man Center, in order not to compromise dormant plans to establish the center on Cyprus.

Caresse did not get the audience that she wanted, but she garnered uplifting rejections. Perhaps the most heartwarming was from Allen Ginsberg, who wrote her a card on September 24, 1968, from his communal farm in Cherry Hill, New York. "You're always such a lovely idealist it's good cheer to hear your vibration from where you are."[10] He was too busy milking goats and cows to attend, but he was with Caresse "in word in spirit." The card reached Rieti stamped $.04 postage due.

Several years earlier, in 1948, at the start of her political activism, Caresse composed a statement that would appear to be out of character. She called it "We, The Murderers." As a member of the "powerful generation of murderers," she said that it was time to "clear the earth for extreme youth and hope" and urged mass suicide for everyone over the age of twenty, or as an alternative, a "voluntary draft, beginning with ours, the murder generation." Men and women of fifty to sixty would be drafted to commit hari-kari.[11] She wanted to present an ultimatum in response to the escalating cold war, and what she considered to be a prelude to a new, more virulent and devastating nationalism.

To support her position, she offered some personal history. She considered herself lucky when it came to world wars:

> My husband volunteered to kill, but was not killed in World War I. My son was called upon to kill but was not killed in World War II. I ignored both wars as best I could. (In World War I[,] I rolled bandages. In World War II[,] I opened an art gallery.) . . . The sight of a uniform nauseates me. . . . As an act of faith in the young [I] am ready to eliminate myself completely rather than continue my responsibility for murder.

There is no indication in what forum Caresse read this statement; perhaps she tried to at Women Against War or Citizens of the World rallies. But she made sure it found a place in her archive.

Caresse had always given her public the impression that she was intent on living life to its fullest, that her answer was "always yes" to new experiences and ideas, but hardly to death. The statement may serve as a record of how far she was willing to go for the cause of pacifism, even if that meant committing an act of violence against herself. Consciously or not, Caresse revealed how oblivious she was to the judgement of others, how indifferent she was to setting herself up for ridicule, how the word "embarrassment" was not part of her vocabulary. Even more importantly, the statement discloses a covert theme to her actions: committing suicide could be proactive, not exclusively a rejection of life. Harry Crosby had thought so, and she did also, or wanted to think she did.

Six years later, Caresse wrote another tract (never published) on suicide, nearly three times the length of the first, entitled "In Defense of Suicide or the Planned Death: A Concept by Caresse Crosby."[12] She confesses that for twenty years, since 1934, she has been preoccupied by the meaning of suicide, that she has "guarded the promise of suicide" in her conscience. She had not been able to reconcile herself to Harry's suicide.

> During the seven years of a believingly perfect marriage I both consciously and subconsciously accepted suicide as the SUMUM AMOR to which we were ardently dedicated and for which I promised myself I was waiting, though never fully convinced and never quite ready.

As she understood it, she lost her faith in suicide because Harry did not wait for her. Her grief as a widow had less to do with Harry's death than with the lost chance of committing with Harry "the almost too beautiful rebellion, the forbidden transit to everlasting awareness." When Harry died, she was not ready to accept the "necessity" of suicide. Now in 1954, she had reasserted her trust in voluntary death with an almost messianic fervor: she wanted "all mankind" to benefit from the belief that suicide could be a "progression," an act of affirmation, not a capitulation to misery and depression.

If indeed Caresse stayed true to "the cult" of suicide (apparently, for Caresse, "cult" and "belief" are interchangeable) for the rest of her life, then her frequent assertion that she always liked to "say yes" becomes more than an expression of enthusiasm for experiencing all life had to offer. No doubt, Caresse was part hedonist. However, by living "each day with the last day as absolute as was the first"—one way that she describes the cult of suicide—she created for herself a sense of "freedom" and "moral well-being." She had fused two powerful instincts: first, the preservation of life through literature, art, and dedication to social progress; second, the pursuit of whatever course of action she chose, however perilous its implications. In her mind, the memory of a perfect seven-year marriage was sustained.

During the last year of her life, her health severely at risk, her financial resources strained, Caresse carried on so that each day was as "absolute" as the last. Although asthma prevented her from visiting New York during the winter of 1969, she spent March 1969 in the Middle East, back to Cyprus, still trying to gather support for World Citizens. (Apparently Jacques Cousteau suggested claiming the off-shore continental shelf as "World Territory in the name of the World Citizen.")[13] But she ended up as a patient in Salvator Mundi, writing to Kay Boyle on May 5, 1969, that she "was tucked up in the hospital with a chronic case of bronchitis, all of April laid low here in Rome." Another person with Caresse's medical problems might have forgone the trip to the Middle East, but caution was not prominent in her manual for living.

Kay Boyle had alerted Caresse to editorial and permissions problems brewing between the Black Sun Press and Two Windows Press. Caresse's friend Sy Kahn, who was teaching at the University of the Pacific in Stockton, California, was putting together an edition of Harry's published and unpublished poems, with tentative permission from Caresse. Don Gray, of Two Windows Press, wanted to extend a contract to Kahn and considered the feasibility of extending the format and content of the project. Gray asked Boyle if she would contribute a piece about Harry for the volume. He also hoped to reprint the precious introductions to Harry's poems by T. S. Eliot, Ezra Pound, Stuart Gilbert, and D. H. Lawrence. Boyle would have nothing to do with the expanded project unless Caresse approved. Like a lion protecting her cub, Caresse halted further progress on the proposed volume.[14] A Two Windows edition of Harry's poems alone, edited by Sy Kahn, was eventually published in 1983, according the format that, from the start, Caresse had understood it would follow.

Rocca was open for the 1969 summer season. Caresse took off half of August to visit Polleen and granddaughter Serena in Ibiza. She was nursing the hope that Polleen, now quite wealthy, might invest in Rocca, even manage it. But Polleen thought her mother should sell the castle and salvage her resources so that she could live out her life in relative comfort. Caresse, however, refused to consider the possibility that she was no longer physically capable of running the castle. When friend and fellow activist Matt Shermer expressed concern over her well-being, she told him not to worry: "I am alive but kicking at the idea I may not live to 2,000 A.D. since the papers say today that by 2,000 we will practically be immortal and love making will go on forever."[15] Affiliated with the American Referendum Association in New York, Shermer was active in various world peace movements and had published *The Sense of People* in 1968, which he dedicated to Caresse for publishing his booklet *You Must Run the World!* in 1951. In addition to inquiring about her health, he had requested permission to quote from the booklet for a radio program on peace in the Middle East and southeast Asia. Caresse was happy to grant his request, but she could not provide the $1,000 he needed to continue his work. She assured him that if there were "any landfall during the Summer," she would pass along some of it to him.

Since Caresse could not last until 2000—that would require her to live to 108—she set her eyes on 1988. To a friend of Helen Simpson's interested in helping her sell the castle, she declared that she intended to live another twenty years and was ready to set up and run a school at Rocca to restore frescoes, for which she needed $100,000 a year.[16] Or she would sell the castle to a foundation for $40,000 a year for fifteen years with one stipulation: "My own 5 room apartment in one of the wings with private entrance I would keep for myself during my lifetime using when I wished." Upon her death, the apartment would revert to the foundation. She insisted that the $600,000 investment would be a good deal for the buyer.

Real estate aside, Caresse planned a be-in at the castle for September 1969, an event that recalled the spirit of the Threshold for Peace happening the previous year. She intended to record and publish "around the world" voices of the young, diverse crowd of participants she hoped to attract. She did not propose here, as she first had twenty years ago, that older generations commit suicide because they had corrupted the world with violence. But she did think that they should step aside and make room for the "young in heart and limb, the strong in mind and spirit to give us guidelines, to turn the dreamers from their apathy, the greedy from their spoils, the mad from their wars."[17] Caresse was guileless. Her rhetoric may have been inflated, but her dedication to advancing world peace was genuine.

She anticipated another summer season at the castle, with plans for art classes, literary happenings, and political rallies. Her old friend Ellen Barry, on her own since the death of her husband, playwright Philip Barry, in 1949, had expressed interest in raising funds to restore the Rocca frescoes. Caresse needed between five and eight painters who wanted to work on "the real thing" and were able to pay $200 a week for a room, breakfast, and instruction. "Too much?" she asked Barry, "or can we get a grant?"[18] She thought the Italian government might pay the salary of the teacher. But by the time Caresse settled into Roloff Beny's apartment in Rome for the fall of 1969, she confessed that if she found a buyer, she would sell the castle.

For a while, Caresse considered the advantages of moving to New York. Josette, now remarried and settled in New York, scouted around for apartments or hotels suitable for Caresse. Josette and Caresse had remained close relatives through the years, even if they had not seen one another much. There had been visits to Washington, D.C., and New York and Rocca, where Josette gave useful suggestions for remodeling—actually rebuilding—the kitchen. Caresse kept Josette informed about her latest projects and the state of her health. Josette had never stopped regarding Caresse as her second mother, often adding "your loving daughter" at the end of her letters. The best housing Josette could find for Caresse was a small midtown hotel on Forty-eighth Street between Third and Lexington—a room, kitchenette, and maid service for $350 a month.[19] Caresse preferred her larger digs in Rome, where there were fewer colder days. During her previous winter in New York, in 1969, she had ended up in the hospital.

Caresse pretended that years of a creative, vigorous life were in front of her and persuaded those around her in Rome to share the illusion. She made plans for travel, books, new editions of *Portfolio,* classes in fresco painting, and peace conferences. But she admitted in a letter to Anaïs Nin that she had "so little stamina" that she could not write "more than a line or two without feeling exhausted." Always the lady, she dressed formally every evening, often sacrificing warm comfort for chilly glamour. When she could not catch her breath at the end of one dinner party, she was rushed to Salvator Mundi hospital. For a week she lay in bed, a tube in her nose for oxygen. Everyone knew she was near the end, including Caresse.[20] She died on January 24, 1970, at the age of seventy-seven. Chronic bronchitis, asthma, and congestive heart failure had finally collected full toll.

The *New York Times* ran an obituary of Caresse on January 25, accompanied by a photograph from 1956, in which she appears as her everyday elegant and vital self. (A more recent photograph would have accomplished the same effect.) She was given credit for cofounding the Black Sun Press; for publishing such authors as Hart Crane, James Joyce, D. H. Lawrence, Ezra Pound, Kay Boyle, Ernest Hemingway, William Faulkner, and Dorothy Parker; and for editing two (out of six) issues of *Portfolio*. A description of *The Passionate Years* makes a flawed, derisive attempt to capture Caresse's personality by listing her accomplishments as a girl scout, and by noting that she was "indirectly responsible for the founding of Alcoholics Anonymous."[21] Caresse's marriage to Bert Young goes unmentioned, and Paris is incorrectly cited as the city where she lived most of life. Her association with Citizens of the World and Women Against War is given one sentence. Overall, the obituary sounds hastily written and suggests that Caresse had been out of the general public psyche for many years.

A small wake was held in Roloff Beny's apartment. Desmond O'Grady, Robert Mann, and Peggy Guggenheim were among those attending. Frances Steloff held a Caresse Crosby Memorial at the Gotham Book Mart on February 18, 1970. Buckminster Fuller served as master of ceremonies. Sixty-four people signed the guest registry.[22] Mrs. Simpson and granddaughter Lorraine de Mun included cards of love and devotion. Old friends like Gretchen and Pete Powel ("the Crouchers"), Dorothy Norman, Sam Rosenberg, Teeny Duchamp, Rufus King, Harry Moore, and Bill Barker were among those who came to celebrate Caresse's contributions to literature and art. Also in attendance was George Minkoff, who published in 1970 what Caresse had long yearned for, an exquisite *A Bibliography of the Black Sun Press*. Anaïs Nin, Henry Miller, and Kay Boyle mailed tape recordings, and Robert Snyder showed his documentary *Always "Yes!" Caresse*. Archbishop Makarios sent a note of sympathy.

"Only with [the] death [of Caresse Crosby], and an end to all the planning and the hope, can the Black Sun Press be said to cease publication," noted Shelly Cox, then director of Special Collections at Morris Library.[23] Although Caresse and Harry started the press together, Caresse was the Black Sun Press right to the end of her life. In *Ladies Bountiful: A Colorful Gallery of Patrons of the Arts*, W. G. Rogers describes Caresse as "erect, aristocratic, fond of company, . . . the master of a ready, sympathetic wit." She knew how to have fun and at the same time help novelists, painters, and poets. "As between helping a needy creator and having a mink coat," she told him, "I'd help the creator and do without the mink."[24] People wanted to know Caresse because they thought she was attractive, exuberant, and useful.

Caresse Crosby had stopped listening to people tell her what to do when she was a teenager. If circumstances were unsuitable to her, she changed them when she could—not hesitating to take advantage of her privilege and class if she needed to. If Caresse failed as a poet and short story writer, she did nevertheless create an entertaining and informative memoir of the first half of her life. She was an insightful and daring publisher, devoted to supporting writers and to producing books that were themselves works of art. She understood the sacrifices writers and artists made to keep themselves alive and went through a good part of her personal wealth to support them. She devoted additional funds and precious energy towards furthering universal peace and justice. Ultimately, she lacked credentials for the political arena, but she was not one to acknowledge defeat.

In general, Caresse preferred the company of men, and although she was not always the best judge of their character, she enjoyed affairs with men, younger and older, to the end of her life. But the man she loved most was Harry Crosby. Although he was not the first person to find Caresse beautiful, charming, and vivacious, Harry recognized and appreciated before anyone else Caresse's rebellious spirit, her talent, and her need to be in the world. Caresse kept his work in print, whitewashed his crimes, and was eager to name buildings and awards in his honor. Alive or dead, Harry was Caresse's lifelong inspiration and tormentor.

Caresse waffled about one thing: death. She resisted Harry's overtures to end their lives together. An atheist and a fatalist, she boasted that a fortune-teller predicted that she would die in her seventy-seventh year. She endorsed suicide for herself and her contemporaries so that a younger, less demoralized generation could lead the world to a more peaceful existence. Yet she told numerous people she had to live longer than seven and half decades if she were going to accomplish all she wanted to. Caresse knew that Harry was not waiting for her on the other side, but she sometimes behaved as if she thought he were watching her, making sure that she carried on their mission.

In an undated letter to Anaïs Nin, Caresse confessed that she approached autobiography with trepidation.

> I flit lightly with an ever present sense of humor even of the ridiculous and I hold my breath with terror lest I might delve too deeply inward—only skimming the hidden memories.

The story of an independent, creative, successful woman should not end on a note about her chronic broken heart, but Caresse invited such speculation. She was too interesting, too accomplished a woman to be remembered chiefly as the widow of Harry Crosby. But his ghost lurks in the background. How much of her life did she devote to proving she had made the right choice when she married Harry Crosby?

Notes
Bibliography
Index

Notes

Abbreviations

Names

KB—Kay Boyle
MC—Malcolm Cowley
CC—Caresse Crosby
HC—Harry Crosby
CCC—Constance Coolidge Crowninshield
CL—Canada Lee
HM—Henry Miller
HTM—Harry T. Moore
DP—David Porter
EP—Ezra Pound
RLS—Richard L. Simon
BY—Bert Young

Texts

CG—Crosses of Gold by Caresse Crosby
GI—Graven Images by Caresse Crosby
PS—Painted Shores by Caresse Crosby
PY—The Passionate Years by Caresse Crosby
WITW—Who in the World (unpublished manuscript by Caresse Crosby)
SOS—Shadows of the Sun by Harry Crosby

Libraries

JHL—John Hay Library, Brown University
ML—Morris Library, Southern Illinois University

1. Spunky Little Rich Girl

1. *PY,* p. 14.
2. *PY,* p. 14.
3. *PY,* p. 14.
4. *PY,* p. 65
5. *PY,* p. 69. In the biographical entry in *World Biography,* CC is described as the daughter of William H. Jacob, but no mention is made of her mother.
6. *PY,* p. 69.
7. A stylized but beautiful portrait of CC by May den Engelsen is the frontispiece for *The Stranger.* CC has short, cropped hair pushed to the side, blue-violet eyes shaped like isosceles triangles, a slash of muted red for lips, pink cheeks, a beige round collar blouse, and a yellow one-button jacket with a red flower. Hugh Ford says that *The Stranger* is CC's response to HC's *Sonnets for Caresse.* CC and HC are the birds of gold and silver harnessed to a "chariot of Hope" in flight towards the sun. See p. 171, *Published in Paris.* The poem was reprinted in the November 1929 edition of *transition.*
8. *PY,* p. 72.
9. Box 27. File 3. ML.
10. CC's great-great-grandmother was Annie Theresa Fulton, the daughter of Robert Fulton. Box 1. File 2. ML. The quotation appears in *The Columbia World of Quotations,* no. 15431.
11. *PY,* p. 87.
12. *PY,* p. 77.
13. *PY,* p. 88.

2. Polly Meets Harry

1. Geoffrey Wolff, *Black Sun,* p. 4. For details about HC's life, I draw largely (but not solely) on this book.
2. Geoffrey Wolff, *Black Sun,* p. 55.
3. Geoffrey Wolff, *Black Sun,* p. 73.
4. See *PY,* p. 94, for CC's full account of their first meeting.
5. *PY,* p. 95.
6. See HC's June 2, 1921, letter to CC, in which he fondly recalls "the countless little incidents [that] have taken place along the road." Box 42. File 9. ML.
7. *PY,* p. 94.
8. HC to CC, June 2, 21, 1920. Box 42. File 9. ML.
9. This is the second stanza of the illuminated "Sonnet for Caresse." See Box 37. File 9. ML.
10. See Box 27. File 3. ML.
11. See HC to CC, June 2, 1921. Box 42. File 9. ML.
12. HC to CC, June 2, 1921. Box 42. File 9. ML.
13. CC claims that the film, *Lilac Time,* starred Norma Talmadge. *Lilac Time*

was produced in 1928, too late for Talmadge to have appeared in it in such a capacity. The film also starred Gary Cooper and Colleen Moore. CC gets the plot of the film right, but that is all.

14. *PY,* p. 104.

15. *PY,* p. 106.

16. HC to CC, c. fall 1921. Box 42. File 9. ML.

17. Dick Peabody wrote a touching note to his children after Christmas 1921 expressing his wish to see them. File 62. Box 6. ML.

18. These reassurances come from the already quoted, forty-page, June 2, 1921, letter that HC wrote to CC. He wanted her to read this letter to herself every day while they were apart.

19. Geoffrey Wolff has documented the events of the months that Polly and HC spent together. See *Black Sun,* p. 97. CC's account in *PY* is rather vague, in part because she collapses the amount of time that passed, particularly the first two months they spent in Paris, May and June 1922. Perhaps she was reluctant to reveal that HC lived with her at the Regina, even while he was sharing rooms with an American at the Metropolitan.

20. CC to HC, on a "Sat" of July 1922. Box 42. File 10. ML.

21. HC to CC, August 1, 1922. Box 42. File 10. ML.

22. CC to HC, August 3, 1922. Box 42. File 10. ML.

23. In *Black Sun,* Geoffrey Wolff cites the August 1, 1922, letter as the source of information about this new line of product, called "Paris le Bain."

24. *PY,* p. 112.

25. HC notes this in a July 30, 1922, diary entry. See p. 28 of HC, *SOS.* In addition to Wolff, this volume serves a source for HC's life, and in passing, of CC's. It is an extremely valuable work since Germain consults the diaries published by the Black Sun Press in three volumes as well as HC's holograph notebooks and the notations both he and CC made on the typescript copy of the notebooks.

26. *PY,* p. 112.

27. See William Wiser's chapter on CC in *The Great Good Place: American Expatriate Women in Paris,* p. 170.

3. How Polly Became Caresse

1. *PY,* p. 127.

2. Polly Drysdale describes this encounter in her unpublished memoir. She is quoted by Anne Conover in *Caresse Crosby: From Black Sun to Roccasinibalda,* p. 4. Wolff also describes this episode in *Black Sun,* p. 103.

3. Billy Peabody to CC, November 22, 1925. Box 62. File 7. ML.

4. January 11, 1924, entry in *SOS,* pp. 44–45.

5. A photograph by CC of the bronze bust appears as a frontispiece to CC's *Poems for Harry Crosby.*

6. See Geoffrey Wolff, *Black Sun,* pp. 119–24, for an extensive discussion of Walter Berry's influence on HC.

7. Many people, including the Crosbys, believed that Wharton had a small apartment of her own in Berry's house, which she used at her convenience, and that she had hoped to marry Berry after her divorce. R. W. B. Lewis claims this was not the case at all. A confirmed bachelor, Berry took over Wharton's lease at 53 rue de Varenne after she moved to Ste. Claire. See Lewis's *Edith Wharton,* pp. 437.

8. *PY,* p. 119.

9. *PY,* p. 82.

10. *PY,* p. 221.

11. See Shari Benstock, *Edith Wharton: No Gifts from Chance,* p. 402.

12. Billy Peabody to CC, n.d. Box 62. File 7. ML.

13. April 17, 1926, *SOS,* p. 102.

14. *PY,* p. 123.

15. *PY,* p. 123.

16. *SOS,* p. 40.

17. See Geoffrey Wolff, *Black Sun,* p. 141.

18. *PY,* p. 136. CC identifies the woman as Lady Abdy. According to Wolff, CC met Ortiz the same night that HC met the Russian painter Polia Chentoff. The Crosbys bought Chentoff's painting "First Communion" and she painted portraits of them both. HC's is the frontispiece to *Chariot of the Sun,* the first book with the Black Sun imprint. On p. 219, Wolff writes that Chentoff and the Crosbys met on November 7, 1927, opening night at the Autumn Salon, but on p. 220, Wolff cites a letter HC wrote to his mother in which he states that he met Ortiz at the Comte Etienne de Beaumont's but does not mention Chentoff (at least not in the section quoted). CC says they met Chentoff in 1928. She later destroyed Chentoff's portrait of HC.

19. "She is both my wife and my child." January 12, 1924, *SOS,* p. 45.

20. July 23, 1924, *SOS,* p. 55.

21. HC to CC, July 2, 1924. Box 42. File 11. ML.

22. Geoffrey Wolff, *Black Sun,* pp. 84–85.

23. November 23, 1924, *SOS,* p. 62.

24. HC to CC, March 31, 1925. Box 42. File 11. ML.

25. CC, "How It Began," n.p. Both CC and HC describe the house as a cube or lump of sugar. HC in *SOS,* July 17, 1925, p. 81; CC in *PY,* p. 130, as well as in above citation.

26. *PY,* p. 131.

27. "Constance Martel" was first collected in a bound manuscript entitled "Poems by Caresse Crosby," dated 1925. Box 2. ML. It appeared in prose form on p. 26 of *Graven Images.*

28. "Harry" appears in *Poems for Harry Crosby.*

29. See "How It Began" and *PY,* p. 130.

30. See Geoffrey Wolff, *Black Sun,* caption for illustration opposite p. 81.

31. *SOS,* November 25, 1925, p. 91.

32. "Polly" does not appear in HC's diary even though HC began writing it before the name change.

4. A Woman of Many Trades

1. *SOS,* April 26, 1926, p. 102.
2. *PY,* p. 143.
3. *PY,* p. 222.
4. *PY,* p. 155.
5. *PY,* p. 142.
6. *SOS,* June 18, 1926, p. 110.
7. See *CG,* p. 62; and *GI,* p. 20.
8. *PY,* 169.
9. *PY,* 156.
10. So CC wrote to Robert Ficter, December 6, 1969. Box 48. File 6. ML.
11. Geoffrey Wolff, *Black Sun,* p. 144.
12. The de Geeteres continued to live on their barge at least through the 1960s. Mary Blume reported in a January 10, 1969, article in the *International Herald Tribune* that Mr. de Geetere, "a slim and bright-eyed 73 1/2-year-old painter of unquenchable high spirits" had recently patented a design for flying saucers, high-tech kites for children.
13. Never published, the four-page manuscript is in the Black Sun Archive at JHL. See Geoffrey Wolff, *Black Sun,* pp. 160–61, for a fuller discussion.
14. See *PY,* pp. 161–65, for an extended description of the de Geeteres.
15. *PY,* p. 162.
16. Geoffrey Wolff, *Black Sun,* p. 161. For a different account of how the Crosbys and the de Geeteres met, see Wolff, p. 159. William Wiser's account in *The Great Good Place,* pp. 178–80, corroborates the account that CC gives in *PY.*
17. For more details about HC's contribution to *transition,* see Eugene Jolas, pp. 235–36.
18. See Geoffrey Wolff, *Black Sun,* pp. 243–47 for a detailed explanation of the origins of their friendship. Wolff says that the first contact between the Crosbys and the Jolases was CC's unannounced visit to *transition*'s offices on the rue Fabert late in 1927.
19. *PY,* p. 248.
20. *PY,* p. 165.

5. Treasures for the Black Sun Press

1. *PY,* p. 147.
2. KB, "The Crosbys: An Afterword," p. 119.
3. I am relying on Joan Mellen's *Kay Boyle: Author of Herself* and Sandra Whipple Spanier's *Kay Boyle: Artist and Activist* for biographical material on KB.

4. Spanier, *Kay Boyle; Artist and Activist,* p. 89 and Mellen, *Kay Boyle: Author of Herself* p. 126.

5. Joan Mellen, *Kay Boyle,* p. 188.

6. KB, *My Next Bride,* p. 164. All quotations are from this edition.

7. *My Next Bride,* pp. 99–100.

8. *My Next Bride,* p. 290.

9. *My Next Bride,* p. 322.

10. *PY,* p. 236.

11. KB: CC and HC. Box 33. File 6, ML.

12. Robert McAlmon and KB, *Being Geniuses Together 1920–1930,* p. 326.

13. *PY,* p. 201.

14. Geoffrey Wolff, *Black Sun,* p. 199 and *PY,* pp. 206–7. Wolff declares that CC's account often corroborates HC's account but that it is "comically romanticized."

15. *PY,* p. 207.

16. Cecil Roberts, *The Bright Twenties.* See pp. 292–96 for a fuller history of this property.

17. *PY,* p. 176.

18. See Geoffrey Wolff, *Black Sun,* pp. 225–27, and letters from HC to Henrietta Crosby July 24, August 3, 17, 1928. Box 44. File 1. ML.

19. Cecil Roberts, *The Bright Twenties,* p. 295. Also see *PY,* p. 231.

20. See Polly Peabody Drysdale's description of Le Moulin in Anne Conover, *Caresse Crosby: From Black Sun to Roccasinibalda,* pp. 27–28 for additional details.

21. See *PY,* pp. 252–53. Among the signatures CC mentions are those of D. H. Lawrence, Salvador Dalí, the Maharanhee of Cooch, Louis Bromfield, and Eva Braun.

22. In *Kay Boyle: Author of Herself,* Joan Mellen captures the atmosphere at the Mill. However, she reports that HC left the scene on New Year's Eve because he could not stand the commotion made by the children. KB herself recalls spending some time with HC on that raucous occasion in *Being Geniuses Together.* See pp. 326–28. HC served McAlmon a special drink he had concocted to inspire "poetic delirium." Wolff corroborates this in *Black Sun,* adding that HC had received a telegram from Josephine Rotch Bigelow that evening. Mellen could have confused this scene with an earlier episode in Gstaad during the Christmas of 1926. See *PY,* p. 171. CC herself writes that she and KB kidnapped Bobby on Christmas Eve. See *PY,* p. 248.

23. Robert McAlmon, *Being Geniuses Together,* p. 308.

24. Hugh Ford describes this occasion, with help from HC's diary, in *Published in Paris,* pp. 186–87. For details surrounding KB's review of *White Buildings,* see Mellen, p. 109.

25. See Langdon Hammer and Brom Weber, p. 403.

26. Hart Crane to CC. Box 36. File 8 ML.

27. *PY,* p. 247.

28. In his biography of Crane, Clive Fisher provides a full and colorful description of Crane's nasty brush with the French legal system. See pp. 406–7.

29. Hammer and Weber, *The Selected Letters of Hart Crane,* p. 388.

30. "One Spring: Notes from the Journal of Caresse Crosby," Paris, 1929. p. 3. Unpublished manuscript. Box 6. File 1. ML.

31. *PY,* p. 241.

32. *PY,* p. 241.

33. See *PY,* p. 247.

34. See Wolff, pp. 201–2, for an amusing account of how HC got the gold to Lawrence.

35. See HTM, *The Life and Works of D. H. Lawrence,* p. 257, for a fuller discussion of the story.

36. "One Spring," p. 19.

37. See *PY,* pp. 230–31. Also see Janet Byrne, *A Genius for Living: The Life of Frieda Lawrence,* p. 335.

38. Two letters from Frieda to CC, one from Vence, the other from Bandol, and one letter from CC to Frieda, all written in 1930 in conjunction with the deaths of D. H. Lawrence and HC, strongly suggest an affectionate cordiality. Box 55. 10. ML.

39. See letters from CC to Lawrence: August 27, September 23, 1929, and letters from Lawrence to CC: August 12, 28, October 15, 23, November 1, 1929. Box 55. File 8. ML.

40. Harry Marks, "By Way of Preface."

41. See Geoffrey Wolff, *Black Sun,* p. 175, and William Wiser, *The Great Good Place: American Expatriate Women in Paris,* p. 168.

42. Geoffrey Wolff, *Black Sun,* p. 248.

43. *PY,* p. 191.

44. See Hugh Ford, *Published in Paris,* p. 188.

45. "One Spring," p. 9.

46. See January 18, 1954, letter from CC to Richard Ellmann. Box 47. File 9. ML.

47. Hugh Ford, *Published in Paris,* p. 189.

48. *PY,* p. 194.

49. William Wiser believes that CC was not aware of the Byzantine relationships in the Paris world of arts and letters. See *The Great Good Place,* p. 190.

50. So Hugh Ford describes the drawing. See *Published in Paris,* p. 192.

51. See Richard Ellmann, *James Joyce,* 1959, p. 627. Ellmann describes Joyce as keeping the Crosbys in a "state of controlled fury" during their editing sessions.

52. See Brenda Maddox, *Nora: A Biography of Nora Joyce,* p. 276.

53. Both Ellmann and Maddox discuss at length Lucia's mental illness. See in particular Ellmann, *James Joyce,* pp. 663–71, and Maddox, *Nora,* pp. 300–318.

54. See CC: Richard Ellmann, January 18, 1954. Box 47. File 9. ML.

55. *James Joyce, Ulysses: An Exhibition of Twenty-Four Inscribed Copies of the First Edition,* p. 1998.

56. See Sylvia Beach to CC, June 19, 1929. Box 31. File 8. ML.

57. Geoffrey Wolff, *Black Sun,* p. 183. I am drawing on Wolff and on the previously mentioned essay by CC, "How It Began," the introduction to *A Bibliography of the Black Sun Press,* edited by George Minkoff, for the background of the relationship between the MacLeishes and the Crosbys.

6. The Death of Harry Crosby

1. Geoffrey Wolff, *Black Sun,* p. 221. He is relying on CC's diaries here. It is not clear what is meant by "violent fights."

2. These letters are contained in Box 1. JHL.

3. CCC: HC, June 30, 1926. Box 1. File 21. JHL.

4. See respectively Box 1. Files 23 and 12. JHL.

5. See HC's letters to CCC in Box 1. Files 4 and 20. JHL.

6. Josephine Rotch Bigelow: HC, November 27, 1929. Box 32. File 7. ML.

7. *SOS,* p. 288.

8. *SOS,* p. 19.

9. *SOS,* p. 292 and p. 286.

10. *PY,* p. 267. CC is probably referring to *American Needlewoman,* the monthly Maine newspaper that was published by Vickery and Hill Publishing Company.

11. *PY,* p. 256.

12. *PY,* p. 257.

13. "One Spring," p. 21.

14. *PY,* p. 175.

15. Geoffrey Wolff, *Black Sun,* p. 230. *SOS,* September 24, 1929.

16. HC, *SOS,* pp. 230–31.

17. These words are in an imaginary letter that appears in "One Spring," p. 12. CC addressed the letter to Halladay. She crossed out this name, replacing it with the initials J. H. P. It is possible that this person was J. H. Philbin, the Jacob family lawyer. See the April 24, 1931, letter from Philbin to "Polly." Box 63. File 9. ML. On pp. 21–22 of "One Spring," CC writes: "I wish I hadnt smoked ["tried opium" had been scratched out and "smoked" written in by hand] opium last night, when one is not happy it only intensifies the malaise."

18. "One Spring," n.p.

19. "One Spring," p. 5.

20. "One Spring," p. 20.

21. "One Spring," p. 14.

22. See *PY,* p. 259, and Geoffrey Wolff, *Black Sun,* p. 287.

23. CC told this to Andreas Brown of the Gotham Book Mart, Inc., August 1, 1969. Brown was editing *SOS,* and CC suggests in the letter that he consult MacLeish about the final entries in the journal. Box 34. File 3. ML.

24. Box 32. File 7. ML. See also Geoffrey Wolff, *Black Sun,* pp. 285–87.

25. *SOS,* p. 258.

26. See notebook 6, p. 29. JHL. Also see HC's Paris, August 19, 1929, will, p. 1. Box 3. File 2. JHL.

27. *PY,* p. 206.

28. Geoffrey Wolff, *Black Sun,* p. 10. Scott Donaldson, in *Archibald MacLeish: An American Life,* p. 92, called the cable that MacLeish sent CC "the most thoughtful of untruths."

29. MacLeish file. Box 57. File 4. ML. According to Joan Mellen in *Kay Boyle,* KB was angry that Geoffrey Wolff reported that the ring was found flattened on the floor. CC had told KB that was not true. KB told Mellen that she herself wore the ring on her own finger. See p. 495.

30. *New York Times,* December 13, 1929, p. 29.

31. Box 53. File 2; Box 31. File 8; Box 33. File 8. ML.

32. Joan Mellen, *Kay Boyle,* pp. 142–43.

33. Box 36. File 9. ML.

34. Box 64. File 10. ML.

35. Notebook 10, p. 127. JHL.

36. Wolff, p. 296. See 295–96 for reactions of others.

37. See Shari Benstock, *Edith Wharton,* p. 403. Benstock is referring to a February 18, 1931, letter from Edith Wharton to Bernard Berenson.

38. Box 48. File 12. ML.

39. CC to André Fontana, May 4, 1954. Fontana's letter to CC is dated April 9, 1955. File 48. Box 12. ML.

40. Geoffrey Wolff, *Black Sun,* p. 297.

41. Billy Peabody to CC, January 23, 1930? Box 62. File 9. ML.

42. CC to Billy Peabody, May 20, 1930. Box 62. File 9. ML.

43. CC to Billy Peabody, June 24, 1930. Box 62. File 9. ML.

44. I am relying on Anne Conover's discussion of Polleen's unpublished memoirs here. See Anne Conover, *Caresse Crosby: From Black Sun to Roccasinibalda,* pp. 53–55.

45. Bernard A. Drabeck and Helen E. Ellis, *Archibald MacLeish: Reflections,* p. 58.

46. Hugh Henle to CC, February 16, 1930. ML.

47. MC, *Exile's Return,* p. 269.

48. *PY,* p. 304.

49. MC, p. 11. MC told CC that he was not able to write about Crane "with complete honesty" as long as Crane's mother Grace was alive. MC: CC, September 7, 1934. Also, MC's estranged wife, Peggy, was having an affair with Crane and was on board the *Orizaba* when Crane jumped over on April 27, 1932. See Clive Fisher, pp. 498–501.

50. See HTM, *The Priest of Love: A Life of D. H. Lawrence,* p. 489, for a longer excerpt from this letter.

51. D. H. Lawrence to CC, January 30, 1930. File 55. Box 8. ML.

52. EP to CC, n.d. File 64. Box 10. ML.
53. See Millicent Bell, "The Black Sun Press: 1927 to the Present," p. 11.
54. "Thee" and "Thy" are replaced by "you" and "your."
55. Hart Crane: CC. Box 36. File 9. ML.
56. CCC to CC, December 1929? File 46. Box 11. ML.

7. Business or Pleasure

1. One of the most important collections of Tauchnitz editions is located in the Todd-Bowden Collection at the British Library.
2. See Walter Phelps Jacob: CC, April 14, 1930. Box 51. File 11. ML.
3. *PY,* 268.
4. *PY,* p. 268.
5. *PY,* p. 269.
6. CC: Mary Jacob, September 6, 1930. Box 51. File 10.
7. CC: Mary Jacob, November 16, 1930. Box 51. File 10.
8. *PY,* p. 273.
9. *PY,* p. 278.
10. Jacques Porel: CC, March 1932. Boxes 3, 4. File 64. ML. Most of the letters in these two thick folders are undated, although there are several like the one just quoted that have an approximate date pencilled in. All quotations from Jacques' letters are from this file.
11. Bobby Fochin, one of CC's lovers during this period, wrote countless letters of devotion to her. See Boxes 10, 11. File 48. ML.
12. T. S. Eliot: CC. Box 47. File 10. ML.
13. Hugh Ford, *Published in Paris,* p. 224.
14. Clive Fisher, *Hart Crane,* p. 425.
15. D. H. Lawrence and Stuart Gilbert wrote the introductions for the other two posthumously published collections of poetry: *Chariot of the Sun* and *Sleeping Together, A Book of Dreams.*
16. EP: CC, 10 November (no year). All letters are in Box 64. File 10. ML.
17. EP: CC, 10 November (no year).
18. EP: CC, 2 August (no year).
19. EP: CC, 7 September (no year).
20. EP: CC, 25 August (no year).
21. *PY,* 265.
22. *PY,* 264. Polleen was not as receptive to EP as CC was. She thought him poorly dressed and unkempt and avoided him when he called at rue de Lille after he tried to kiss her on the mouth. See Anne Conover, *Caresse Crosby: From Black Sun to Roccasinibalda,* p. 55.
23. *PY,* 265.
24. CC reminisces further about her friendship with EP in *WITW,* the unpublished sequel to *PY.* See pp. 1–6. Box 4. File 6. ML.

25. William Watt gave me his impressions of CC in two letters, one dated May 4, 2002, the other May 24, 2002. Descriptions of CC and of "Agora," the journal Watt wanted to start under the mentorship of CC and EP, are contained in these two letters.

26. A full account of CC's efforts to release EP from St. Elizabeths appear in chap. 11, *WITW.* Box 4. File 6. ML.

27. See CC: Ernest Hemingway, February 17, 1930. Box 50. File 11. ML.

28. *PY,* p. 297. According to CC, Hemingway had overextended his funds by purchasing a painting by Juan Gris.

29. See Leonard J. Leff, *Hemingway and His Conspirators,* p. 151, for more background to the history of this story.

30. See p. 174 of Joan Mellen's *Kay Boyle* for a vivid description of KB's eventual meeting with Carnevali in Bazzano.

31. Fadiman's report, dated March 18, 1933, can be found in Box 67. File 10. ML. RLS included it with a letter to CC dated March 20, 1933. Specifically commenting on the manuscript of the story "Gentleman, I Address You Publically," Fadiman says that it "is about fairies and lady lovers." He reviewed the book for *The New Yorker* in November 1933.

32. See Joan Mellen, *Kay Boyle,* pp. 175–76 for an extensive discussion of this event.

33. In an August 2, 1967, letter to CC, KB mentions that she never would have allowed Ann Watkins to take her proposal to Simon and Schuster, as CC suggests that she does in *PY,* p. 327.

34. See Joan Mellen, *Kay Boyle,* p. 213.

35. See Joan Mellen, *Kay Boyle,* p. 175.

36. Letters from RLS to CC are in Box 67. File 10. ML.

37. RLS alludes to these events in a January 11, 1933, letter to CC.

38. RLS: CC, January 11, 1933.

39. Copies of CC's letters to RLS are not among her papers in ML. RLS refers to a "thick envelope" of letters from her in an October 10, 1932. In an October 17 letter, he mentions "those darling letters [that you sent] to me daily."

40. See the allusion that RLS makes to this statement in an November 1, 1932, letter to CC.

41. RLS refers to his fond memories of Fleur in a March 22, 1933, letter. In *PY,* p. 194, CC relates a story about how Picasso asked her for one of Narcisse's black offspring. CC agreed to give him one, but when Fleur was born, the only female and the only black one in the litter, CC knew that she would never part with her.

42. See RLS: CC, March 6, 1933, for confirmation of the length of the time they spent together.

43. *PY,* p. 301.

44. *PY,* p. 302.

45. On p. 303 in *PY,* CC reported that RLS visited with Frank Harris, who was "on or near his deathbed." She must have confused Harris, whose three-volume *My Life and Loves* had been banned in the United States and England because of its explicit sexual scenes, with another author. Harris died in 1931.

46. RLS: CC, March 6, 1933.

47. RLS: CC, March 6, 1933.

48. *PY,* p. 301.

49. CC to "Diana Darling," November 22, 1933. Neither Diana nor CC's companion is identified. The letter can be found in Box 6. File 4. ML.

50. Sandra Whipple Spanier reports that KB told her that this volume is now "a collectors' item, selling for over $4000." *Kay Boyle: Artist and Activist,* p. 232, n. 36.

51. René Crevel: CC. Box 37. File 4. ML.

52. See March 31, 1952, letter to CC from Carlos Lynes Jr., who was writing a biography of Crevel at the time he wrote to CC. Box 56. File 13. Also see letter CC wrote to John W. Cameron. Box 34. File 9. ML.

53. January 30, 1953, letter from CC to Carlos Lynes Jr. Box 56. File 13. ML. This might be the "recent philistine encounter" that bitterly upset CC and Crevel shortly before Crevel's death.

54. See Meredith Etherington-Smith's *The Persistence of Memory: A Biography of Dalí,* p. 189, and Ian Gibson, *The Shameful Life of Salvador Dalí,* pp. 401–2.

55. Meredith Etherington-Smith discusses this episode on p. 155, *The Persistence of Memory: A Biography of Dalí.* CC discusses it in *PY,* p. 287.

8. Atlantic Crossings

1. *PY,* p. 309.

2. *PY,* p. 310.

3. CC: KB, September 10, 1931. Box 33. File 9. ML.

4. KB: CC, undated letter ("Sunday") written from Villa Coustille, Col-de-Villefranche, Nice.

5. In *The Shameful Life of Salvador Dalí,* Ian Gibson reports that in his autobiography, *The Secret Life of Salvador Dalí,* Dalí does not give CC proper credit for helping them get across the Atlantic. See his discussion on p. 391.

6. *PY,* p. 329.

7. *PY,* p. 331.

8. See Ian Gibson, *The Shameful Life of Salvador Dalí,* pp. 392–93 for fuller discussion.

9. Meredith Etherington-Smith describes this party in greater detail in *The Persistence of Memory: A Biography of Dalí,* on p. 187. See also Ian Gibson, *The Shameful Life of Salvador Dalí,* pp. 397–98.

10. *PY,* p. 312.

11. Emlen Etting to CC, May 11, 1932. Box 48. File 2. ML.

12. This description appears in a blurb for Cinema 16, a nonprofit organiza-

tion created by Amos and Marcia Vogel, and originally devoted to 16mm experimental film. The copy of the blurb along with a March 1954 article in *Holiday* called "Cinema 16" by Al Hine is in Box 48. File 2. ML.

13. *PY*, p. 313.

14. *PY*, p. 313.

15. See George Minkoff, *A Bibliography of the Black Sun Press*, 1970, p. 44.

9. Mind Over Matter

1. CCC: CC, July 22, 1936. Box 36. File 3. ML.

2. CCC: CC, July 22, 1936. Box 36. File 3. ML.

3. *PY*, p. 334.

4. *PY*, p. 335.

5. BY. Box 72. Files 2–4. ML.

6. *PY*, p. 341.

7. CC: BY, August 1940? ML.

8. CC: BY, April 20 [1939?], ML.

9. CC: BY, April 20 [1939?], ML.

10. BY: CC, n.d.

11. BY: CC, n.d.

12. CC: BY [illegible date].

13. See Gibson, *The Shameful Life of Salvador Dalí*, pp. 456–61 for a discussion of Dalí's political perspective and for his stay at Hampton Manor.

14. HM, *Henry Miller: Letters to Emil*, p. 100.

15. Gunther Stuhlmann, ed. *A Literate Passion: Letters of Anaïs Nin and Henry Miller 1932–1953*, p. 83.

16. In *The Happiest Man Alive: Henry Miller*, Mary V. Dearborn identifies CC as "a friend of Nin's whom HM had come to know well in Paris." See p. 210.

17. *The Diary of Anaïs Nin*, vol. 3 *1939–1944*, ed. Gunther Stuhlmann, p. 15.

18. Anaïs Nin: CC, September 6, 1967. Box 60. File 8. ML. Also see p. 54 of *Anaïs Nin: Anaïs: An International Journal*, vol. 2 (1984), for selected correspondence between Nin and CC.

19. Nin, *Incest: The Unexpurgated Diary of Anaïs Nin 1932–1934*, p. 307.

20. Gunther Stuhlmann estimates that this letter was written in August 1967. See p. 53 of *Anaïs: An International Journal*, vol. 2 (1984), p. 54.

21. See Deirdre Bair, *Anaïs Nin*, p. 427, for a fuller discussion.

22. Deirdre Bair, *Anaïs Nin*, p. 427.

23. CC: Anaïs Nin, October 10, 1968. Bill Barker believes that Anaïs Nin was never a guest at Hampton Manor. In an interview with me on July 28, 2001, in Hudson, New York, Barker said that Nin's description was so well done that CC did not have the heart to dispute it.

24. *The Diary of Anaïs Nin*, vol. 3 *1939–1944*, ed. Gunther Stuhlmann, p. 237.

25. Meredith Etherington-Smith, *The Persistence of Memory: A Biography of Dalí*, p. 263.

26. *PY,* p. 350.
27. Tone Price to CC, November 24, 1941. Box 65. File 3. ML.
28. This brief diary can be found in Box 6. File 3. ML.

10. Old Friends, New Friends

1. *WITW,* p. 3. CC had intended to quote from Polleen's unpublished manuscript "Occupied Territory," but she provides no text.
2. Polleen: CC, October 29, 1943, letter. Box 62. File 4. ML.
3. See Billy's April 15, 1943, letter. Box 62. File 8. ML.
4. *WITW,* p. 3. Billy told CC about this mission after the war.
5. *WITW,* p. 2.
6. *PY,* p. 277.
7. Bruce Kellner, ed. *The Harlem Renaissance,* p. 341.
8. *WITW,* p. 3.
9. Bernard A. Drabek and Helen E. Ellis, p. 45.
10. Bernard A. Drabek and Helen E. Ellis, p. 46.
11. Scott Donaldson, *Archibald MacLeish: An American Life,* p. 177. The MacLeishes took another apartment on 8 rue Emile Augier because it was available for a longer period.
12. In *Uphill with Archie,* his memoir about growing up as the son of Archibald MacLeish, William MacLeish reports that his father told him many times about how the Crosbys published his work in Paris. Coincidentally, in 1970, William MacLeish became friends with Bert Bigelow, who had been married to Josephine Bigelow when HC killed her. A civil rights and anti-nuclear-power activist, Bigelow was head of Meeting School, where MacLeish's daughter Meg was a student. See p. 222.
13. *WITW,* p. 3.
14. *WITW,* p. 7.
15. Bruce Kellner, *The Harlem Renaissance,* p. 216.
16. James V. Hatch, *Black Theater USA,* p. 393.
17. *WITW,* p. 8.
18. Interview with Walter Phelps Jacob, August 9, 1992, at his home in Cape Elizabeth, Maine.
19. The play is on file at ML. Box 6. File 6.
20. *WITW,* p. 6.
21. Gerald J. Pollinger: CC, September 28, 1960. Box 63. File 13. ML.
22. In a letter dated May 22 [1940s], Dorothea Tanning wrote to CC that she had sent CL a card announcing the opening but that he did not come. Box 69. File 2. ML.
23. *WITW* chap. 11, p. 6.
24. CL: CC. CL greets CC with "Dearest My Baby" in this undated letter. Box 58. File 2. ML.

11. A Woman of Influence

1. She records their names in her one-time-only journal where she talks about missing Billy.

2. *WITW,* p. 5.

3. From *PS.* Illustrated with three watercolors by François Quelvée. Editions Narcisse, 2 rue Cardinale, Paris. 1927. ML.

4. *WITW,* p. 1.

5. Zoray Kramaer: CC, March 2, 1942. Box 54. File 7. ML.

6. See Anton Gill's biography of Peggy Guggenheim, *Art/Lover,* p. 329, for confirmation of their first meeting. Gill describes CC as a "rich socialite who had been one of the great figures of the Left Bank American society in Paris in the 1920s."

7. *WITW,* p. 5.

8. Pete Powel: CC, n.d. ["Summer 1943" pencilled in] Box 65. File 2. ML.

9. DP: CC, June 17, 1943. Box 64. File 5. ML.

10. Pete Powel: CC, June 14, 1943. Box 65. File 2. ML.

11. See "G Place Gallery," p. 3, and *WITW,* pp. 8, 9.

12. *WITW,* p. 9.

13. Anne Conover, *Caresse Crosby: From Black Sun to Roccasinibalda,* p. 89.

14. See HM: CC, December 28, 1943. Box 59. File 3. ML.

15. CC: HM, August 19, 1968. Box 59. File 5. ML.

16. See HM: CC, May 3, 1944. Box 59. File 3. ML.

17. HTM, "The Answer is 'Yes'": Remembering Caresse Crosby, *Anaïs,* vol. 2, pp. 59–60. The entire piece (pp. 59–63) is HTM's fond summary of recollections about CC.

18. Selden Rodman, "Enthusiasm and Compassion," *Anaïs,* vol. 2, pp. 58–59. Rodman thinks that Sylvia Beach is responsible for introducing him to CC. He also reports that at the time, he did not know he was dining in such distinguished company.

19. Program notes are in Box 66. File 6. ML.

20. HTM, "The Answer is 'Yes'": Remembering Caresse Crosby, *Anaïs,* vol. 2, p. 60.

21. See "The Mercurial Canada Lee, pp. 22–65, in Glenda E. Gill, *White Grease Paint on Black Performers, 1935–1939.*

22. Anaïs Nin: CC, June 11 1968. Earlier, on May 8, 1968, Nin wrote CC that "today you would be all the more loved for it [her romance with CL]." Box 60. File 8. ML.

23. HTM, "The Answer is 'Yes'": Remembering Caresse Crosby," p. 60.

24. Anne Conover, *Caresse Crosby: From Black Sun to Roccasinibalda,* p. 93.

25. See Romare Bearden: CC, October 16, 1944. Box 31. File 9. ML.

26. Romare Bearden: CC, n.d. ["ca. 1945" pencilled in]. Box 31. File 9. ML.

27. Romare Bearden: CC, n.d. Box 31. File 9. ML.

28. "'Temptations of St. Anthony' Banned in Boston, Shown Here," *The Evening Star,* October 11, 1946. p. B-2. File 6. Box 7. ML.

29. See Humphrey Carpenter's *A Serious Character: The Life of Ezra Pound,* p. 736. Carpenter quotes from a letter by Charles Olson who describes the event.

30. *WITW,* p. 5.

31. See E. Fuller Tobey, *The Roots of Treason: Ezra Pound and the Secret of St. Elizabeths,* p. 206.

32. Humphrey Carpenter, *A Serious Character: The Life of Ezra Pound,* p. 809.

12. Back in the Avant-Garde

1. *WITW,* p. 2.

2. HTM, "The Answer is 'Yes'": Remembering Caresse Crosby," p. 60.

3. See CC: HTM, May 8, 1945, and HTM: CC, May 17, 1945. Box 59. File 3. ML.

4. Box 5. Files 2, 3. ML.

5. Stephen Kraft, a colleague of Lazzari's at the American University in Washington, D.C., related his experience as a volunteer for *Horses* in a May 7, 2002, letter to me as well as in a May 30, 2002, telephone conversation.

6. See August 4, 1945, letter MacLeish wrote to Lacoste. Box 57. File 4. ML.

7. See *Paris Post* article quoted in Conover, p. 116.

8. "The Full Armor of Light," introduction to *Portfolio I,* 1945. Box 8. File 1. ML.

9. *WITW,* p. 6.

10. See Billy Peabody to CC, July 19, 1944. Box 62. File 10. ML.

11. HTM: CC, October 3, 1945. Box 59. File 2. Also quoted in Anne Conover, *Caresse Crosby: From Black Sun to Roccasinibalda,* p. 117.

12. See Frances Steloff: CC, March 4, 1954. Box 68. File 6. ML.

13. CC: HM, January 14, 1946. Box 58. File 3. Also quoted in Conover, p. 119.

14. CC: HM, January 14, 1946. Box 59. File 2. Also quoted in Conover, p. 119.

15. Ian Hamilton, *Robert Lowell,* p. 131.

16. See CC: Man Ray. Box 57. File 8. February 12, 1946.

17. Anne Conover, *Caresse Crosby: From Black Sun to Roccasinibalda,* p. 120.

18. Kenneth Rexroth to Selden Rodman, May 22, 1946. Kenneth Rexroth Collection. Special Collections. University Research Library. UCLA.

19. Kenneth Rexroth to CC, May 22, 1946. Box 66. File 2. ML.

20. Kenneth Rexroth to CC, December 12, 1948. Box 66. File 2. ML.

21. *WITW,* p. 2.

22. *WITW,* p. 3.

23. Box 9. File 1. ML.

24. Tom Clark, *Charles Olson: The Allegory of a Poet's Life,* p. 140.

25. Tom Clark, *Charles Olson: The Allegory of a Poet's Life,* p. 115.

26. Tom Clark quotes a November 8, 1952, letter that Olson wrote to his wife, Connie, where he describes CC as "empty," but his later letters to CC suggest that he had revised this opinion. See Box 61. File 1. ML.

27. See chap. 32 of *PY* for a full and amusing description of the entire trip.
28. *PY*, p. 292.
29. *WITW*, p. 1.
30. *WITW*, p. 4.
31. *WITW*, p. 15.
32. *WITW*, p. 19.
33. *WITW*, p. 6.
34. CC: to Bill Peabody, March 18, 1954. Box 62. File 10. ML.
35. Takis wrote several touching letters to CC during the 1950s in which he mourns his separation from Greece, reports on his progress in London and Paris, and thanks CC for the money she sent him.
36. Eleni Vlachos, *Kathimerini,* May 24, 1947, as quoted in Conover, p. 131.
37. CC: Derek Patmore, January 15, 1948. Box 61. File 10. Also quoted in Conover, p. 134.
38. *WITW*, p. 8.

13. Mondialization

1. See the time line CC created for "A Personal History of World Citizenship." ML.
2. See "A Personal Decade of World Citizenship 1945–1955," a brief essay included with a proposal for a 350-page book about CC's efforts on behalf of "world citizenship." The book would contain illustrations, photographs, and documents of World Citizen activities and publications. Box 14. File 2. ML.
3. Rufus King Sr. would become chairman of the criminal justice section of the American Bar Association and practice law with the law firm of Downey Rice. He served on a presidential commission on law enforcement and was a national leader of the movement to decriminalize narcotics.
4. *WITW*, chap. 12, p. 1.
5. *WITW*, chap. 12, p. 1.
6. "A Personal Decade of World Citizenship 1945–1955," p. 2. Box 14. File 2. ML.
7. See Anne Conover, *Caresse Crosby: From Black Sun to Roccasinibalda,* p. 141.
8. Blair eventually worked for CBS in Paris. See his June 12 [1961?] letter to CC. CC noted in one of many chronologies that she compiled for *WITW* that she was fired from the position of reporter, however temporary it was to begin with. Box 35. File 10. ML.
9. *WITW*, chap. 16, p. 2.
10. *WITW*. The chapter sequence breaks down around here. This material comes from "Chap 13" (handwritten by CC on top), p. 1.
11. I am drawing on my biography of Rexroth, *A Life of Kenneth Rexroth,* pp. 200–202, for an itinerary and general description of this trip.
12. Box 66. File 2. ML. Bill Barker confirmed the affair in his July 29, 2001, interview.
13. Kenneth Rexroth: CC, April 6, 1953, and September 9, 1956, respectively.

14. This is one version of several "documents" that CC composed. Box 11. File 3. ML.

15. Joseph C. Grew: CC, March 18, 1950. Box 50. File 2. ML.

16. See materials related to CC's political activism in Box 6. File 4. ML.

17. See Box 48. File 12. ML.

18. CC: E. H. Foley Jr., October 31, 1949. Box 48. 12. ML.

19. See Box 10. File 4. ML.

20. Bill Barker talked to me about his friendship with CC and her life in general during the July 28, 2001, interview.

21. *WITW*, chap. 15, p. 3.

22. *WITW*, chap. 15, p. 5, 6.

23. See Box 10. File 4. ML.

24. Polleen Peabody: CC, November 9, 1949. Box 62. File 4. ML.

25. CC: Michael Howard, November 1, 1951. Box 11. File 1. ML.

26. William Jay Smith conveyed his impressions of CC to me in a telephone interview on May 10, 2002.

27. See "Tentative list of contents" for *WITW*, Box 5. File 2.

28. See transcript of "Radio Broadcast from Rome, August 1952." Box 20. File 4. ML.

29. For an example see "Facing Disaster," September 1950. Box 6. File 1, or "Radio Address," Delhi, March 1951. Box 20. File 4. ML.

30. "Declaration" (October 1, 1953). Box 12. File 3. ML.

31. "A Suggestion on the Architectural Program for the Symbolic Center of the 'Citizens of the World' in Delphi, Greece, July 1952" by Demetrios Pikionis. Box 11. File 5. ML.

32. Athens, May 29, 1953. Box 12. File 2. ML.

33. "Press Extracts." Box 13. File 3. ML.

34. See Anaïs Nin, *The Diary of Anaïs Nin,* vol. 6 , pp. 137–44, for a detailed summary of these events. Nin had originally intended this piece to be included in Lawrence Lipton's short-lived West Coast magazine *Eve.*

35. See Case No. 2389/1953 of the Council of State. Box 12. File 3. ML.

14. Fame

1. MC: CC, September 7, 1934. Box 36. File 2. ML.

2. HTM, "The Answer is 'Yes,'" p. 61.

3. CC: MC, November 19, 1949. Box 36. File 2. ML.

4. CC: MC, December 7, 1949. Box 36. File 2. ML.

5. MC: CC, December 14, 1949. Box 36. File 2. ML.

6. *PY* was also published by in England by Alvin Redman (1955), Southern Illinois University Press (1968), and Harper (1979).

7. Excerpts of these 1953 reviews appear on the back cover of the November 1968 Arcturus edition published by Southern Illinois University Press.

8. William Peabody File. Box 62. File 10. ML.

9. In my interview with Bill Barker on July 29, 2001, Barker reported that CC told him about Polleen's wishes concerning Billy's estate.

10. See CC: Josette Peabody, January 28, 1957. Box 61. File 11. ML.

11. Box 31. File 5. ML.

12. CCC: CC, August 28, 1954. Box 46. File 11. ML.

13. Millicent Bell: CC, November 9, 1953. Box 31. File 14. Also see CC's description of Berry, *PY,* p. 116: "He was enormously elongated, slim as straw and as *sec;* his small head poised erect above a high wing collar was bird-like in its sudden turnings and its bright quick glance."

14. CC: Millicent Bell, October 31, 1954. Box 31. File 14. ML.

15. For this description of CC's lecture at Brown University and of her physical appearance, I am relying on Jane Baltzell's account "The Answer Was Always 'Yes'" published in a 1954 issue of Brown University's literary magazine. All quoted material in this paragraph and the two that follow is from that essay unless otherwise indicated.

16. Joan Mellen, *Kay Boyle,* p. 387.

17. CC: KB, April 6, 1956. Box 33. File 12. ML.

18. KB: CC, January 17, 1957. Box 33. File 12. ML.

19. Barker interview, July 28, 2001. Tanning sent a postcard to CC in care of Barker expressing delight at the prospect that CC would be coming. File 69. Box 2. ML.

20. The poem was last reprinted in *Collected Poems of Kay Boyle.*

21. Box 29. File 1. ML.

15. A Thirty-Year Plan

1. See February 16, 1965, letter written by A. R. A. Hobson to CC: Box 51. File 2. ML.

2. See CC: Harvey Fite, May 31, 1960. Box 48. File 8. ML.

3. See HC, *Devour the Fire: Selected Poems of Harry Crosby;* and Kahn, "Hart Crane and Harry Crosby: A Transit of Poets."

4. Snyder was also awarded a Diploma of Merit from the Edinburgh Film Festival for *A Visit with Pablo Casals,* Special Award for the Best Folkloric Documentary, Bilbao, the Cine Golden Eagel for *Bayanihan Philippine Dance Company,* and the Gran Premio Bergamo for *The Hidden World.* As part of his "Life Encounters" series, he had made documentaries about Willem DeKooning, HM, Buckminster Fuller, and Anaïs Nin.

5. Box 21. File 2. ML.

6. See the rough copy of a letter CC wrote to Alexander Xydis on July 29, 1964. Box 16. File 4. ML.

7. Alfred H. Barr Jr.: CC, February 6, 1963. Box 31. File 7.

8. CC: Rufus King, November 16, 1962. Box 15. File 8. ML.

9. CC: His Excellency the Ambassador of Greece, Washington, February 21, 1963. CC was in St. Croix, U.S. Virgin Islands, when she wrote this letter to "Aleco"

(Alexander Xydis). Her family in Boston was in all likelihood the Crosbys. Box 72. File 1. ML.

10. CC relates this incident in the same February 21, 1963, letter to Ambassador Xydis.

11. CC: Perry Culley, American Embassy, Paris. May 2, 1964. Box 16. File 2. ML.

12. See Anne Conover, *Caresse Crosby: From Black Sun to Roccasinibalda,* p. 164, for affirmation of their first meeting. In my interview with him, Bill Barker confirmed that Fuller and CC had an affair.

13. Linda Hamalian, *A Life of Kenneth Rexroth,* p. 62.

14. HTM, "The Later Caresse Crosby: Her Answer Remained 'Yes,'" p. 14.

15. In an April 26, 2002, telephone interview with me, Professor Paul Schleuter reminisced about this party. At the time, Schleuter was a graduate student, HTM's first doctoral candidate.

16. Buckminster Fuller: CC, June 17, 1966. Box 18. File 5. ML.

17. CC quotes a passage from an April 22, 1966, letter that she wrote to Makarios in which she expresses her wish to include Dr. Kuchuk in the negotiations with the hope of "interesting the artists and the youth of Turkey as well as the Turkish Cypriots." See CC: Buckminster Fuller, June 23, 1966. Box 18. File 5. ML.

18. Box 16. File 2. ML.

19. Fuller: CC, June 17, 1966. Box 18. File 5. ML.

20. Fuller: CC, September 29, 1969. Nearly a year and a half earlier, Noguchi offered to design a garden around the dome at Kyrenia. Box 17. File 2. ML.

21. The origins of the Cyprus Peace Plan were related by CC in a *Resume* on the plan. See Box 16. File 9. ML. For a fuller account of the Cyprus Peace Plan, see Conover, chap. 14, pp. 162–81.

22. See Jacqueline Bograd Weld, *Peggy the Wayward Guggenheim,* chaps. 48 and 49, for a full and lively description of activities at Guggenheim's palazzo.

23. The photograph appears on p. 100 in Carole P. B. Vail, *Peggy Guggenheim: A Celebration.* CC was sometimes compared to another contemporary, Nancy Cunard, because they both ran fine letterpresses, wrote memoirs, spent personal fortunes (though CC was by far the less affluent), and liked sex. CC and Cunard met only twice, CC told Hugh Ford in response to a February 2, 1967, letter that he wrote to CC. Box 48. File 12. ML. Cunard died in 1965.

16. How to Run a Castle

1. Walter Phelps Jacob: CC, January 23, 1956. 51. File 11. ML.

2. Leonard Jacob: CC, May 1, 1959. Box 51. File 8. ML.

3. CC: William Chapman, March 21, 1963. Box 35. File 7. ML.

4. See Diane Barker: CC, November 10, 1959. Box 31. File 6. ML. Although they passed as husband and wife, Diane and Bill were not legally married. Interview with Bill Barker, July 28, 2002.

5. Gregory Corso: CC [1959]. Box 36. File 4. ML.

6. Ferlinghetti did take a look at the books which he received in February 1960 but decided against publishing them. See his February 25, 1960, letter to CC. Box 48. File 6. ML.

7. Box 31. File 4. ML.

8. See Robert Mann: CC, August 26, 1963. File 57. Box 8. ML. Details of Mann's agenda for the castle and CC are contained within this five-page letter.

9. CC: Frances Steloff, November 10, 1961. Box 68. File 6. ML.

10. See CC: Man Ray, July 29, 1961; Man Ray: CC, September 16, 1961; CC: Man Ray, September 23, 1961. Box 57. File 8. ML. The pastels were exhibited in Milan at the Galleria Schwarz in 1971.

11. See Robert Mann: CC, August 26, 1963. File 57. Box 8. ML.

12. HTM, "The Later Caresse Crosby: Her Answer Remained 'Yes,'" p. 14. HTM doubted there were black faculty at SIUC. Personal letters and memorabilia were purchased posthumously from CC's estate in 1971.

13. CC: Sharon ("Bobby") Vail, August 18, 1964. ML. At KB's insistence, CC also turned away Robert Gessner, professor of film studies at New York University. He had broken off an affair with KB, creating great bitterness. See KB: CC, August 23, 1966. Box 33. File 13. ML.

14. The telegram, dated November 16, 1964, and correspondence are in Box 31. File 10. ML.

15. This letter is undated. Box 31. File 10. ML.

16. CC: Julian Beck and Judith Malina, March 30, 1965. Box 31. File 10. ML.

17. Julian Beck. CC: Box 31. File 10. ML.

18. Robert Mann: CC, March 8, 1966. File 57. Box 8. ML.

19. Box 28. File 3. ML. Dr. Brandenburg also noted that CC's fingers appeared deformed, that there was "clubbing of her fingers." December 13, 1965, letter to Dr. Louis F. Bishop, CC's doctor in New York.

20. Box 6. File 4. ML.

21. Interview with Walter Phelps Jacob. August 9, 1992.

17. Keeping the Faith

1. See Desmond O'Grady's recollection of this occasion in Humphrey Carpenter, p. 884.

2. In his interview with me, Bill Barker stated that EP admired CC for maintaining her integrity. Barker and Mann drove EP and Olga Rudge to the castle from the Rome airport. They stayed for ten days.

3. See CC: EP, August 17, 1961. Merano. File 64. Box 10. ML.

4. See W. G. Rogers, *Wise Men Fish Here: The Story of Frances Steloff and the Gotham Book Mart,* for a sensitive history of Ms. Steloff and her bookstore.

5. Frances Steloff: CC, May 6, 1968. Box 6. File 68. ML.

6. Steloff, p. 25.

7. CC: Betty Allen, October 23, 1969. Box 30. File 8. CC met Allen in London when she spent Christmas 1968 with Polly and family.

8. HTM, "The Later Caresse Crosby," p. 14.

9. Box 17. File 6. ML. Artists and writers who lent their names to the Committee for the Arts include Roloff Beny, KB, Norman Cousins, Marcel Duchamp, Peggy Guggenheim, Dorothy Norman, Elsa Schiaparelli, Cyril Connolly, and Anaïs Nin.

10. Allen Ginsberg: CC, September 24, 1968. Box 49. File 12. ML.

11. Box 6. File 2. ML.

12. Box 12. File 7. ML.

13. Box 18. File 2. ML.

14. See KB: CC, April 22, 1969, and CC: KB, May 5, 1969. In a May 13, 1969, letter to KB, Don Gray explained that he had never intended to develop the project without CC's approval. Box 33. File 14. ML.

15. CC: Matt Shermer, July 4, 1968. Box 17. File 5. Shermer introduced CC to journalist and novelist Vincent Sheean, best known for *Personal History,* a perceptive interpretation of events to come in the 1940s. Sheean had hoped to stay at Rocca while completing a novel set in imperialist Rome, but his dates did not coincide.

16. CC to Dr. Boris Pregal: July 15, 1968. Box 17. File 5. ML.

17. Box 18. File 2. ML.

18. CC: Ellen Barry, February 3, 1969. Box 31. File 6. In the same letter CC announced that *PY* had just been published in paperback and reminded Barry that she and her husband, Philip, were in it. CC tells a funny story about the spectacle they all made in 1930 driving to a Cannes casino in the Barry's new red Mercedes Benz. The car was so low slung that it kept getting stuck in the gutter. See *PY,* p. 272.

19. Josette Spiero: CC [late 1960s]. Box 61. File 11. ML.

20. Anne Conover's interview with Robert Mann and her correspondence with Desmond O'Grady are a source for details of CC's last evening at home and her week in the hospital. See *Caresse Crosby: From Black Sun to Roccasinibalda,* p. 215.

21. *New York Times,* January 25, 1970, p. 68. In 1924, Dick Peabody, Caresse's first husband, had established a clinic for alcoholics. See Geoffrey Wolff, p. 102.

22. Box 28. File 5. ML.

23. Friends of ML, *The Black Sun Press,* Supplement to *ICarbS* 3.2, p. 21.

24. W. G. Rogers, *Ladies Bountiful: A Colorful Gallery of Patron of the Arts,* p. 60. See also pp. 5–9.

Bibliography

Alpern, Sar, Joyce Antler, Elisabeth Israels Perry, and Ingrid Winther Scobie, eds. *The Challenge of Feminist Biography: Writing the Lives of Modern American Women.* Urbana: University of Illinois Press, 1992.

Bair, Deirdre, *Anaïs Nin.* New York: Putnam, 1995.

Bell, Millicent. "The Black Sun Press: 1927 to the Present." *Books at Brown.* Providence: John Hay Library, 1995.

Bell, Susan Groag, and Marilyn Yalom. *Revealing Lives: Autobiography, Biography, and Gender.* Albany: State University of New York Press, 1990.

Benstock, Shari. *Edith Wharton: No Gifts from Chance.* London: Hamish Hamilton, 1994.

———, ed. *The Private Self: Theory and Practice of Women's Autobiographical Writing.* Chapel Hill: University of North Carolina Press, 1988.

———. *Women of the Left Bank, 1900–1940.* Austin: University of Texas P, 1986.

Boyle, Kay. "The Crosbys: An Afterword' *ICarbS* Spring/Summer (1977): 117–25.

———. *Collected Poems of Kay Boyle.* Port Townsend: Copper Canyon Press, 1991.

———. *My Next Bride.* 1934. London: Virago, 1986.

Byrne, Janet. *A Genius for Living: The Life of Frieda Lawrence.* New York: HarperCollins, 1995.

Carpenter, Humphrey. *A Serious Character: The Life of Ezra Pound.* New York: Dell, 1988.

———. *Geniuses Together: American Writers in Paris in the 1920s.* New York: Houghton Mifflin, 1988.

Clark, Tom. *Charles Olson: The Allegory of a Poet's Life.* New York: Norton, 1991.

The Columbia World of Quotations. New York: Columbia University Press, 1996.

Conover, Anne. *Caresse Crosby: From Black Sun to Roccasinibalda.* Santa Barbara: Capra, 1989.

Cosslett, Tess, Celia Lury, and Penny Summerfield, eds. *Feminism and Autobiography.* London: Routledge, 2000.
Cowley, Malcolm. *Exile's Return.* New York: Viking, 1956.
Crosby, Caresse. *Crosses of Gold.* Paris: Albert Messein, 1925.
———. *Graven Images.* Boston: Houghton Mifflin, 1926.
———. "How It Began." Intro. to *A Bibliography of the Black Sun Press,* ed. George Robert Minkoff. Great Neck, NY: Minkoff, 1970.
———. *Impossible Melodies.* Paris: Editions Narcisse, 1928.
———. *Painted Shores.* Paris: Editions Narcisse, 1927.
———. *The Passionate Years.* Carbondale: Southern Illinois University Press, 1968.
———. *Poems for Harry Crosby.* Paris: Black Sun, 1931.
———. *The Stranger.* Paris: Editions Narcisse, 1927.
"Crosby, Caresse." *World Biography.* Institute for Research in Biography, 1954.
Crosby, Harry. *Devour the Fire: Selected Poems of Harry Crosby.* Ed. Sy Kahn. Berkeley: Two Windows, 1983.
———. *Shadows of the Sun: The Diaries of Harry Crosby.* Edward Germain, ed. Santa Barbara: Black Sparrow, 1977.
Dearborn, Mary V. *The Happiest Man Alive: Henry Miller: A Biography.* New York: Simon and Schuster, 1991.
Donaldson, Scott. *Archibald MacLeish: An American Life.* Boston: Houghton Mifflin, 1992.
Drabeck, Bernard A., and Helen E. Ellis. *Archibald MacLeish: Reflections.* Amherst: University of Massachusetts Press, 1986.
Ellmann, Richard. *James Joyce.* New York: Oxford University Press, 1959.
Etherington-Smith, Meredith. *The Persistence of Memory: A Biography of Dalí.* New York: Random House, 1992.
Fisher, Clive. *Hart Crane: A Life.* New Haven: Yale University Press, 2002.
Ford, Hugh. *Published in Paris: American and British Writers, Printers, and Publishers in Paris, 1920–1939.* New York: Macmillan, 1975. Yonkers: Pushcart, 1980.
Furguson, Robert. *Henry Miller: A Life.* New York: Norton, 1991.
Gibson, Ian. *The Shameful Life of Salvador Dalí.* New York: Norton, 1977.
Gill, Anton. *Art/Lover: A Biography of Peggy Guggenheim.* New York: HarperCollins, 2002.
Gill, Glenda E. *White Grease Paint on Black Performers, 1935–1939.* American University Studies. Series 9 History. Vol. 40. New York: Peter Lang, 1988.
Gould, Warwick, and Thomas F. Staley. *Writing the Lives of Writers.* London: Macmillan, 1998.
"G Place Gallery." *Art Digest* 18.4 (November 15, 1943): 3.
Hamalian, Linda. *A Life of Kenneth Rexroth.* New York: Norton, 1991.
Hamilton, Ian. *Robert Lowell.* New York: Random House, 1982.
Hammer, Langdon, and Brom Weber. *O My Land, My Friends: The Selected Letters of Hart Crane.* New York: Four Walls Eight Windows, 1997.
Hatch, James V. *Black Theater USA.* New York: Free, 1974.

Heilbrun, Carolyn. *Writing a Woman's Life.* New York: Norton, 1988.
Homberger, Eric, and John Charmley, eds. *The Troubled Face of Biography.* New York: St. Martin's, 1988.
Iles, Teresa, ed. *All Sides of the Subject: Women and Biography.* New York: Teachers College Press, 1992.
Irigaray, Luce. *Speculum of the Other Woman.* Trans. Gillian C. Gill. Ithaca: Cornell University Press, 1985.
James Joyce, Ulysses: An Exhibition of Twenty-Four Inscribed Copies of the First Edition. New York: Glenn Horowitz Bookseller, 1998.
Jolas, Eugene. "Harry Crosby and *transition.*" *In Transition: Writing and Art from "transition" Magazine 1927–1930.* New York: Doubleday, 1990.
Kahn, Sy. "Hart Crane and Harry Crosby: A Transit of Poets." *Journal of Modern Literature* 1 (1970): 45–56.
Kellner, Bruce, ed. *The Harlem Renaissance.* Westport, CT: Greenwood, 1984.
Kirschstein, Bette H. *Life Writing/Writing Lives.* Malabar, FL: Krieger, 2001.
Koch, David V., Alan M. Cohn, and Kenneth W. Duckett, eds. *ICarbS* 3.2 (Spring–Summer 1977).
Kolodny, Annette. "A Map for Rereading: Or, Gender and the Interpretation of Literary Texts." *New Literary History* 11 (1980): 451–67.
Leff, Leonard J. *Hemingway and His Conspirators.* Lanham, MD: Rowman and Littlefield, 1997.
Lewis, R. W. B. *Edith Wharton.* New York: Harper and Row, 1975.
MacLeish, William H. *Uphill with Archie: A Son's Journey.* New York: Simon and Schuster, 2001.
Maddox, Brenda. *D. H. Lawrence: The Story of a Marriage.* New York: Simon and Schuster, 1994.
———. *Nora: A Biography of Nora Joyce.* New York: Fawcett, 1988.
Marcus, Linda. *Auto/Biographical Discourses.* Manchester: Manchester University Press, 1994.
Marks, Harry. "By Way of Preface." *The Black Sun Press.* Providence: John Hay Library, 1930.
McAlmon, Robert. *Being Geniuses Together, 1920–1930.* Rev. ed., New York: Doubleday, 1968. Rev. with supplementary chaps. and an afterword by Kay Boyle, San Francisco: North Point, 1984.
Mellen, Joan. *Kay Boyle: Author of Herself.* New York: Farrar Straus, 1994.
Miller, Henry. *Henry Miller: Letters to Emil.* Georges Wickes, ed. New York: New Directions, 1989.
Moore, Harry T. "The Later Caresse Crosby: Her Answer Remained 'Yes.'" *D.C. Magazine: A Literary Retrospective.* Ed. Richard Peabody. Washington, DC: Paycock, 1981. 13–14.
———. *The Life and Works of D. H. Lawrence.* New York: Twayne, 1951.
———. *The Priest of Love: A Life of D. H. Lawrence.* Carbondale: Southern Illinois University Press, 1974.

———. "The Answer Is 'Yes': Remembering Caresse Crosby." *Anaïs.* Vol. 2. Los Angeles: The Anaïs Nin Foundation, 1984.

Nin, Anaïs. *The Diary of Anaïs Nin.* Vol. 1, *1931–1934.* Vol. 2, *1934–39.* Vol. 3, *1939–1944.* Vol. 6, *1955–1966.* New York: Harcourt, Brace, Jovanovich, 1931–1966.

———. *Incest: The Unexpurgated Diary of Anaïs Nin 1932–1934.* New York: Harcourt Brace, 1992.

Peabody, Richard, ed. *D.C. Magazines: A Literary Retrospective.* Washington, DC: Paycock, 1981.

Roberts, Cecil. *The Bright Twenties.* London: Hodder and Stoughton, 1970.

Rodman, Selden. "Enthusiasm and Compassion," *Anaïs.* Vol. 2. Los Angeles: The Anaïs Nin Foundation, 1984.

Rogers, W. G. *Ladies Bountiful.* New York: Harcourt, Brace: 1968.

———. *Wise Men Fish Here: The Story of Frances Steloff and the Gotham Book Mart.* Tarrytown, NY: Booksellers House, 1965.

Schumacher, Michael. *Dharma Lion: A Biography of Allen Ginsberg.* New York: St. Martin's, 1992.

Snyder, Robert. *Always Yes! Caresse.* Documentary film. Pacific Palisade: Master's and Masterworks, 1963.

———. *Anaïs Nin Observed: From a Film Portrait of a Woman as Artist.* Chicago: Swallow, 1976.

Spanier, Sandra Whipple. *Kay Boyle: Artist and Activist.* Carbondale: Southern Illinois University Press, 1986.

Steloff, Frances. "Talk of the Town." *New Yorker* August 16, 1969. 23–26.

Stuhlmann, Gunther, ed. *Anaïs: An International Journal* 2 (1984).

———. *A Literate Passion: Letters of Anaïs Nin and Henry Miller 1932–1953.* New York: Harcourt Brace, 1987.

Tobey, E. Fuller. *The Roots of Treason: Ezra Pound and the Secret of St. Elizabeths.* New York: Harcourt Brace, 1984.

Vail, Karole P. B. *Peggy Guggenheim: A Celebration.* New York: Solomon R. Guggenheim Foundation, 1998.

Wagner-Martin, Linda. *Telling Women's Lives.* New Brunswick: Rutgers University Press, 1994.

Weld, Jacqueline Bograd. *Peggy: The Wayward Guggenheim.* New York: Dutton, 1986.

Wickes, George. *Americans in Paris.* Garden City: Doubleday, 1969.

Wiser, William. *The Great Good Place: American Expatriate Women in Paris.* New York: Norton, 1991.

Wolff, Geoffrey. *Black Sun: The Brief and Silent Eclipse of Harry Crosby.* New York: Random House, 1976.

Index

Linda Hamalian is a professor of English at William Paterson University of New Jersey, where she teaches twentieth-century literature and serves as the director of the Graduate Program in English. She is the author of *A Life of Kenneth Rexroth,* editor of Rexroth's revised and expanded *An Autobiographical Novel,* and coeditor of *Solo,* a collection of short stories.